MW00398492

"In *Hearers and Doers*, Kevin Vanhoozer shows us what it looks like when the Christian church 'does' the truth, when our making of disciples includes the waking of disciples—waking us up to the metaphors and myths of our secular age so we can follow Christ with faithfulness and passion. A splendid book that brings together biblical exegesis, theological reflection, and cultural analysis—all for the sake of the church."

Trevin Wax
director for Bibles and reference at LifeWay Christian Resources;
author of *Eschatological Discipleship* and *This Is Our Time*

"This delightful book provides pastors with a rich vision for church renewal. Rather than propose a new technique or program, Kevin Vanhoozer gives a deeply theological account of how disciples can participate in the triune God's work. *Hearers and Doers* is a superb book for those who want to recover a pastor-theologian vocation, written by a trusted theological mentor and guide for many. Highly recommended!"

J. Todd Billings
Gordon H. Girod Research Professor of
Reformed Theology, Western Theological Seminary

"It has become cliché to say that North American Christianity is a mile wide and an inch deep, but it's true. While expressions of evangelical Christianity are widespread in American culture and society, the actual depth and substance of our lives is, sadly, rather thin. We can fill big churches, but we struggle to grow godly men and women who are both hearers and doers of the word! Enter Kevin Vanhoozer and this marvelous book, *Hearers and Doers*. As a pastor who, like Kevin, loves Scripture, theology, and the church, I can say that this is just the tonic we need. Discipleship driven by substantive scriptural reflection on the truth revealed in Christ—what a novel idea! Get two copies of this book: one for you and one for a friend. Highly recommended!"

Todd Wilson
president, The Center for Pastor Theologians

"In *Hearers and Doers*, Kevin Vanhoozer's goal is to help pastors to form Christian believers and communities who not only hear but do what God says to them in Scripture. He discusses broadly the biblical principles that govern our growth in grace in the context of the many cultural influences that encourage or discourage conformity to Jesus Christ. The author is quite knowledgeable about both culture and Scripture so as to contrast the disciplines of the Christian life with the indulgences this world offers. The book gives us a huge amount of help, as we seek to understand the roles of the Bible, the church, and the Holy Spirit in our sanctification. Vanhoozer writes with clarity and grace. I recommend the book highly."

John M. Frame
professor of systematic theology and philosophy emeritus,
Reformed Theological Seminary (Orlando)

"Praise God! A gifted theologian who writes to edify the church and encourage pastors! May his tribe increase! Kevin Vanhoozer is a rare bird—one who knows when to be creative and when to adhere to the faith once for all entrusted to the saints. Here that combination is on full display as he presents exercises for 'bodybuilding,' grounded in the critical role of biblical doctrine in discipleship for fostering strong and healthy church bodies. This book stimulated my imagination and inspired me with the privilege and responsibility of being a pastor."

Bill Kynes
pastor, Cornerstone Evangelical Free Church (Annandale, VA)

"Kevin Vanhoozer has written a book 'for such a time as this.' We are not just facing a crisis of biblical literacy or a crisis of spiritual formation. It is deeper than that: our imaginations—the eyes of our hearts—have been taken captive by rival visions of the good and beautiful life. Vanhoozer challenges all those concerned with the care of souls to become 'eye doctors,' to help those under our care read the Bible in a way we never have so as to see the world with new eyes. If you're like me and find such a challenge beautiful but daunting, compelling but you don't know where to begin—begin by reading this book, which is filled with wisdom and practical prescriptions."

Rankin Wilbourne
senior pastor, Pacific Crossroads Church
(Los Angeles); author of *Union with Christ*

"In an age where theology is often overlooked and discipleship ignored, Kevin Vanhoozer has given the church a masterpiece on what it means to know and follow Jesus. Vanhoozer offers a vision of discipleship that is holistic—involving culture, practices, tradition, and the imagination—but that highlights the importance of doctrine and Scripture in the calling to become like Christ. In *Hearers and Doers*, we have a world-class theologian who has written a clear and compelling message about one of the most important topics. I hope every pastor reads this book, and I know that it will help Christ's people to be conformed to his image."

Jeremy Treat
pastor for preaching and vision at Reality LA;
adjunct professor of theology at Biola University;
author of *The Crucified King* and *Seek First*

"Written for the pastor, this book is a must-read for anyone concerned with Christian discipleship—and right now just about every Christian I know has concerns about the state of Christian discipleship. Wedding discipleship with cultural analysis and theological scriptural engagement, Vanhoozer joins together what the contemporary church has far too long put asunder. The result is a powerful, practical, and grace-filled vision of discipleship that our local churches today desperately need to live into their callings to form disciples who inhabit, proclaim, and embody the kingdom of God all the time, everywhere."

Kristen Deede Johnson
professor of theology and Christian formation,
Western Theological Seminary (Holland, MI)

"Pick up, read (listen), and heed (do). Kevin Vanhoozer consistently directs our attention to the importance of theology for discipleship, demonstrating how practical—and vital—doctrine is to understand and live out what is in Christ. This book, his third for the pastor-theologian, follows closely the grain of the previous two, effectively building on them by demonstrating the need for canonical fitness and establishing the importance of transformed imaginations to cultivate wisdom and to grow in Christ through the Spirit. This book is a must-read for pastors seeking to develop disciples who can articulate and live their faith."

Karl "KJ" Johnson
director, C. S. Lewis Institute of Chicago

"There is one perpetual mandate, mission, and ministry given by the Lord Jesus Christ to the church: the Great Commission with the great privilege of making disciples. With Kevin Vanhoozer as a teacher and guide, we have a master theologian-pastor instructing and modeling for pastor-theologians the full-orbed ministry of engaging in the joyful task of discipleship. He does so by emphasizing both Scripture and doctrine, hearing and doing, informing minds and forming habits, the individual and the church, biblical story and cultural context. I give thanks to the Lord for this book, and I am prayerfully excited to see how it will be used among God's people in the church to the end that all members and the whole church will truly be fit for purpose—to be a fitting image of the Lord Jesus Christ for the glory of God."

Greg Strand
executive director of theology and credentialing, Evangelical Free Church of America; adjunct professor of pastoral theology, Trinity Evangelical Divinity School

Doers

&

Hearers

Hearers and Doers

A PASTOR'S GUIDE TO MAKING DISCIPLES THROUGH SCRIPTURE AND DOCTRINE

KEVIN J. VANHOOZER

LEXHAM PRESS

Hearers and Doers: A Pastor's Guide to Making Disciples through Scripture and Doctrine

Copyright 2019 Kevin J. Vanhoozer

Lexham Press, 1313 Commercial St., Bellingham, WA 98225
LexhamPress.com

Print ISBN 9781683591344
Digital ISBN 9781683591351

Lexham Editorial: Elliot Ritzema, Jeff Reimer, Danielle Thevenaz
Cover Design: Eleazar Ruiz
Typesetting: Abigail Stocker

CONTENTS

PREFACE

Hearers and Doers is intended to help pastors fulfill their Great Commission to make disciples, with emphasis on the importance of teaching disciples to read the Scriptures—"every word that comes from the mouth of God" (Matt 4:4)—theologically. The bulk of the book spells out more fully what "theologically" means in this context and why reading Scripture theologically is the royal road to discipleship. Here I need only to call attention to the fact that genuine faith in Jesus Christ as Lord and Savior involves both hearing (understanding) and doing (obedience) as well as heartfelt trust.

Early on in my writing career I adopted a policy of writing one book for the church for every book I wrote for the academy. Of these, this is the third in my unofficial trilogy on the vocation of the pastor-theologian as one who builds up the church of Jesus Christ.[1] An earlier book was intended to convince pastors and laypeople alike of the importance of gaining cultural literacy—the ability to understand what's happening in contemporary

---

1. The other two books are my *Faith Speaking Understanding: Performing the Drama of Doctrine* (Louisville: Westminster John Knox, 2014) and *Pictures at a Theological Exhibition: Scenes of the Church's Worship, Witness and Wisdom* (Downers Grove, IL: IVP Academic, 2016). This is not to be confused with a book I coauthored with Owen Strachan urging pastors to reclaim their vocation as theologians, *The Pastor as Public Theologian: Reclaiming a Lost Vision* (Grand Rapids: Baker Academic, 2015).

culture and how it affects us—for the sake of reclaiming Christian cultural agency: the ability to leave one's mark on culture rather than passively submit to cultural conditioning.[2]

The interests represented by these books—the pastor as theologian, theology as practical understanding, the importance of understanding culture and the prevailing "social imaginary" (I explain this in ch. 1), and the urgent need to make the biblical narrative the church's control story—converge in the present work, with its focus on the necessity of doctrine for discipleship. *Hearers and Doers* continues to tease out the way gospel and culture relate and commends reading the Bible theologically to sustain a Christian counterculture: a being-together in Christ. The emphasis on *doing* is meant to remind us that making disciples involves more than knowing things. Head knowledge, either of Scripture or doctrine, is not enough to make disciples. In and of itself, head knowledge gets no further than Dietrich Bonhoeffer's "cheap grace"—a belief in the forgiveness in Christ without repentance that admires Christ but stops short of following him. Bonhoeffer describes it as "baptism without church discipline, Communion without confession ... grace without discipleship."[3]

It remains to be seen how our digital age and the social media that dominate it will affect the church's disciple-making, and young people are hardly the only ones being spiritually formed by this culture. Perhaps it's because I am married to someone from another culture (France) and have lived in two others (England and Scotland), but I became acutely aware of the formative nature of culture on a person's way of

---

2. Kevin J. Vanhoozer, Charles A. Anderson, and Michael J. Sleasman, eds., *Everyday Theology: How to Read Cultural Texts and Interpret Trends* (Grand Rapids: Baker Academic, 2007).

3. Dietrich Bonhoeffer, *The Cost of Discipleship* (London: SCM, 1959), 44–45.

thinking, experiencing, and doing things long before I came across postmodernity's focus on the kinds of *situatedness* (for example, historical, cultural, socioeconomic, ethnic) that allegedly affect our reasoning about reality. I do not believe that culture is uniformly evil, but I do think that it is a powerful means of spiritual formation. John Calvin rightly stipulated that self-knowledge is not possible without knowledge of God, but today we should probably add that self-knowledge also requires knowledge of the social world we inhabit.

In spite of its importance, culture too often flies under the radar of disciple-making. I think the reason is that we fail to recognize how culture forms us not only by making explicit claims or value judgments (though it often does this too) but also subconsciously—for example, by creating pictures of the good life and conditioning us to think these pictures are "normal."[4] Culture also forms us by catching us in its web—the electronic (inter)net—and by inculcating certain habits through common practices that shape our life together. Books by Tony Reinke and Andy Crouch alert us to this everyday electronic culture and remind us that you cannot serve both God and Google.[5] Though I am greatly concerned about young people in the church, and the parents who should be on the front line of their spiritual formation, the present book is especially for pastors and other

---

4. I'm thinking of the power of what Charles Taylor terms the "social imaginary" in his magisterial study of the modern world, *A Secular Age* (Cambridge, MA: Belknap Press of Harvard University Press, 2007). For a concise summary of Taylor's ideas, see James K. A. Smith, *How (Not) to Be Secular: Reading Charles Taylor* (Grand Rapids: Eerdmans, 2014). For an application of Taylor's ideas to church ministry, see the collection of essays edited by Collin Hansen, *Our Secular Age: Ten Years of Reading and Applying Charles Taylor* (Deerfield, IL: The Gospel Coalition, 2017).

5. Tony Reinke, *12 Ways Your Phone Is Changing You* (Wheaton, IL: Crossway, 2017); Andy Crouch, *The Tech-Wise Family: Everyday Steps for Putting Technology in Its Proper Place* (Grand Rapids: Baker Books, 2017).

church leaders who seek to parent the parents by teaching the practical skill of hearing and doing Scripture via Christian doctrine and discipleship.[6]

Hearers and Doers is not the first book to address the nature and method of discipleship, yet three emphases may distinguish it from others:

1. Its argument that the best way for pastors to "take every thought captive to obey Christ" (2 Cor 10:5) is, first, to wake up their churches to the peculiar powers and principalities of contemporary culture by exposing the pictures and stories that capture our imaginations and program our lives and, second, to set out the more glorious truth of the gospel, thus redeeming the imagination and reorienting disciples so that they can walk in the truth.

2. Its insistence on reading Scripture theologically as a principal means for becoming spiritually fit (hence "through Scripture and Doctrine" in the subtitle).

3. The way in which it highlights the ironic juxtaposition of our culture's obsession with physical fitness and the church's relative neglect of its members' spiritual fitness. I have previously used "diet" as a metaphor for how doctrine encourages spiritual

---

6. For parents looking for a guide to discipling their children, I recommend Dillon T. Thornton's *Give Them Jesus: Raising Our Children on the Core Truths of the Christian Faith* (New York: FaithWords, 2018). For parents looking for a guide to helping their children understand contemporary culture, I recommend John Stonestreet and Brett Kunkle, *A Practical Guide to Culture: Helping the Next Generation Navigate Today's World* (Colorado Springs: David C. Cook, 2017).

fitness.[7] Here I expand the image and relate it to
exercise and health as well. The overall aim is to
help pastors view the church as a "fitness culture"
and discipleship as the process of rendering believers *fit for purpose.*

I want to thank several groups who over the past couple of
years served as "hearers" and, if not quite "doers," then interlocutors of the original lectures on doctrine and discipleship that
form the basis for the present book. As a senior fellow in systematic theology for the C. S. Lewis Institute, it has been my privilege to speak regularly at the Fellows Program in Chicago, under
the able leadership of Karl "KJ" Johnson. The C. S. Lewis Institute
exists to develop wholehearted disciples of Jesus Christ who are
able both to articulate and live out their faith. I'm grateful to Dan
Osborne, too, for his invitation to address the Pastor Fellowship
of the Northeast Ohio chapter of the C. S. Lewis Institute in
Youngstown, Ohio. Thanks go to Al Fletcher for his invitation
to address the 2016 Annual Meeting of the American Baptist
Churches of Maine, and to Jack Hunter for the opportunity to
speak at the New Orleans Baptist Association's Fall Meeting in
2018. I am grateful to Jerry Andrews for inviting me to San Diego
to be the keynote speaker at the 2017 Theology Conference of
the Fellowship Community (which Jerry acknowledges is "the
most redundant title in all Christendom"), a "covenanted biblical community" of pastors within the Presbyterian Church
(USA). Finally, I'm grateful to Bob Hansen and Judy Bradish for
their invitation to teach (again) in the "Christian Perspectives"
adult Sunday school class that has been going for fifty-two years

7. See my *The Drama of Doctrine: A Canonical-Linguistic Approach to Christian Theology* (Louisville: Westminster John Knox, 2005), 374–76.

(and counting) at The Orchard, an Evangelical Free Church of America congregation in Arlington Heights, Illinois.

This book would never have seen the light of day without Thom Blair, an instructional designer at Faithlife, who persuaded me to record the material in part 2 for a Logos Mobile Education course, and Jesse Myers of Lexham Press, who convinced me to turn the lectures into a book. I owe my editor Elliot Ritzema a special debt of gratitude for his many insightful comments and suggestions for revising the manuscript. Finally, I am grateful to Ryan Fields for reading the final draft with the eyes of a pastor-theologian, and for offering numerous ideas for improving the argument.

Introduction

FROM DOCTRINE (CHRIST FOR US) TO DISCIPLESHIP (WE FOR CHRIST)

But the one who looks into the perfect law, the law of liberty, and perseveres, being no hearer who forgets but a doer who acts, he will be blessed in his doing. (Jas 1:25)

What does it mean to be biblical? This has become my life question, and it matters for three reasons: first, because the Bible is divine discourse; second, because we need to know Scripture in order to answer the key christological question, Who is Jesus Christ for you today? and third, because we need to know the Bible in order to respond rightly to the follow-up question, *Who are we, for Jesus Christ, today?*[1] In short: what it means to be biblical is inextricably related to what it means to

---

1. John G. Stackhouse Jr., *Making the Best of It: Following Christ in the Real World* (Oxford: Oxford University Press, 2008), 5. Stackhouse's question is a variation of Bonhoeffer's famous reference to "who Christ really is, for us today" (Letter to Eberhard Bethge, April 30, 1944, in Dietrich Bonhoeffer, *Letters and*

be Jesus' disciples, and what form this discipleship should take in the twenty-first century.

All three questions directly relate to how and what I teach in the theology courses that my seminary students, many of whom intend to be pastors, have to take. But why? What does learning doctrine have to do with discipleship or being biblical? In an age of ever-decreasing MDiv credit hours, why spend precious classroom time on theology? What does systematic theology have to do with church ministry and the Christian life? In short, why should pastors study theology?

THE DIVINE CURRICULUM

James 1:22–25 provides the short answer with its metaphor of the wise and foolish lookers. Those who look into the mirror of (that is, listen to) Scripture see themselves as they truly are: children of light, "in Christ." However, if one simply hears the truth but fails to do it, it is like forgetting your true identity. In other words, simply hearing but not doing the truth is like having amnesia. It's an unstable mental condition: you're less likely to behave like a child of the King if you've forgotten you belong to the royal family. Doctrine, like Scripture, teaches disciples who they are "in Christ." Disciples have to understand, and remember, whose Way they belong to.

The longer answer involves saying what the church, and church ministry, is for. If we take the long biblical view, we see that the purpose of the church, like Israel, the first people of God, is to be "a chosen race, a royal priesthood, a holy nation" (1 Pet 2:9). Much of the books of Numbers and Deuteronomy deal with the forty-year period in which the Lord God sought

---

Papers from Prison, ed. Eberhard Bethge, rev. ed. [New York: Touchstone, 1997], 279).

to form Israel into a holy nation, a people worthy of citizenship in the promised land.

The curriculum the Lord God set Israel was hardly a walk in the park. It was rather a forty-year course of wilderness camping and caravanning. This was no aimless wandering, however. The Lord God was teaching Israel how to walk by faith, not by sight. It was the ultimate outdoor education program, a bit like Outward Bound, but for an entire people. Outward Bound's mission is "to change lives through challenge and discovery" and to form "more resilient and compassionate citizens."[2] It was the brainchild of Kurt Hahn, who believes that the sea, mountains, and desert can provide a kind of training that no academic institution can match. These landscapes teach the technical skills necessary for survival, the personal virtues necessary for life, and the interpersonal teamwork necessary for life together. "You are needed" is the watchword: Outward Bound expedition members are "crew, not passengers."

The church, like Israel, is a set-apart people with a set-apart mission: to proclaim, embody, and inhabit the kingdom of God. To use Augustine's image: the church is the city of God, and the purpose of church ministry is to help members live lives worthy of citizens of the gospel (Phil 1:27). Church members are on an Upward Bound expedition, and they too are crew, not passengers. The church's expedition through the world, like Israel's expedition through the wilderness, is the Lord God's way of forming a holy nation.

Discipleship has never been a cakewalk. To follow the cruciform way of Jesus is to wander in the wilderness, as Israel did for forty years, a precursor of Jesus' own forty-day desert trial.

---

2. "Our Mission," Outward Bound, https://www.outwardbound.org/about-outward-bound/outward-bound-today/ (accessed June 23, 2018).

There are streams in the desert, to be sure, but no rose gardens. Yet the church is upward bound because its members' citizenship is in heaven (Phil 3:20). If we keep in mind Augustine's image of the church as the city of God, then theology—the teaching that undergirds living for God as his city—is part and parcel of the Christian's civic responsibility. Theology teaches how to live the good life in light of the good news to the glory of the God alone who is good (Mark 10:18). The Puritan theologian William Ames defines theology more as "that good life whereby we live to God than as that happy life whereby we live to ourselves."[3] Of course, the truly happy life—blessedness—is the good life lived unto God, in friendship and fellowship with the blessed Trinity (1 John 4:13–16). The crucial point is that theology is an eminently practical affair, more *living with* than *writing about* God.

Jesus' Great Commission is all about theology in the sense that I have just defined it. The Great Commission clearly involves more than evangelism. Jesus directs church leaders to "make disciples of all nations" (Matt 28:19). This involves baptizing them in God's Triune name and teaching them to observe everything Jesus has commanded (Matt 28:20). In the early church, baptism was often the graduation ceremony that followed a course of catechism, a question-and-answer form of instruction in the basics of the Christian faith. Those preparing to be baptized were taught what God had done in Christ. Their baptism then showed who they were in Christ: members of his body who had died to the old way of living and were raised to life in Christ's Spirit. Baptism is the port of entry into discipleship and involves much more than signing on the dotted line of church

---

3. William Ames, *The Marrow of Theology* (Grand Rapids: Baker Books, 1968), 77.

membership. To be baptized as a disciple is to enter a way of life, bound to Christ (Eph 6:6) and upward bound to God.

C. S. Lewis knew what church ministry is ultimately for: "The Church exists for nothing else but to draw men into Christ, to make them little Christs. If they are not doing that, all the cathedrals, clergy, missions, sermons, even the Bible itself, are simply a waste of time. God became Man for no other purpose. It is even doubtful, you know, whether the whole universe was created for any other purpose."[4] Lewis is exactly right, though he could have added biblical interpretation and theology to his list of time-wasting activities—*if* they do not result in the building-up of disciples.

The church does other important things as well. Most notably, it organizes and conducts worship services. Yet it does so in large part to form people into those who can worship in spirit and in truth (John 4:24), people who know how to present their bodies "as a living sacrifice, holy and acceptable to God" (Rom 12:1). We worship rightly when we live in ways that demonstrate the supreme worthiness of God and God's word. God does not desire ritual sacrifice; instead, he wants his people to know and love him (Hos 6:6).

FOLLOWING THE WAY OF JESUS

This, then, is the topic of the present book, and the answer to the question, Why should pastors study theology? So that they can better know whom they worship, and learn how to form others into true worshipers who know how to worship, and to walk, in spirit and truth (John 4:22-24). Theology serves the

---

4. C. S. Lewis, *Mere Christianity* (New York: Touchstone, 1996), 199.

church largely because *doctrine serves discipleship*. So does biblical interpretation when done the right way.

The notion that doctrine and the theological interpretation of the Bible are practical may seem counterintuitive. Indeed, the picture of abstract, impractical doctrine is often the default assumption of those who dismiss theology as merely academic, and seminaries as "cemeteries." This prejudice against doctrine speaks to the low level of theological literacy in many churches.[5] Praise choruses and moralistic sermons are not enough to feed our malnourished imaginations. Inspirational thoughts work well on greeting cards, not as the main point of sermons. My hope is that the present book will help pastors recover Calvin's vision for theology as a help to reading the Bible in ways that enliven and encourage disciples to walk its way of wisdom. Let me go further: I believe the church today ministers most practically when it teaches people to read the Bible theologically, that is, to hear and do God's word.

Why does doctrine matter? Primarily because without it, we could not answer Jesus' question to his disciples, "Who do you say that I am?" (Matt 16:15). Christian doctrine sets forth in speech who Jesus Christ is (Christology), why he had to suffer (sin), how his death on the cross effected salvation (atonement), how we relate to him (pneumatology), how we benefit from his death (soteriology), how the Spirit assembles the firstfruit of the new creation in Christ (ecclesiology), and what happens when he returns (eschatology). In order to say who Jesus is, we also need the doctrines of God, the Trinity, and creation, because his

---

5. I acknowledge that theologians are often to blame for this. For example, it's disappointing that there is no entry on discipleship in the *New Dictionary of Theology: Historical and Systematic*, 2nd ed. (Downers Grove, IL: IVP Academic, 2016).

story does not start with his birth to Mary, but with his eternal fellowship with the Father in the Spirit and with all things being made through him. Finally, because Jesus Christ is true God and true man, we also need to say something about the doctrine of humanity. Virtually every topic in systematic theology is necessary if we are to respond rightly to Jesus' question.

We are now in a better position to see how doctrine (the answer to the question, Who is Jesus Christ for us today?) is related to discipleship (the answer to the question, Who are we for Jesus Christ today?). To make disciples we have to know what it is for humans to exist in, for, with, and through Jesus Christ.

Jesus himself cared about making disciples; he called disciples to make disciples: "Go therefore and make disciples of all nations, baptizing them in the name of the Father and of the Son and of the Holy Spirit, teaching them to observe all that I have commanded you" (Matt 28:19). That Jesus cares about discipleship means he also cares about theology, that is, about helping those he calls to discern and follow "the Way" (Acts 9:2). Churches need to know their doctrine because we live in a pluralistic society that offers many "ways" to live. Christians need to know what Jesus meant when he claimed to be "the way, and the truth, and the life" (John 14:6), for a disciple is essentially one who walks in this Way. The church is the social embodiment of this Way, and theology, at its core, is about knowing and loving this Way, the Way of the Father's Son, in the Spirit, into the wilderness—and back again, to the Father.

Theology is about learning how to live out Christ's life in us (Gal 2:20), a life that includes cruciform wisdom (1 Cor 2:2) and resurrection power (Phil 3:10). It is about helping the church to understand the biblical story of which it is a part. Indeed, the church is, in one sense, the conclusion to the whole sweeping narrative of Scripture inasmuch as the church is a microcosm of what God is doing to remake creation in Jesus Christ through the Holy Spirit.

Theology is about making disciples by teaching believers how to walk in this newness: "Jesus' summons is a summons to life."[6] Theology sets out the new reality in Christ and urges disciples to step into it—in other words, to step out in faith, with understanding, on the Way of Jesus Christ. Theology has acquired a bad reputation largely because theologians have not always made it clear how practical—how good for walking—it is. I'm going to ask you to think about Christian theology in a way that might be new to you, though really it is an attempt to retrieve an earlier way of doing theology—for the church! Before it became a university department, theology was done in, for, and by the church, and it was done to help people mature in the knowledge of Jesus Christ.

FROM HEARING TO DOING

How exactly does learning doctrine lead to learning how we can be for Jesus Christ today? In Matthew 4:19 Jesus comes across two brothers, Simon and Andrew, who happened to be fishermen, and he says to them, "Follow me, and I will make you fishers of men." To be a "fisher of men" is to engage in evangelism, a proclamation of the good news that the Jesus crucified for our sins is alive and seated at the right hand of God, Lord of all. The aim of evangelism is to make converts, people who believe the gospel, repent of their former way of life, a bonfire of the vanities, and face a new direction—Christward. A convert is one who has repented of the past, turns around, and faces the future

---

6. John Webster, "Discipleship and Calling," *Scottish Bulletin of Evangelical Theology* 23 (2005): 138.

with faith in Jesus. A disciple is one who does not simply face a new direction but begins to walk in it. A disciple is a convert in motion, on the way. Jesus cared about making and *growing* disciples, helping them to mature.

Some converts, though they may be facing in the right direction, have not yet learned to walk. They need to be taught the basic principles of Christianity—the ABCs—which the author of Hebrews likens to milk (Heb 5:12–13). In contrast, more advanced teaching is "solid food ... for the mature" (Heb 5:14). A good pastor, like a parent, wants to provide nurturing fare: "Or which one of you, if his son asks him for bread, will give him a stone?" (Matt 7:7). Similarly, which pastor, if his congregants ask him for abundant life, will give them a truism? What disciples truly need is the know-how to live by "every word that comes from the mouth of God" (Matt 4:4).

Making disciples involves more (but not less) than informing minds or forming habits. It also involves transforming imaginations, that is, the primary ways they see, think about, and experience life. This is an enormously challenging, immensely rewarding, and strategically vital task. What is a pastor to do? *Hearers and Doers* is an attempt to answer this question and to provide concrete guidance for pastors.

THE PLAN OF THE BOOK

In part 1 I examine the problems and possibilities for discipleship today. I argue that everyone is always following someone else's words, whether in the form of images (metaphors) or stories, and that these words are potentially disciple-making insofar as they arrest the imagination and hold it captive (ch. 1). I then examine the words, images, and stories about wellness, nutrition, and fitness that dominate large swaths of contemporary culture, and suggest that secular culture is itself a powerful disciple-making force that pastor-theologians need to understand and, when need be, call out (ch. 2).

Thanks be to God: the Bible frees the captive imagination, enabling disciples to wake up to the false images that hold us captive and walk instead in the truth of what they see in the mirror of Scripture. Jesus, Paul, and James all agree that hearing alone without doing falls short of genuine discipleship. Moreover, doing the truth involves more than being moral. Discipleship is less about ethics than it is about eschatology, by which I mean the breaking-in of the kingdom of God in Christ. This awakening to the new reality announced in the gospel requires a biblically formed imagination (ch. 3).

Pastors have the privilege and responsibility of freeing captive imaginations by preaching the gospel and teaching Christian doctrine. Scripture and doctrine are the primary means for making disciples because they cultivate Christian literacy: what every Christian needs to know in order to become a competent citizen of the gospel. Training is required—in particular, training in reading Scripture rightly, which among other things involves seeing oneself as a participant in a God-driven drama of redemption. In this and in other ways, Scripture informs belief and behavior, *and* transforms the imagination to make one wise and fit for purpose (ch. 4).

In part 2 I give pastors tools and suggestions with which to make the vision sketched in part 1 visible. Accordingly, each chapter proposes three theological "core exercises" designed to help pastors train disciples to make God's word the primary imaginative framework and plausibility structure for their daily lives and respond to it with belief, obedience, and trust.

I begin by urging pastors to reclaim their Protestant Reformation heritage. This involves seeing disciples, as well as the church itself, as creatures of the word. Everything starts with seeing the church theologically, as it really is—a people God has gathered through his Son and Spirit. The pastor must be a theologian: someone who can relate life in general, and the lives of his congregation, to what Scripture shows us the Father doing in Christ through the Spirit to renew creation. A brief survey of four key Reformation principles helps to orient pastors to their vocation as ministers of God's word. I encourage pastors today to recover *sola Scriptura*, and in particular insist that "Scripture alone" should rule the church's social imaginary. Indeed, if there is anything fresh in my approach to this well-worn topic, it may be my insistence that *sola Scriptura* has a role to play in making disciples. If the imagination pertains to what Paul calls the "eyes of the hearts" (Eph 1:18), then pastors ought to be eye doctors who correct the astigmatisms and myopias of the local church (ch. 5).

One false picture of Christianity is that it is primarily about an individual's relationship to God. While it is true that we relate to God as individuals, modern individualism has distorted and blown this out of all proportion, eclipsing God's concern for the church as a gathered community. The story of Scripture is about God's purpose to form a holy nation, which means the disciple is a member of a company. In chapter 6, I present doctrine as a kind of theatrical direction that helps disciples both understand the whole story of salvation and their particular part in it. Doctrine makes disciples by helping people become fit for the purpose of playing their parts as followers of Jesus. I also argue that the local church and its regular worship practices are themselves a crucial training ground for Christian life and for learning how local bodies can make "Christly gestures."

One of the great challenges of making disciples today is the skepticism about institutions and about knowledge claims in general. So many churches believe and behave in different ways, yet they all claim to be following Jesus. Which path should a would-be disciple follow? In response, in chapter 7 I make the perhaps counterintuitive argument that the best way to remain Protestant, and to uphold the supreme authority of Scripture, is to make *catholic* disciples—men and women who become part of the whole (universal) church, and are thus attuned to the remarkable consensus reflected in the Great Tradition, something the Protestant Reformers cared about and maintained. I contend that local Bible churches belong to this catholic church, and that the catholic church is simply the sum total of local Bible churches. What's at stake is the *kind* of disciples we're making: should they be rugged individuals, where everyone reads the Bible in a way that is right in his or her own eyes, or members of the communion of saints?

After arguing for the importance of Scripture, doctrine, the liturgy, and tradition, in chapter 8 I turn my attention to the content of discipleship: Christlikeness. Being a disciple involves more than admiring Christ, or even imitating his example; it involves becoming like him (Matt 10:25). I argue that this is not a matter of becoming mirror images but rather *fitting* images, that is, people who embody the mind of Christ everywhere, always, and to everyone. After reviewing a number of key ideas, I go on to suggest that doctrine should be the disciple's diet and that the local church is an evangelical fitness culture, a place to make disciples *fit* for the purpose of being fitting images of Christ. Making disciples involves not only learning but also *putting on* Christ. Here, too, I suggest three core exercises for improving the disciple's core strength.

The book concludes by contrasting the life of the archetypal self-made man with that of the follower of Jesus, and with a final exhortation to make disciples fit for the purpose of glorifying God in all they do and say.

PART ONE

Warming Up:
Why Discipleship Matters

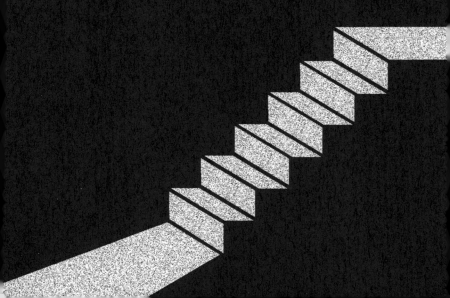

1

THE ROLE OF
THEOLOGY IN
MAKING DISCIPLES

Some Important Preliminaries

Two very different films frame the concern of the present book.

The 2008 Pixar animated film *Wall-E* offers pointed social commentary. Like many science-fiction films, its story is set in the future, but what motivates it is a very present environmental concern.

The film depicts a traumatized earth and a future society of consumers who have so depleted the world of its resources and, in the process, created so much rubbish that it is not darkness that covers the earth but debris—piles and piles of it (in contrast to the robot-hero, Wall-E, who recycles). In fact, there's so much garbage on the earth that all of humanity has to take to space in search of a new place to live, a new world with new raw materials to consume. However, a good planet is hard to find, and old habits die hard, so, after seven hundred years of life on board their "Executive Starliners," where all tasks have become automated and there is no garden to keep, the humans have developed into full-time consumers who do nothing but eat and enjoy asocial media. They are too bloated even to get up off their deck chairs. One critic says that the film describes humankind as "obese, infantile consumers who spend their days immobile in hovering lounge chairs, staring at ads on computer screens—in other words, Americans."[1] Ironically, the human passengers aboard the *Axiom* are more robotic than Wall-E, for they passively allow themselves to be programmed by whatever program, or advertisement, they happen to be watching. They are sleeping with their eyes wide open, glued to their electronic devices. Sound familiar?

The second film, *Cold Souls*, is a "metaphysical tragicomedy" that also comes wrapped in science fiction. It appeared a year later and features Paul Giamatti as an anxious New York actor (a fictionalized version of himself) who has trouble disassociating himself from the characters he plays, a problem that takes a significant emotional toll. As he struggles with his current role, in Chekhov's emotionally fraught play *Uncle Vanya*, whose protagonist is stuck in a melancholic funk, Paul decides to avail himself of a high-tech company that promises to deliver a life free of angst by extracting his soul and then putting it into deep-freeze storage. The idea is that, once divested of their souls, people can enjoy relief from all the emotional burdens and existential sorrows that afflict and weigh them down. Accordingly,

---

1. Dana Stevens, "Robot Wisdom: Wall-E Reviewed," *Slate*, June 26, 2008, http://www.slate.com/articles/arts/movies/2008/06/robot_wisdom.html. Another critic sees the film as a daring attack on "a culture of consumption" (Joe Romm, "Wall-E Is an Eco-dystopian Gem—an Anti-consumption Movie (from Disney!)," ThinkProgress, July 16, 2008, https://thinkprogress.org/wall-e-is-an-eco-dystopian-gem-an-anti-consumption-movie-from-disney-eacc10a75b76/).

he undergoes the procedure, piercing to the division of soul and body, only to discover that his soul resembles a puny chickpea. Being soulless helps neither his marriage nor his acting, however, so he returns to the company and leases a Russian poet's soul to give more authenticity to his performance of Chekhov's play. His acting improves, but his marriage doesn't. Eventually, Paul decides to get his own soul back, only to discover that it has been stolen by someone who thinks *she* can become a better actor by implanting Paul's soul. The film depicts humans as tormented souls who move through life searching, unsuccessfully, for meaning.

These two films may not represent the state of the art in thinking about bodies and souls, but they do represent the state of contemporary social imaginings about what it is to be human and in what human flourishing consists. Elsewhere I have sounded the alarm about how the imaginations of many churchgoers are being held captive by secular pictures of human flourishing and the good life.[2] It is an alarm worth sounding again, for what rules our imaginations—the pictures and stories that yield self-understanding and give coherence to everyday life—orients us to the world and directs our steps toward success. The time, energy, and money we spend during our roughly fourscore years on the world's stage is largely a function of the stories and images of human flourishing in which we believe and put our trust.

---

2. See my "The Discarded Imagination: Metaphors by Which a Holy Nation Lives," in *Pictures at a Theological Exhibition: Scenes of the Church's Worship, Witness and Wisdom* (Downers Grove, IL: IVP Academic, 2016), 17–46.

KINGDOM PICTURES
ISRAEL LIVED BY

Consider the kings of Israel. Each of them had a certain picture of what he wanted his kingdom to be. No doubt many of these pictures were influenced by the many kingdoms that surrounded Israel. Where else would they get their pictures of "successful" kings? Indeed, the Israelites got the very idea of having a king in the first place because everyone else seemed to be doing it. The elders of Israel approached Samuel with just this logic: "We want a king over us. Then we will be like all the other nations, with a king to lead us and to go out before us and fight our battles" (1 Sam 8:19-20 NIV). Interestingly, some of Jesus' disciples were in danger of making the same error when they thought the kingdom of heaven he came proclaiming would reinstate the kind of Davidic earthly monarchy marked by military might and political power (John 18:36). Even after his resurrection, his disciples' imaginations were still captive to certain stereotypes and misconceptions of the kingdom: "They asked him, 'Lord, will you at this time restore the kingdom to Israel?'" (Acts 1:6). I wonder: how different are disciples today?

Back to Israel's kings and concept of kingdom. As I was saying, the imaginations of most of the kings after David and Solomon, especially in the northern kingdom, were captive to secular pictures of what successful kingdoms were supposed to look like. The basic error of these Israelite kings was to trust in human resources (fighting men, chariots, silver, gold) instead of the word of the Lord. To place one's ultimate trust in anything but the Lord God is to commit idolatry, ascribing worth to the worthless (mute and impotent images made of wood and stone). What is of particular significance is how the misleading royal/social imagination led to the wrong kind of walking. This description of Jehoram is typical: "And he walked in the way of the kings of Israel. ... And he did what was evil in the sight of the Lord" (2 Kgs 8:18). Or again: "But Jehu was not careful to walk in the law of the LORD, the God of Israel, with all his heart" (2 Kgs 10:31). It gets worse: "He [Ahaz] did not do what was right in the eyes of the LORD his God ... but he walked in the way of the kings of Israel. He even burned his son as an offering, according to the despicable practices of the nations" (2 Kgs 16:2–3). A false picture of kingship held them captive, though they were of course personally responsible for their idolatry.

Not all the kings were evil. Josiah, for example, discovered the words of the covenant with the LORD God, and this fueled his imagination enough to work important reforms (2 Kgs 23). In reminding Israel's kings of God's word, the prophets were purveyors of what Walter Brueggemann calls a "counter-reality," a different way of thinking about and socially embodying power, success, and justice.[3]

In the end, however, it was not enough simply to listen to the word God spoke through the prophets. The hearing fell on hearts hardened by a false picture of what a successful nation looked like. What counted was what Israel did, and the kings, representing the whole nation, did not walk in the way of the LORD. In an event of poetic justice, Israel eventually got a king like the other nations—the king of Assyria, who captured the capital, Samaria, and took all the Israelites from the northern kingdom away. The Bible is clear about the cause-and-effect relationship: "And this [exile] occurred because the people of Israel had sinned against the LORD their God ... and had feared other gods and walked in the customs of the nations" (2 Kgs 17:7–8). The holy nation had defiled itself.

---

3. Walter Brueggemann, *The Prophetic Imagination*, 2nd ed. (Minneapolis: Fortress, 2001), 83.

THE CHURCH AS
HOLY NATION

The church, like Israel, is called to be a "holy nation" (1 Pet 2:9). Peter also calls the church a "chosen race" and a "royal priesthood." The church is not only an assembly of individuals but also a social reality—but of what kind? Church history is full of suggestions: everything from "Holy Roman Empire" to "counterculture." In this book, I want to focus on the striking biblical image of the church as the corporate *body* of Jesus Christ, composed of many *embodied* persons. What body image rules how we think about the church? Many may be tempted to think of the church as only another earthly institution whose dynamics can be studied, explained, and improved on by psychologists, sociologists, or those with PhDs in institutional management.

The apostle Paul, for his part, is more interested in body-building. And so, he thinks, is the Lord Jesus Christ: "He gave the apostles, the prophets, the evangelists, the shepherds and teachers, to equip the saints for the work of ministry, for building up the body of Christ" (Eph 4:11–12). Church leaders do this partly by building up the individuals that are its members. What disciples do with their bodies contributes to the building up of the body of Christ. Moreover, contra popular opinion, our bodies are not our own, to be used anyway we like. They are rather temples of the Holy Spirit, constructed on the basis of Jesus' pouring out his own body for our sake: "You are not your own, for you were bought with a price" (1 Cor 6:19–20). Pastors are to engage in bodybuilding to God's glory by awakening disciples to the reality that their bodies are members and instruments of Christ's: "So glorify God in your body" (1 Cor 6:20).

Making disciples, then, involves more than converting souls. It involves bodybuilding, that is, edifying the church. We build the church by building up the body one member at a time. However, it is not yet clear what pictures and which images we ought to have in mind to guide us in thinking of building up the body. How exactly do we glorify God in our bodies? Who can tell us what to do with our bodies?

There is probably no more damaging picture distorting our present-day lives, and our understanding of the God of the gospel, than "love." Love is often depicted as a desire to be fulfilled (romanticism) or as accepting people for who they are (inclusivism) or as loyalty to one's own people group (tribalism). The love stories produced by Hollywood suggest that fulfilling love's desire is an unadulterated good—even if it may involve adultery, if the marriage is stale and unfulfilling. Love is presented as an intrinsically good emotion, never mind the sexes, genders, and increasingly, numbers of people involved. Some believe that love must be "free" of all obligations, especially the social bondage of monogamous marriage. Given this romanticized, sentimentalized, and politicized image, it should be no surprise that many view the Bible's portrait of God as a jealous judge to be past its sell-by date.

As we'll see in chapter 2, there are plenty of other images—particularly of wellness, health, and fitness—in secular culture. Our pictures of human flourishing are as ancient as their contemporaries. Salus was the Roman goddess of welfare, health, and prosperity. *Salus* is also the Latin term for "salvation." Should citizens of the church, a holy nation, be disciples of Salus and worship at her shrine with her other devotees? Christians today must take care not to repeat ancient Israel's mistake, adopting idolatrous practices out of a desire to be like the other nations. The church today may not be in danger of worshiping idols made of wood and stone, but it is in danger of trusting the wrong things—programs, techniques, ideologies, even theologies—instead of fearing the Lord, walking according to his word, and pursuing *salus* in Christ.

TRANSFORMING THE SOCIAL IMAGINARY "IN ACCORDANCE WITH THE SCRIPTURES"

One of the key prophetic tasks of theology is to free the church, a holy nation, from idols. This includes false ideologies and metaphors and stories that guide and govern a people's way of life. That's the negative task of theology: to call out false beliefs and false practices *and* the false ways of imagining the world that fund them. Pastor-theologians therefore need to have at least a basic understanding not only of the Scriptures but also of the context disciples inhabit. The cultural context deeply influences the way people experience, interpret, think about, and seek to live out the gospel. To Socrates' adage "Know thyself" we must add, "Know thy culture."

The philosopher Charles Taylor, in his book *A Secular Age*, helpfully draws attention to the importance of the *social imaginary* for understanding our present cultural context. A social imaginary is the picture that frames our everyday beliefs and practices, in particular the "ways people imagine their social existence."[4] The social imaginary is that nest of background assumptions, often implicit, that lead people to feel things as right or wrong, correct or incorrect. It is another name for the root metaphor (or root narrative) that shapes a person's perception of the world, undergirds one's worldview, and funds one's

---

4. Charles Taylor, *A Secular Age* (Cambridge, MA: Belknap Press of Harvard University Press, 2007), 171.

plausibility structure.[5] For example, the root metaphor of "world as machine" generates a very different picture than "world as organism." To "know thy culture," then, we have to become more specific: "Know thy worldview, and the root metaphor that generates and governs it."

Sociologist Peter Berger first called attention to how the modern and postmodern world pictures made religious traditions and the idea of the sacred seem less plausible.[6] The emphasis here is on "social" rather than "intellectual": a social imaginary is not a theory—the creation of intellectuals—but a storied way of thinking. It is the taken-for-granted story of the world assumed and passed on by a society's characteristic language, pictures, and practices. A social imaginary is not taught in universities but by cultures, insofar as it is "carried in images, stories, and legends."[7] People become secular not by taking classes in Secularity 101 but simply by participating in a society that no longer refers to God the way it used to. "God" makes only rare appearances in contemporary literature, art, and television.

Social imaginaries, then, are the metaphors and stories by which we live, the images and narratives that indirectly indoctrinate us. Yes, we have all been indoctrinated: filled with doctrine or teaching. The doctrines we hold, be they philosophical, political, or theological, feel right or wrong, plausible or implausible, based largely on how well they accord with the prevailing social imaginary or world picture. What I have called above the "negative task" of theology is to critically reflect on the way in which the church embodies the prevailing social imaginaries

---

5. On the idea of a root metaphor, see Stephen C. Pepper, *World Hypothesis: A Study in Evidence* (Berkley: University of California Press, 1970), ch. 5.

6. Peter Berger, *The Sacred Canopy* (Garden City, NY: Doubleday, 1967).

7. Taylor, *A Secular Age*, 172.

of the day rather than the biblical imaginary—the true story of what the Triune God is doing in the world. Pastor-theologians do not fight against flesh and blood, but against social powers and ideological principalities.

One important way theology helps church leaders to make disciples is by better enabling them to critically examine the images and stories by which Christians live in light of the biblical images and stories by which they ought to live. Chief among these is, of course, the story of Jesus Christ, the climax of the story begun in the Old Testament concerning Adam, Abraham, and Israel.

The apostle Paul is worth imitating in this regard, for he clearly saw how the story of Jesus' lordship differed from, and subverted, the prevailing Roman story of Caesar's lordship, going so far as to identify his own personal story with Jesus' passion narrative: "I have been crucified with Christ" (Gal 2:20). For Paul, there was only one image and one story that ought to govern the Christian life: the gospel. *Theology serves the church by helping to shape its collective imagination so that its image of its body life, and everything else, is governed by the gospel message at the heart of the master story that unifies Scripture*: what God was doing by anticipation in Israel, and ultimately in Christ, to provide light to the nations, reconcile all things to himself, and renew creation. This is a very different picture of *salus* than that offered by the Roman goddess or by today's spiritual gurus.

Jesus was a master storyteller, and the stories he told were designed to transform the disciples' social imaginary. He wanted his disciples to be hearers and doers who understood what they were doing in terms of the stories he told and the story of the Messiah he was living out. Consider what he said and did on the night he was betrayed. He took bread, gave thanks, broke it, gave it to the disciples, and said, "This is my body, which is given for you. Do this in remembrance of me" (Luke 22:19; cf. 1 Cor 11:24).

The Lord's Supper is a striking image that is easily misunderstood. According to one second-century dialogue, some Romans thought Christians practiced a form of cannibalism.[8] They simply could not make sense of the Supper according to their social imaginary, which did not consider weakness or self-sacrifice a virtue. Of course, Christians hear and understand the Supper as an image that points to a very different story. To participate in the Lord's Supper is to "proclaim the Lord's death until he comes" (1 Cor 11:26) and to celebrate the result of that death, namely, the incorporation of people from all tribes and classes into a single communion. This is not cannibalism but a grace-enabled communalism: to partake of the body of Christ is to celebrate one's incorporation into Christ and thus into the family of God. One cannot discern the body (see 1 Cor 11:29), and hence the real meaning of the Supper, however, apart from the social imaginary generated and governed by the gospel.

The gospel is the theme and climax of the storied social imaginary and plausibility structure that constitutes the church, informs its beliefs, and rules its practices. No other social imaginary is as subversive of ethnic, religious, and class distinctions as is the Christian gospel. Because all who trust in Christ as their Lord and Savior are members of one body, "There is neither Jew nor Greek, there is neither slave nor free, there is no male and female, for you are all one in Christ Jesus" (Gal 3:28). In an era when nations close borders against nation, when people groups within the nations rage, the church's practice of

---

8. See Minucius Felix, *Octavius* 30, *Ante-Nicene Fathers*, ed. Alexander Roberts, James Donaldson, and A. Cleveland Coxe (Buffalo, NY: Christian Literature, 1885), 4:192, rev. Kevin Knight, New Advent, http://www.newadvent.org/fathers/0410.htm. See also Athenagoras, *Plea for the Christians* 35.

multiethnic fellowship in Christ stands out—when, that is, it's actually practiced.

The church has its own story to live by—the gospel of Jesus Christ. Think of theology as *critical reflection on the stories by which the church lives and which it lives out.* These stories, alas, are as often nonbiblical as they are biblical, hence theology's responsibility to sort out what is of culture only and what is genuinely of the gospel. If the church is to make disciples, it needs to do theology to make sure it is helping people to follow the gospel rather than some Madison Avenue campaign for luxury cars or some cleverly devised Hollywood myth of forbidden love (see 2 Pet 1:16).

The biblical story of salvation must not be confused with the false gospel of physical *salus.* Pastors must remain vigilant, guarding not only the orthodoxy of statements of faith but also the imaginations of their congregants. The next chapter therefore conducts a case study in helping pastors discern the signs— and social imaginaries—of the times. Sleepers, awake!

2

WHOSE FITNESS?
WHICH BODY IMAGE?

*Toward Understanding the Present
North American Social Imaginary*

There is only one gospel, but four authorized accounts. The story of Jesus is true, though it is imagined in four ways, and the church is the richer for it. The rest of the New Testament is apostolic reflection on the gospel and its implications. This includes the letters of Paul, all of which have what Richard Hays calls a "narrative sub-structure."[1] Paul's theology owes everything to the evangelical imaginary that Jesus is Lord.

If I had to sum up in one sentence what Paul is trying to do in most of his letters, I would say that he is setting forth a new imaginary grounded in the new reality inaugurated in Jesus Christ, then asking church members to live in accordance with this reality. There is no other gospel precisely because there is

---

1. Richard B. Hays, *The Faith of Jesus Christ: The Narrative Substructure of Galatians 3:1–4:11*, 2nd ed. (Grand Rapids: Eerdmans, 2002).

no other reality, no other reliable way to meaning, truth, salvation, eternal life, and fellowship with God.

Paul was astonished, however, at how quickly the early church was deserting the gospel of Jesus Christ (Gal 1:6). This was every bit as shocking as Israel's defection from her covenant with the Lord God. The sobering question is whether the present-day church is also tempted to desert the gospel. Eugene Peterson's paraphrase of Galatians 1:6–7 sounds as though Paul might have written it yesterday: "I can't believe your fickleness—how easily you have turned traitor to him who called you by the grace of Christ by embracing a variant message! It is not a minor variation, you know; it is completely other, an alien message, a no-message, a lie about God."[2] The no-message is in fact an alternative social imaginary, a set of pictures and stories of the good life, and of the church, that lead away from Christ instead of toward him.

There is only one gospel—the good news of Jesus Christ—but there is unfortunately an abundance of *fake* news: bogus messages about the good life; counterfeit gospels. Theology helps the church make disciples by exposing the lie—the false social imaginaries that often hold even church members captive (the negative, critical task)—and by redirecting them to the way, truth, and life of Jesus Christ (the positive, indicative task).

To make disciples we have to wake disciples—wake them to the metaphors and myths of which secular culture is an expert purveyor. This chapter explores the well-documented North American obsession with the health, fitness, and well-being of our physical bodies. This social imaginary, which places such value on the physical body, stands in striking contrast to the

2. Eugene H. Peterson, *The Message: The New Testament in Contemporary Language* (Colorado Springs: NavPress, 1993), 459.

widespread indifference to the health, fitness, and well-being of the body of Christ—and to the importance of what individual church members do with their own physical bodies to glorify God.

Viewing the church as the body of Christ is a well-known biblical metaphor suggested by Jesus himself. This alone should give us pause. Jesus taught in parables—metaphors extended into narratives. A parable describes the kingdom of God in terms of images drawn from elsewhere: "The kingdom of God is like ..." The point, not to be missed, is that Jesus himself understood the power of metaphors and stories (the stuff of social imaginaries) in making disciples. Richard Hays says that New Testament ethics is largely a matter of having one's moral vision shaped by imaginative stories. For Hays, thinking biblically involves "metaphor-making, placing our community's life imaginatively within the world articulated by the texts."[3]

The process of making disciples involves both deprogramming (exposing, critiquing, and correcting the pictures and stories we live by) and reprogramming (replacing the "old self" and the social imaginaries that funded our former way of life with the social imaginary generated by Scripture and the gospel). Accordingly, I will first expose some of the most important and powerful cultural myths of our day, some of which hold even Christians captive. This is the first step in taking every thought, and social imaginary, captive to obey Christ (2 Cor 10:5).

To begin making disciples, then, we must get clear on the picture that currently holds the social imagination, and some churches too, in its grip. Accordingly, this chapter analyzes three

---

3. Richard B. Hays, *The Moral Vision of the New Testament: A Contemporary Introduction to New Testament Ethics* (San Francisco: HarperSanFrancisco, 1996), 299.

strands of a cultural cord as concerns our image of the body: the medical strand, the diet strand, and the fitness strand.

MEDICINE AND HEALTH
CARE: MAKING WELL

Get well soon. What used to be a greeting card is now a philosophy of life. In the past, people went to the doctor or to the hospital when they were sick. These days, they're as likely to pursue "wellness" even when they're not ill—say, by spending a weekend in a spa. Everyone wants to be well, of course. One of the first things foreign-language students learn to say is "How are you?" It's a concern we see in the Bible too.

When Jacob traveled to visit his uncle, the first thing he asked when he arrived was, "Is it well with him?" (Gen 29:6). The Hebrew term behind "well" is *shalom*, one of the richest and most important terms in the Old Testament, occurring more than two hundred times. It can apply to either individuals or groups and connotes peace, soundness, harmony, and completeness. "Peace" is not simply the absence of conflict but something altogether more positive: wholeness. To wish someone well (*Shalom!*) is to express concern for their general welfare. Ultimately, God alone is the source of true *shalom*.

The Septuagint, the Greek translation of the Old Testament, often uses *eirēnē* (peace) to translate *shalom*. Paul's claim in Ephesians 2:14 is thus all the more impressive when, after mentioning the blood of Christ, he declares, "For he himself is our peace." I also find it striking that Jesus, instead of asking, "How are you?" says instead, "Peace to you" (Luke 24:36) or "Go in peace" (Luke 8:48). We also find references to being made well in the New Testament. The woman who had suffered from a discharge of blood for twelve years said to herself, "If I only touch his garment, I will be made well" (Matt 9:21). And she was. The term Matthew uses in this context is *sōzō*, which also means "to save." *Salus*, a Latin term we have already encountered, meaning "health," is the origin of our English word *salvation*. In the New Testament, context helps to ascertain which sense or senses of the term is in view, the physical and/or spiritual. It is important not to lose sight of the spiritual dimension, and the indispensability of Jesus Christ: "For he himself is our wellness" (cf. Eph 2:14).

An analysis of the role of wellness in contemporary culture helps us see how far we have moved beyond the biblical picture. Modern culture has both secularized and paganized the concept of wellness, either shrinking the notion of *shalom* to the level of the physical and the individual or expanding it to the level of the spiritual and cosmic. This change in the social imaginary of what it means to be well has repercussions, not only in our concept of the good life, but also in our concept of the good news of Jesus Christ.

In the twenty-first century, *wellness* has become a national obsession, and big business. A handful of scholars suggest that the pursuit of well-being defines our present age, where the "workout ethic" has replaced the Protestant "work ethic."[4] Consider the Global Wellness Institute (GWI), a nonprofit organization whose mission is "to empower wellness worldwide by educating public and private sectors about preventative health and wellness."[5] Their vision is to be "the recognized global wellness authority" for businesses and organizations dedicated to ensuring optimal well-being to people around the globe. You

---

4. See, for example, Carl Cederström and André Spicer, *The Wellness Syndrome* (Cambridge: Polity, 2015); William Davies, *The Happiness Industry: How the Government and Big Business Sold Us Well-Being* (London: Verso, 2015).

5. From "About Us," Global Wellness Institute, https://globalwellnessinstitute.org/about-us/ (accessed June 28, 2018).

have to applaud their ambition of wanting to influence "the overall wellbeing of our planet and its citizens." One of their initiatives is the "Wellness Moonshot"—an international team of wellness leaders committed "to eradicate chronic, preventable disease worldwide by uniting the health and wellness industries." Since 2007, the GWI has also commissioned research on wellness, such as *The Global Wellness Economy Monitor 2017*.

I recommend visiting the GWI webpage titled "History of Wellness."[6] It is not simply informative, but revealing. You'll learn, for example, that the English term *wellness* originally meant the opposite of *illness* and dates from the 1650s. While they acknowledge that the concept of wellness has ancient roots, the article notes that the word gained considerable traction only starting in the second half of the twentieth century, with the publication of books like John Travis's 1981 *The Wellness Workbook: How to Achieve Enduring Health and Vitality*. It was not until the twenty-first century, however, that wellness entered the social vocabulary and collective unconscious. Several American universities now encourage new students to sign "wellness contracts" when they arrive on campus.

If you want to know what fuels the present-day social imaginary, follow the money: the GWI estimates that global wellness fuels a $3.7 trillion economy, more than three times larger than the global pharmaceutical industry (beauty and anti-aging programs and products alone amounted to almost $1 trillion). The sectors include the spa industry, wellness tourism, anti-aging, workplace wellness, and alternative medicine. The latter covers wellness practices such as acupressure, aromatherapy, biofeedback, chiropractic, massage, meditation, tai chi, and yoga. These

---

6. "History of Wellness," Global Wellness Institute, https://globalwellnessinstitute.org/industry-research/history-of-wellness/ (accessed June 28, 2018).

are the everyday practices that seem normal to a secular social imaginary that understands wellness as does the World Health Organization: "as a state of complete physical, mental and social well-being."[7]

Hotels have for some time now offered various fitness options, but increasingly wellness has become the reason for traveling. So-called wellness tourists made 691 million "wellness trips" in 2015, spending in excess of $500 billion, according to the GWI. For example, a resort in Phuket, Thailand, offers four wellness immersion programs, including digestive cleanses and mental awareness sessions. Instead of staying well while you travel, wellness has become both purpose and destination.

If you want to profit from other people's desire for wellness, check out the GWI web page on global wellness trends, where you will find a list of the wellness initiatives destined to become big business in the years ahead. One new trend is the pursuit of *extreme* wellness, using "biohacking" (the tag line: "building a better you through biology") and cutting-edge procedures like DNA/biomarker testing to come up with a "hyper-personal road-map." This is just one of many enhancement technologies that offer the tantalizing possibility of being *better* than well.

Deepak Chopra goes one step further. He believes that a person can attain "perfect health"—a condition "that is free from disease, that never feels pain, that cannot age or die."[8] Chopra's stroke of brilliance is to combine New Age mysticism with quantum mechanics to promote "quantum healing" (much to the consternation of real physicists)—and to write inscrutable,

---

7. From the preamble to the "Constitution of the World Health Organization," World Health Organization, October 2006, http://www.who.int/governance/eb/who_constitution_en.pdf.

8. Deepak Chopra, *Perfect Health: The Complete Mind/Body Guide*, rev. ed. (New York: Three Rivers Press, 2000), 7.

irrefutable sentences like "We are the eyes of the universe looking at itself."[9]

The wellness movement has its share of critics, though pastors and theologians are conspicuous by their absence from this
particular choir. They shouldn't be, for *wellness* has become part
of the warp and woof of the American social imaginary. What's
the "good news" of the wellness movement? That you can make
yourself well—save yourself—by following this or that program.
To the extent that it has become an ideal picture that orients people's hopes and lives and encourages self-help salvation, wellness has become an American idol, a false gospel.[10] Pastors can
come to a better understanding of the current American social
imaginary by attending to some of its critics.

The most prominent critic is probably Barbara Ehrenreich,
who refers to "an epidemic of wellness" in the subtitle of her
book *Natural Causes*.[11] The book is part cultural history and part
social critique. Her aim is to identify the toxin that has infected
the American imagination, leading us to believe the fantasy that
we can overcome the ravages of sickness and death through
medical technology and preventative medicine. The book details
the lengths we have gone in pursuit of wellness and offers sharp
critiques of the wellness industry and the aforementioned "bio-
hacks" that promise immortality through genetic engineering.
In Ehrenreich's account, Americans are sheep who follow, and
pay for, every trend that promises wellness and eternal life. She

---

9. Deepak Chopra, Twitter, September 25, 2014, 12:20 a.m., https://twitter.
com/deepakchopra/status/515038027367059456?lang=en (accessed July 13, 2018).

10. Some would add, an ideology: a package of ideas, values, and practices that serve the interest of those industries that profit by it. Others worry
about the new "biomorality"—"the moral demand to be happy and healthy"
(Cederström and Spicer, *Wellness Syndrome*, 5).

11. Barbara Ehrenreich, *Natural Causes: An Epidemic of Wellness, the Certainty
of Dying, and Killing Ourselves to Live Longer* (New York: Twelve, 2018).

is shocked that so many Americans now keep step with this culture of wellness, submitting to tests and treatments and following an arduous self-improvement regimen.

Why is this a problem? The short answer is: biology. Ehrenreich has a PhD in cellular immunology, and this has strengthened her commonsense conviction that our bodies ultimately defy our control. We can neither will ourselves to grow taller nor to live longer. While certain bad choices like smoking can shorten our lives, even those who make good choices will eventually die of natural causes. Ehrenreich cites the example of Jerome Rodale, who in 1950 founded *Prevention*, a magazine devoted to promoting practices that stave off disease. Just minutes before he died from a heart attack at the age of seventy-two, Rodale boasted, "I've decided to live to be a hundred."[12] In Ehrenreich's opinion, the wellness industry caters to rich people who can afford to be narcissists. Here, I fear, she may be too optimistic: more and more middle-class Americans are buying into the cult of the body and the culture of well-being at any cost.

Those who follow the gospel of wellness are in danger of denying reality, namely, the limits of their own bodies and their unavoidable deaths. Ehrenreich's book is an exposé that calls out as a lie the notion that we can control our own bodies and our fates. She also calls out the wellness Pharisees who display a self-righteous superiority toward those who do not take part in their health-seeking practices. Ehrenreich thinks there's something fundamentally wrong with spending more and more of one's life simply trying to prolong it. The meaning of life must

12. A *New York Times Magazine* article published just months before he died referred to the "organic gospel according to Rodale": Wade Green, "Guru of the Organic Food Cult," *New York Times Magazine*, June 6, 1971, https://www.nytimes.com/1971/06/06/archives/guru-of-the-organic-food-cult-guru-of-the-organic-food-cult.html.

involve more than the lengthening of life. This is one reason why Ehrenreich has grown skeptical of modern medicine.

In this, she is hardly alone. Elisabeth Rosenthal, author of *An American Sickness: How Healthcare Became Big Business and How You Can Take It Back*, believes the health-care system has become dysfunctional to the point that its economic rules now challenge commonsense sayings like "A lifetime of treatment is preferable to a cure." She writes, "In the past quarter century, the American medical system has stopped focusing on health or even science. Instead it attends more or less single-mindedly to its own profits."[13]

A second critical voice is that of Carl Elliott, a bioethicist and author of *Better than Well: American Medicine Meets the American Dream*. On the surface, his book is about enhancement technologies, but, as he states in the introduction, the underlying issue is the nature of identity: "In short, we need to understand the complex relationships between enhancement technologies, the way we live now, and the kinds of people we have become."[14] Elliott is concerned that modernity has encouraged individuals to be the heroes of their own stories, breaking from the socially embodied traditions in which they were raised and free to remake themselves in whatever image takes their fancy (usually that of a celebrity). In technology we trust. Think, for instance, of pharmaceutical enhancements, like steroids, that make athletes "better than well." Cosmetic enhancements (plastic surgery, Botox, breast implants, etc.) are another example.[15] There is no

---

13.   Elisabeth Rosenthal, *An American Sickness: How Healthcare Became Big Business and How You Can Take It Back* (New York: Penguin, 2017), 1.

14.   Carl Elliott, *Better than Well: American Medicine Meets the American Dream* (New York: Norton, 2003), xxi.

15.   For a fascinating social history of cosmetics, see Kathy Peiss, *Hope in a Jar: The Making of America's Beauty Culture* (University Park: University of Pennsylvania Press, 2011).

physical need for such changes, only a desire for psychological well-being. Elliott comments, "Today, enhancement technologies are not just instruments for self-improvement, or even self-transformation—they are tools for working on the soul."[16]

Please don't misunderstand: I welcome new medical discoveries, and I marvel at what modern medicine is now able to do. My concern, however, is the effect of secularization and medicalization on our concept of what it is to be well. This critique is articulated well by Atul Gawande, himself a physician and professor at Harvard Medical School, in his best-selling book *Being Mortal: Medicine and What Matters in the End.* Gawande indicts a medical establishment that does not know what to do with death and dying. There is no treatment for mortality. Nevertheless, this has not stopped them from making mortality a medical experience: "Lacking a coherent view of how people might live successfully all the way to their very end, we have allowed our fates to be controlled by the imperatives of medicine, technology, and strangers."[17]

Gawande's book discovers another ingredient in the present social imaginary's conception of wellness: independence. According to received medical wisdom, if you lack the eight "Independent Activities of Daily Living"—shopping, housekeeping, cooking, laundering, medicating, phoning, traveling, and handling your finances on your own—you may need to get thee to an assisted living facility. Wellness means independent living, yet our reverence for wellness takes no account of the reality of what happens in life. At some point, each one of us will no longer be independent, which prompts a difficult question: "If independence is what we live for, what do we do when it can

---

16. Elliott, *Better than Well*, 53.
17. Atul Gawanda, *Being Mortal* (New York: Metropolitan, 2014), 9.

no longer be sustained?"[18] Thanks to modern medicine, we have experienced not only a biological transformation (most of us live longer) but also a cultural transformation in how we conceive the good life.

Is it possible to do *dependent* living *well*? Neither the medical establishment nor society in general (or, for that matter, the church) has to date come up with a good answer.[19] Gawande's book is ostensibly concerned with death, but the moral pertains to more than mortality: "Medical professionals concentrate on repair of health, not sustenance of the soul."[20] In a culture that has medicalized what used to be the fundamental problem— meaningfulness and mortality—there is now a spiritual vacuum. Nurture abhors a vacuum, as does culture: hence the many wellness gospels now being peddled.

What *wellness* means is currently up for grabs. As I conclude the survey of this first cultural strand, contrast the secular picture of wellness we have been investigating with John's expansive prayer for Gaius: "Beloved, I pray that all may go well with you and that you may be in good health, as it goes well with your soul" (3 John 2). John speaks so warmly to Gaius because he has just received a report that Gaius is "walking in the truth" (3 John 3). This, I suggest, is the theological meaning of wellness: to live in accordance with true doctrine about Jesus Christ. Knowing the story of Jesus Christ, his cross, resurrection, ascension, and heavenly session, is the proper context for determining whether we are doing well as mortal beings. Horatio Spafford

18. Gawande, *Being Mortal*, 23.

19. See Gawande: "In the absence of what people like my grandfather could count on—a vast extended family constantly on hand to let him make his own choices—our elderly are left with a controlled and supervised institutional existence, a medically designed answer to unfixable problems, a life designed to be safe but empty of anything they care about" (*Being Mortal*, 108–9).

20. Gawande, *Being Mortal*, 128.

probably had 3 John 2 in mind when in 1876 he penned the words to the hymn "It Is Well with My Soul." The lyrics to the opening stanza are well known:

> When peace like a river, attendeth my way,
> When sorrows like sea billows roll;
> Whatever my lot, Thou hast taught me to know
> It is well, it is well, with my soul.

What may be less known is that Spafford wrote these words after passing the place where all four of his daughters had drowned in a shipwreck.

"Get well soon" rings hollow to the man on his deathbed. Yet for Christians, the idea of *dying well* is not a contradiction in terms. On the contrary: Puritans and others wrote entire manuals on the *ars moriendi*, the "art of dying." Indeed, one of the most important things disciples ought to learn from Jesus is how to die well.[21] Paul was an exemplary disciple of Jesus in taking up his cross, which is why he could declare, "I die every day!" (1 Cor 15:31). This only makes sense in light of another statement: "For to me to live is Christ, and to die is gain" (Phil 1:21). Discipleship is indeed the process of making people well, but gospel wellness—the wellness of soul and resurrected body—is a far cry from what is offered up by the priests of modern wellness culture.

We turn now from wellness to diet, the second aspect of today's social imaginary, and from the body cult to the cult of food.

---

21. See John Swinton and Richard Payne, eds., *Living Well and Dying Faithfully: Christian Practices for End-of-Life Care* (Grand Rapids: Eerdmans, 2009); and Matthew Levering, *Dying and the Virtues* (Grand Rapids: Eerdmans, 2018).

DIET AND NUTRITION: SHAPING UP

"Man shall not live by bread alone" (Matt 4:4). "Amen!" say proponents of the low-carb Atkins diet. Once upon a time, Robert Atkins, a cardiologist and nutritionist, had thousands of disciples. *Time* magazine named him one of its ten most influential people in 2002. He had a heart attack the same year and died the next. In 2005, Atkins Nutritionals filed for bankruptcy. Today, the Atkins plan is classified as a "fad diet." The original marketing was great; the science behind it, not so much. Atkins's fundamental premise was that restricting carbohydrates is essential to weight loss. Alas, a calorie by any other name converts to fat.

It is a cautionary tale, told all too often. Of making many diet books there is no end (cf. Eccl 12:12). Probably the best way to become a best-selling author is to write a diet book with a title like *Ten Easy Steps to Lose Ten Pounds in Ten Weeks*. Who could resist easy steps to a significant goal? There is no shortage of formerly fat soothsayers ready to sell their surefire secrets to successful dieting. The author Edith Wharton writes of Henry James's ill health due to his unfortunate adherence to a dangerous diet program called "Fletcherizing," named after its misguided inventor. Horace Fletcher was one of the earliest health-food enthusiasts of the twentieth century. The central idea behind the diet was simplicity itself: chew your food a hundred times, then spit it out. This way, you get the nutrients but not the bulk. The "Great Masticator" (as Fletcher came to be known) counted among his disciples not only Henry James, but also (for a time) Upton Sinclair and John D. Rockefeller. Wharton writes of the diet's effect on James: "The system resulted in intestinal atrophy, and when a doctor at last persuaded him to return to a normal way of eating he could no longer digest, and his nervous system had been undermined by years of malnutrition."[22]

It has been said that you are what you eat, but we could add: you are how you diet. Jesus warned his disciples about false prophets and false christs who will try to lead Christians astray (Mark 13:21–22). James was a devotee to a food cult, a disciple to a particular doctrine about what constitutes good diet. James's fate reminds us that there is false doctrine in the realm of diet as well as theology. It also reminds us that here, too, the consequence of false doctrine is death.

Kima Cargill, editor of *Food Cults: How Fads, Dogma, and Doctrine Influence Diet*, rightly states that dietary practices and nutritional beliefs "do not just serve physical health—they serve a great many psychological functions as well ... [including] a sense of agency and empowerment, as well as pride in self-care."[23] Belonging to a food cult also affords psychological benefits: (1) it offers a medium for group identity and cohesion, and (2) it functions as a substitute for religion in secular Western culture: "Food cults arguably replace what religion once did by prescribing ... food rules and rituals. Like religion, they provide meaning in confusing situations, giving us moral guidelines and comfort."[24] Whatever else we may want to say about them, members of food cults are hearers who *do*. Whether or not what they do is actually good for them, however, depends on the soundness of the doctrines they follow.

---

22. Edith Wharton, *A Backward Glance* (New York: Charles Scribner's Sons, 1964), 365.

23. Kima Cargill, "The Psychology of Food Cults" in *Food Cults: How Fads, Dogma, and Doctrine Influence Diet*, ed. Kima Cargill (Lanham, MD: Rowman & Littlefield, 2017), 7.

24. Cargill, "Psychology of Food Cults," 12.

Dieting and nutrition, like medicine and health care, have become big business. So has raising and preparing food. The market for slimming plans, drugs, health foods and drinks, and of course diet books has exploded. One observer writes, "The diet industry is all about exploitation and profit. The slimming drugs available to us now are just the latest in a long line of imaginative, often spurious, diet preparations."[25] False prophets yield huge profits.

Who among the clamor of competitive voices should we trust? Is it true that you can cheat death with the antioxidant power of pomegranate juice?[26] The American social imaginary about what constitutes good diet has swayed back and forth for decades, and there is still considerable angst over which nutritional doctrines to follow, as the sampling of book titles attests: Hillel Schwartz, *Never Satisfied: A Cultural History of Diets, Fantasies, and Fat;*[27] Harvey Levenstein, *Fear of Food: A History of Why We Worry about What We Eat;*[28] and Susan Yager, *The Hundred Year Diet: America's Voracious Appetite for Losing Weight.*[29] The struggle to occupy the high ground involves not only business and the competition for food dollars but politics as well: Whose

---

25. Louise Foxcroft, *Calories and Corsets: A History of Dieting Over 2,000 Years* (London: Profile, 2011), 195–96.

26. I take this example of a false promise from Leihann R. Chaffee and Corey L. Cook, "The Allure of Food Cults: Balancing Pseudoscience and Healthy Skepticism," in Cargill, *Food Cults*, 22.

27. Hillel Schwartz, *Never Satisfied: A Cultural History of Diets, Fantasies, and Fat* (New York: Free Press, 1986).

28. Harvey Levenstein, *Fear of Food: A History of Why We Worry about What We Eat* (Chicago: University of Chicago Press, 2013).

29. Susan Yager, *The Hundred Year Diet: America's Voracious Appetite for Losing Weight* (New York: Rodale, 2010).

say about dietary requirements counts, and whose interests does it serve?[30]

In an age of conflicting interpretations, many twenty-first-century Westerners are placing their faith in science. The food scientist acts like a prophet, calling society back to healthy eating habits. The medical doctors who worked on what is to date "the most comprehensive study of nutrition ever conducted" (according to the subtitle of *The China Study*) argue that we are leading our youth down a dangerous dietary path that will lead to disease earlier and earlier in their lives: "*Very few people truly know what they should be doing to improve their health.*"[31] They have identified three problems: breakfast, lunch, and dinner. The underlying issue is that we are a fast-food nation, surrounded by ads for junk food, who don't even know where our food comes from. In the foreword to the book, John Robbins writes: "It's easier to find a Snickers bar, a Big Mac, or a Coke than it is to find an apple."[32] Even the scientists sound evangelistic: "The provocative results of my four decades of biomedical research, including the findings from a twenty-seven-year laboratory program … prove that eating right can save your life."[33] The main claim: "People who ate the most animal-based foods got the most chronic disease."[34] Every diet has its critics, however, and this one is no exception.[35]

---

30. See further Marion Nestle, *Food Politics: How the Food Industry Influences Nutrition and Health*, rev. ed. (Berkeley: University of California Press, 2013).

31. T. Colin Campbell and Thomas M. Campbell II, *The China Study: The Most Comprehensive Study of Nutrition Ever Conducted and the Startling Implications for Diet, Weight Loss and Long-Term Health* (Dallas: Benbella, 2006), 1.

32. John Robbins, foreword to Campbell and Campbell, *The China Study*, xvii.

33. Campbell and Campbell, *The China Study*, 2.

34. Campbell and Campbell, *The China Study*, 7.

35. See, for example, Denise Minger, "The China Study: Fact or Fallacy?," July 7, 2010, https://deniseminger.com/2010/07/07/the-china-study-fact-or-fallac/.

Another recent example of the close relationship between diet and discipleship is Valter Longo's *The Longevity Diet: Discover the New Science Behind Stem Cell Activation and Regeneration to Slow Aging, Fight Disease, and Optimize Weight*.[36] The title promises just about everything someone living in a secular age could hope for. Even better, it comes with the backing and authority of science. Longo is a biogerontologist (someone who studies the biology of aging) who has experimented with giving longevity diets to mice, who allegedly live up to 40 percent longer. His claim: "What you eat is the primary choice you can make that will affect whether you live to 60, 80, 100, or 110."[37] The goal is to live to a ripe old age, an aim that gives rise to one of the most ironic euphemisms I have ever come across: "dying healthy."[38] His advice is similar to that of the *China Study* authors: aim for a diet that is close to 100 percent plant- and fish-based. Of course, for the diet to work you can't simply be a hearer, but a doer. Information alone is not transformative. Diets don't work without discipleship.

Aye, there's the rub. For diets to work, one has to actually follow them. That's why I prefer *The Mayo Clinic Diet*. Like Richard Watson's *The Philosopher's Diet* (my second-favorite diet book), the authors know that losing weight is less a matter of following faddish trends or restrictive programs than it is of becoming a certain kind of person. You have to first know what is good for you, and, second, be able to sustain that activity:

Minger is author of *Death by Food Pyramid: How Shoddy Science, Sketchy Politics, and Shade Special Interests Ruined Your Health … and How to Reclaim It!* (Malibu, CA: Primal Blueprint, 2013).

36. Valter Longo, *The Longevity Diet: Discover the New Science Behind Stem Cell Activation and Regeneration to Slow Aging, Fight Disease, and Optimize Weight* (New York: Avery, 2018).

37. Longo, *Longevity Diet*, 39.

38. Longo, *Longevity Diet*, 39.

"To lower your weight 20 pounds or more and keep that lower weight is to change your life."[39] Accordingly, *The Mayo Clinic Diet* is organized around two parts: part 1, "Lose It!" and part 2, "Live It!"

What people have to lose is not weight but certain *habits*. In a nice turn of phrase, *The Mayo Clinic Diet* puts it like this: "The most critical element of weight loss is what *you* bring to the table—*your own personal drive to succeed*."[40] One of the most helpful chapters in the book is written by a behavioral psychologist. Taking a page from Martin Luther on temptation, he writes: "Having an urge [to eat] is OK. Giving in to the urge is the problem."[41] It helps to know that "urges" last only twenty minutes or so.

Jesus' famous saying with which I began this section is a quotation from Deuteronomy 8:3. The phrase is part of a long speech by Moses that we might call his "Great Commission" to Israel. After forty years of wandering in the wilderness, they had arrived on the threshold of the promised land. In chapter 7, Moses warned the Israelites about becoming like the other nations. For Moses, the wellness of Israel depended on a particular diet: the observation of the commands of the Lord. This is the original context for the saying that Jesus later quotes: "Man does not live by bread alone, but man lives by every word that comes from the mouth of the LORD" (Deut 8:3).

The parallel with the contemporary situation of the church is striking. By whose words will Christians order their lives?

---

39. Richard Watson, *The Philosopher's Diet: How to Lose Weight and Change the World*, rev. ed. (Boston: Nonpareil, 1998), 10.

40. *The Mayo Clinic Diet* (Intercourse, PA: Good Books, 2012), 13.

41. *The Mayo Clinic Diet*, 33. Martin Luther's original: "You can't stop the birds [temptations] from flying over your head, but you can stop them from making a nest in your hair."

We get our English term *diet* from the Greek *diaiasthan*: "a way of living." A diet is a regulated and disciplined way of living built on certain beliefs and assumptions (doctrines) about the means to attain a specific good end like weight loss. And, speaking of Greeks, Hippocrates understood the connection between diet and discipline: "Man cannot live healthily on food without a certain amount of exercise."[42] Self-discipline goes a long way—if one is on the right path. One of the most successful diet books ever written, Luigi Cornaro's *The Art of Living Long*, made a similar point 450 years ago. Cornaro's first rule was: regain self-control (he was himself a repentant former glutton).

Disciples of Jesus Christ must live by every word that comes from the mouth of God—and on a diet of sound doctrine (I'll return to this in chapter 7). There is no shortcut, either in dieting (physical health) or discipleship (spiritual health). The church must resist the temptation to become a fast-food holy nation. Physical obesity is a health concern, as is gluttony, the deadly sin with which it is associated (Phil 3:19), but a diet of false doctrine is even more dangerous.

Members of Christ's body must ask themselves two questions: Whose diet, in the sense of a way of life, should we follow, and how can we become the kind of people that will indeed follow it? This is where I part company with *The Philosopher's Diet* and its assumption that to follow the diet of philosophy— that is, to pursue the good life—one need only use one's reason and volition, as if we could will ourselves into good shape. By way of contrast, Jesus says, "My food is to do the will of him who sent me" (John 4:34). Dieting here is obedient doing, but willpower alone is not enough to stay the course: disciples of Jesus

---

42. Cited in Foxcroft, *Calories and Corsets*, 15.

Christ require the grace of Christ, and the indwelling Spirit that unites us to his life.

EXERCISE AND TRAINING: BECOMING FIT

A third aspect that is presently influencing people's ideas about the way to pursue the good life and achieve healthy bodies pertains to exercise and training. As we shall see, the Bible has something important to say about this strand of our contemporary cultural cord too.

You know a picture holds you captive when you're willing to pay billions of dollars for it. Today, millions of Americans spend billions of dollars on gym and health-club memberships. Those who can afford to often have personal trainers. Shelly McKenzie, author of *Getting Physical: The Rise of Fitness Culture in America*, writes, "Understanding the historical underpinnings of exercise culture sheds light on our current beliefs about fitness and its role in our lives."[43] Exercise has become complicit, she argues, in our medicalized age in which all health-seeking behaviors are meritorious. Like some vegans, some joggers think their exercise routine make them more righteous than their nonexercising neighbors: "In the modern era, health is often seen as a personal accomplishment"[44]—call it "justification by workouts." In sharp contrast to the past, training today often seems to be an end in itself: the fit body has "become a new form of physical capital" in the fitness-industrial complex.[45]

Eric Chaline's *The Temple of Perfection*, a history of the gymnasium, is aptly named, for the gym is the place where people

---

43. Shelly McKenzie, *Getting Physical: The Rise of Fitness Culture in America* (Lawrence: University Press of Kansas, 2013), 2.

44. McKenzie, *Getting Physical*, 8.

45. McKenzie, *Getting Physical*, 8.

go to sculpt the human body and approximate it to its ideal form. Chaline notices similarities between organized religion and the gym: the faithful of both church and gym go to special buildings, eat special food, and take part in shared rituals. The gymnasium is "the place where the body is transformed through physical practices, specifically different forms of exercise."[46] So too is the church.

In the broader culture, exercise and fitness did not figure prominently in the social imaginary until the invention at the beginning of the twentieth century of mass-market cameras, which allowed people to see themselves as others saw them. People began to go to the gym not to achieve military readiness, but for an aesthetic or therapeutic purpose: to look or feel better. Some cultural historians link this change to modern individualism and narcissism: improving one's health and appearance was now part and parcel of the individual's pursuit of his or her self-actualization. Others have linked the obsession with physical fitness to the postmodern desire to make the real a copy of the (ideal) image.[47] What is so interesting is not simply the fact that gyms and health clubs have become a multi-billion-dollar business, but that the notion that our bodies are the canvas on which we exercise our will to power. That our bodies are our own, to do with what we desire, is an important piece of the contemporary social imaginary, even though it denies Paul's "You are not your own" (1 Cor 6:19). Working out becomes one more form of consumerism, where what we are buying into is the

---

46. Eric Chaline, *The Temple of Perfection* (London: Reaktion, 2015), 9.

47. See further Barry Glassner, "Fitness and the Postmodern Self," *Journal of Health and Social Behavior* 30 (1989): 180–91. Glassner observes, "Many of the exercise machines found in health clubs and for home use are simulacra. ... Like the bodies to which their users aspire, they are technologically induced copies of copies" (184).

conceit that we can through workouts make ourselves over into something beautiful.

Weight-loss programs became increasingly popular starting in the mid-twentieth century. Marketers, magazines, and movies provided the body images that began to populate the social imaginary. Baby boomers awoke in the 1960s to discover that thin was in, leading one wag to opine that "thinness was now part of the American dream."[48] What we need to appreciate is the power of culture in forming our ideas of the beautiful. That 1960s American culture associated thinness with status, style, and sex appeal was one important factor in the creation of a new fitness industry. The reason for its success "lay not in governmental promotion but in consumer culture."[49] Of course, consumerism is a two-edged sword: "There is no way of estimating how many tons of excess weight are being added to the American waistline by the pizza parlor or by that more modern institution, the Pancake House," complains author Peter Wyden in his book *The Overweight Society*.[50]

It may be hard to believe, but the health benefits of exercise were not widely recognized until fairly recently. One important milestone was a 1949 study that showed how men of a similar social class had significantly different rates of heart attacks based on the amount of their physical activity. The study compared bus drivers and bus conductors and discovered that the latter had a lower incidence of heart disease, presumably because they had to move around continuously, while the drivers merely sat.[51] Television also helped colonize the social

48. Peter Wyden, *The Overweight Society* (New York: Pocket Books, 1965), vii.

49. McKenzie, *Getting Physical*, 56.

50. Wyden, *The Overweight Society*, 17.

51. See J. N. Morris et al., "Coronary Heart-Disease and Physical Activity of Work," *Lancet* 262, no. 6796 (1953): 1111–20.

imagination. The *Jack LaLanne Show*, a television program that
featured the star inviting viewers to exercise along with him
(he divided his viewers into "sitters" and "doers"!), ran for
thirty-four years, from 1959 to 1985. Even so, society found it as
difficult to reach a consensus as to how to define, and prescribe,
exercise as they did fitness in general.

Science was able to weigh in on the therapeutic (for health)
rather than merely aesthetic (for appearance) benefits of exercise. Research on smoking, drinking, stress, and physical activity demonstrated the influence of lifestyle on health. "Executive
health" emerged as a medical subspecialty in response to the
cardiac crisis among affluent CEOs whose only work took place
while sitting at a desk. Jogging (a.k.a. "running") took off in the
1960s and was successful because it could be done anywhere, by
anyone, anytime. In the 1980s, running became not simply cultural but a cultic ritual, with some runners turning their circuit
into a mode of spiritual worship.[52] To body and food cults, add
fitness cults.

If the 1980s were the fitness decade, the health club was its
temple of perfection, a "modern shrine dedicated to the perfect-
ibility of the human body."[53] Health clubs have been described
as fitness culture's consecrated spaces for the cult of the body:
"The fitness body is a highly desirable but entirely manufactured
artefact that could not exist in a prehistoric status of nature."[54]
It was also in the 1980s that fitness centers became perhaps the
first "third place" in which to socialize and form community.
However, at the turn of the millennium, a *Time* magazine article

---

52. See further Fred Rohe, *The Zen of Running* (New York: Random House,
1975); Larry Shapiro, *Zen and the Art of Running: The Path to Making Peace with
Your Pace* (Avon, MA: Adams Media, 2009).

53. Chaline, *Temple of Perfection*, 224.

54. Chaline, *Temple of Perfection*, 206.

titled "The Shape of the Nation" reported a government finding that 80 to 90 percent of Americans were still not getting enough exercise, and this despite "the new blessed trinity" of "the trim, the taut, and the wholly toned."[55] As one social historian wryly observed, "This suggests that the idea of fitness was more popular than the actual practice of exercise."[56]

Here is the basic paradox. Culture is formative, and we live in a fitness culture, but most people are (probably) not fit. Why should this be if, as I have been arguing, culture is such a powerful formative force? My answer: what culture forms is not our bodies in the first instance, but our minds and hearts. The image of the fit body projected by our fitness culture has indeed taken the social imaginary captive, and the power this image exercises does indeed condition our thinking about the body, and fitness, though it does not condition the body itself or cause us to exercise. For this, a choice must be made, a step taken. The problem is that there are too many shortcuts to wellness, health, and fitness now on the market. Call it cheap grace: the preaching of wellness without realism, diet without discipline, and fitness without exercise.

The most significant challenge to becoming fit has to do with defining what fitness is, for there is no consensus about what it means—but not for lack of trying. In the 1950s, physicians Hans Kraus and Sonja Weber developed a series of fitness tests for children to investigate the causes of backaches in adults. The results were shocking: the 8 percent of European children who failed the test were overshadowed by the whopping 56 percent of American children who failed it. The dismal results prompted

---

55. Anastasia Toufexis, "The Shape of the Nation," *Time*, June 24, 2001, http://content.time.com/time/magazine/article/0,9171,142502,00.html.

56. McKenzie, *Getting Physical*, 177.

President Eisenhower to establish the President's Council on Youth Fitness, a precursor to John F. Kennedy's better-known President's Council on Physical Fitness. The presidents feared that postwar prosperity had created a suburban middle-class lifestyle of ease and automation that contributed to children growing soft and lazy. In the words of a US senator at the time: "Mighty Rome collapsed when it lost its physical health. A flabby nation physically becomes a flabby nation mentally and spiritually."[57] The subtext: America's baby boomers might not be fit enough to protect us!

One of the chief aims of the council was to sell the idea of fitness to the public. An article that appeared in *Sports Illustrated* in 1956 weighed in on the difficulty of the task: "All the experts can say is that to be fit means to be able to carry on your daily life comfortably and have energy and strength left over for emergencies. This tells us little, because whose daily life are they talking about and what is the minimum fitness everyone should have?"[58]

As in so many areas, the ancient Greeks were examining the question of what fitness is long before us. The first gymnasia date back to the first Olympic games, centuries before the birth of Jesus. These ancient sporting competitions were originally part of military training (think, for example, of wrestling and the javelin, as well as foot and chariot races). Of course, people were training for war even before the ancient Greeks: "And the king of Babylon brought captive to Babylon all the men of valor, 7,000, and the craftsmen and the metal workers, 1,000, all of

---

57. George H. Bender, "Physical Fitness Problem Faces Young Americans," *This Week in Washington* (constituent newsletter), August 27, 1955, 1 (President's Council on Physical Fitness Records).

58. Dorothy Stull, "Conference at Annapolis: First Blow for Fitness," *Sports Illustrated*, July 2, 1956, 22–24.

them strong and fit for war" (2 Kgs 24:16).[59] But this is not all. In the fifth century BC, there were gymnasia in several major Greek cities, and they served not simply to train athletes and soldiers but to educate and to help citizens achieve *aretē* (virtue).[60]

The United States Armed Forces agree that fitness is not merely physical. In an important supplementary issue of the journal *Military Medicine* devoted to the notion of Total Force Fitness (TFF), first introduced by the Department of Defense in 2009, Admiral Michael Mullen, Chairman of the Joint Chiefs of Staff (2007–2011), set out the vision, goal, and rationale: "I see total fitness as a point of balance between readiness and well-being. ... A total force that has achieved total fitness is healthy, ready, and resilient; capable of meeting challenges and surviving threats."[61] Fitness requires continuous performance, recovery, and resilience of the whole person. Total fitness covers eight domains, encompassing mind and body: physical, medical, nutritional, environmental, psychological, behavioral, social, and spiritual. TFF "is not something someone achieves twice a year for a test. It is a state of being."[62] The goal of TFF is fourfold: maintain health, enhance performance, reduce risk, and improve resilience. The program defines physical fitness as "the ability to physically accomplish aspects of the mission while remaining

59.   See also 2 Chr 25:5, "Fit for war, able to handle spear and shield"; and 2 Chr 26:11, "Uzziah had an army of soldiers, fit for war."

60.   For more on the gymnasium, the "most important social institution" in ancient Greece, see Chaline, *Temple of Perfection*, 15–49.

61.   Michael Mullen, "On Total Force Fitness in War and Peace," *Military Medicine* 175 (August Supplement 2010): 1. See also "Total Force Fitness: Your Roadmap to Peak Performance," Uniformed Services University, Consortium for Health and Military Performance, February 26, 2018, https://www.hprc-online.org/articles/total-force-fitness-your-roadmap-to-peak-performance.

62.   Murray, "On Total Force Fitness," 2.

healthy/uninjured." We can call this being *fit for purpose*, where the purpose is the ability to carry out the mission.

In 2013, the Rand Corporation published a series of books commissioned by the US Air Force to study fitness and resilience as part of the Armed Forces' new holistic approach. The Air Force defines spiritual fitness as *"the ability to adhere to beliefs, principles, or values needed to persevere and prevail in accomplishing missions."*[63] The emphasis is on core personal values that reflect belief in ultimate meaning or purpose, not necessarily God or the supernatural. One of the factors prompting this study is the rise of suicide among the ranks of the military. Evidence suggests that spiritual fitness may protect against suicide. It certainly contributes to resilience, which the Air Force defines as "the ability to withstand, recover, and/or grow in the face of stressors and changing demands." It is fascinating to see how the contemporary social imaginary of what is involved in fitness—a mind-body holism—has affected even the Department of Defense.

This trend toward a kind of mind-body holistic fitness explains the new emphasis on mindfulness, balance, and flexibility, in contrast to earlier decades' emphasis on strength and endurance. CrossFit is a fitness regimen with its own registered trademark and thirteen thousand affiliated gyms nationwide specializing in high-intensity interval training. On the company's website, founder and CEO Greg Glassman defines fitness in terms of "increased work capacity across broad time and modal domains."[64] "Across ... modal domains" explains the

---

63. Douglas Young and Margaret T. Martin, *Spiritual Fitness and Resilience*, Rand Corporation, 2013, 5, https://www.rand.org/content/dam/rand/pubs/research_reports/RR100/RR100/RAND_RR100.pdf.

64. "What Is CrossFit?," CrossFit, https://www.crossfit.com/what-is-crossfit (accessed July 2, 2018).

name CrossFit: the program aims at fitness *across* a number of sports and activities. As to why fitness matters or what it is for, the CrossFit website says the program "prepares trainees *for any physical contingency*." As we shall see in part 2, there is something to be said for being able to improvise what is required in any situation. This is discipleship: knowing how to follow Jesus *in any situation*.

Exercise—any bodily activity that contributes to physical fitness and overall health—remains "a mode of ensuring one's readiness for work,"[65] whether the work in question is soldiering, sales, or surgery. Further, our contemporary fitness culture "relies on the premise that the solution to the nation's physical inactivity can be found in the individual, even though it's apparent that sedentary lifestyles are a societal problem. ... Today, we perceive health [and particularly fitness] as a personal accomplishment."[66] It turns out that the current social imaginary is in some respects asocial: We think of personal well-being instead of that of our family unit. We think about our own diet more than the people we dine with. We think about fitness in terms of my individual routine instead of its being a part of a larger communal rhythm.

If fit bodies are the answer, what is the question? In ancient Greece, the gymnasium answered the question, How can we prepare our young men to be warriors? The burning questions in mid-twentieth-century North America were, for men, How can I stave off heart disease? and for women, How can I measure

---

65. McKenzie, *Getting Physical*, 180.

66. McKenzie, *Getting Physical*, 180.

up to cultural norms of beauty? The dictionary definition of "fit" is "suitable by nature or by art to an end" (as a theologian, I want to add, "or by divine design"). The raises the key question: For what *purpose* do we struggle to become fit? For many today, our physical bodies are our most important identity statement, replacing even political or religious affiliation.

Being *fit* is like being *useful*: nothing is useful *in general*; rather, particular things have particular uses. What is the purpose for making the effort to become fit? Some might say that fitness is its own reward, but what they mean is that self-actualization is a self-evident end. That depends on the self that is actualized, which forces the challenging question, What kind of person do we want to become, and why? and the even tougher question, *What is the meaning of life?* Enter the pastor-theologian, and an alternative social imaginary.

In this chapter, we have been examining three formative aspects of contemporary culture: its ruling images of wellness, good diet, and fitness. Pastors, too, ought to be concerned with wellness, though they know that things will ultimately be well only when rightly related to Christ. Pastors, too, ought to be concerned with the diet of their congregation, particularly if we stretch the term to include what kind of reading and entertainment church members imbibe on a regular basis. And pastors should know that churches, like gyms, exist in part for training purposes (see 2 Tim 3:16), specifically, to train a fit body—the local congregation.

What makes the church unique is the kind of fitness in view and the means by which we obtain it. Make no mistake: a church vested in making disciples must become a fitness culture.

Everything depends on pastors having a clear grasp of the purpose for which we declare a disciple *fit*. It is to that question that we now turn our attention.

3

FROM HEARING TO DOING

First Steps in Making Disciples "Fit for Purpose"

The previous chapter provided an overview of our contemporary fitness culture as a way of waking us up to the formative role played by social imaginaries. We saw that a certain picture of wellness, nutrition, and fitness both generates a multi-billion-dollar industry and shapes large sections of how we live as a society. It does so because it dictates the pictures we live by and, to a large extent, the desires of our hearts.

The church is itself a gym with its own fitness culture. This is not my idea, but the apostle Paul's. He describes Timothy, a pastor, as one "trained in the words of the faith and of ... good doctrine" (1 Tim 4:6). Some translations say "nourished" instead of "trained" (the Greek term *entrephō* connotes both senses), and this simply underlines the point: Timothy himself was discipled through constant exposure to Scripture and a diet of doctrine.

Paul then exhorts Timothy to have nothing to do with other social imaginaries ("profane myths and old wives' tales," 1 Tim 4:7a NRSV) and instead "train yourself for godliness" (1 Tim 4:7b). The Greek for "train" is *gymnazō*. There you have it: the church is to be a gym for training in godliness. Disciples need a diet of Scripture and doctrine in order to get the nourishment necessary for training. And training is necessary "because orthodoxy (believing correctly) turns hypocritical apart from orthopraxy (behaving correctly)."[1] That's the big picture: pastors make disciples by training them to be fit for the purpose of godliness.

Before I begin to fill out this picture, it is important to remember that, while pastors may "make" (that is, train) disciples, only God can "wake" (that is, create) them. Discipleship is about becoming who we are in Christ, and this is entirely a work of God: "Therefore, if anyone is in Christ, he is a new creation" (2 Cor 5:17). Jesus calls his disciples *ex nihilo* (out of nothing). We no more decide to be disciples than we decide to be born, because to become a disciple is to be born not of the flesh, but born again, from above (John 3:3–7; cf. Acts 11:16).

Conversion and repentance involve a radical reorientation and renewal, which only makes sense in light of the work of the Triune God. Discipleship therefore cannot simply be a function of church programs. We need a theology of discipleship "to make sure that in talking about the church and its mission we keep talking about God."[2] Everything begins with a gracious divine initiative, with God's call that gathers a people to be his people, a holy nation. To put it in more technical theological terms: Christian discipleship is rightly understood and rightly

---

1. Robert H. Gundry, *Commentary on the New Testament: Verse-by-Verse Explanations with a Literal Translation* (Peabody, MA: Hendrickson, 2010), 840.

2. John Webster, "Discipleship and Obedience," *Scottish Bulletin of Evangelical Theology* 24, no. 1 (2006): 18.

practiced only when we remember that it is part of the economy (i.e., the historical outworking) of God's grace.[3] Yet there is still something important for disciples to *do*, and the God who calls and assembles his church also calls particular people to help disciples understand the economy of grace and what it commands them to do. Paul says that the risen and ascended Christ "gave gifts to his people" (Eph 4:8), namely, "that some would be ... shepherds and teachers, to equip the saints for the work of ministry, for building up the body of Christ" (Eph 4:11–12). The gifts of Scripture and doctrine serve the same edifying purpose.

HEARING AND DOING: ON AUTHORITY AND TRUTH, OBEDIENCE AND FREEDOM

In perhaps the most famous *Arabian Nights* story, Aladdin discovers a magic lamp that, when rubbed, produces a genie who invariably responds, "Your wish is my command." It is the classic response of a servant to his master: "To hear is to obey." But in real life there is often a gap, sometimes a yawning chasm, between hearing and obeying. Not everyone is as fortunate as Aladdin: sometimes servants hear, and do half-heartedly; at other times, they hear and do not do at all. Jesus told his own, equally compelling stories that illustrate the all-important difference between hearing and doing.

The Gospel of Mark introduces Jesus as a teacher who astonished his hearers, "for he taught them as one who had authority" (Mark 1:22). He taught in the synagogue and, later, offered free seaside lectures (Mark 2:13; 4:1). The form of Jesus' teaching is significant: "And he was teaching them many things in

---

3. From *oikonomia* (Eph 1:10; 3:2, 9) meaning "plan," "stewardship," or, more literally, "household law."

parables" (Mark 4:2). A parable is an extended metaphor ("the kingdom of God is like ..."), a metaphorical narrative—a story in which something extraordinary happens that subverts the ordinary way people think about things. The first such story Mark recounts is the parable of the sower, which is about different kinds of hearers, represented by the different kinds of soil on which the seed of God's word falls. Even the disciples did not understand it at first, and this despite Jesus' obvious hint at the end: "He who has ears to hear, let him hear" (Mark 4:9). The parable they are to hear is itself about hearing God's word. In particular, the parable explains the kind of hearing Jesus is after: a hearing in which God's word takes root in a singular and wonderful way. Indeed, this is the extraordinary element in the parable: that a word-seed can multiply its growth a hundredfold.

This is also a parable of the kingdom of God. Jesus subverts his hearers' conventional picture of a kingdom as something that can be established by swords and soldiers. Jesus instead proclaims a kingdom established by the right reception of the gospel—the right kind of hearing—rather than military conquest. Jesus' parables of the kingdom challenge the prevailing social imaginaries of power, be it ancient Roman imperialism or present-day geopolitics. Jesus taught with authority precisely by announcing a new picture to live by. To hear rightly is to correctly grasp the content of Jesus' teaching, namely, the strange new world of the kingdom of God.

One qualification for being a disciple of Jesus is to be able to follow Jesus' stories. Yet hearing, even with understanding and apparent agreement, is not enough.[4] Toward the end of his longest lesson, the Sermon on the Mount, Jesus makes an explicit contrast between hearing and doing: "Everyone then who hears

---

4. A point poignantly made by Jesus' parable of the two sons (Matt 21:28–32).

these words of mine *and does them* will be like a wise man who built his house on the rock. ... And everyone who hears these words of mine and *does not do them* will be like a foolish man who built his house on the sand" (Matt 7:24, 26). True disciples must be hearers *and* doers of Jesus' words. The Greek term for the rock on which one builds—bedrock—shows up again later in Matthew 16:18, where Jesus says he will build his church "on this bedrock." In other words, he who would build Jesus' church on a rock rather than sand must build it on the bedrock of Jesus' words.[5] This is confirmed in Luke's Gospel where, just after the parable of the sower, Jesus says, "My mother and my brothers are those who hear the word of God and do it" (Luke 8:21).

As rabbi or Master, Jesus did not want his followers simply to listen to his lessons and then continue living as before. To hear and *not* do is both to flout the authority of Jesus' words and to flaunt oneself as lord. Moreover, to hear and *not* do is the opposite not only of obedience but also of learning. No one learns to swim or ride a bike simply by reading an instruction manual. Jesus desires followers who both listen and learn.

When Jesus spoke about hearing and doing, he was thinking about authority, wisdom, and freedom. The wise person acts in accordance with the way things are, which means in accordance with what God says. This is also the way of freedom, for to live wisely means living along the grain of the created order. Jesus is our Master, yes, but he commands that we be *free*: "For freedom Christ has set us free" (Gal 5:1). This is why Jesus says that his yoke is easy and his burden light (Matt 11:30): to follow Jesus is to set out on a freedom trail. Before I unpack that claim, though, let us consider two other important biblical texts that associate hearing, doing, and discipleship.

---

5. See Gundry, *Commentary on the New Testament*, 29.

In Romans 2 Paul addresses Jews who rely overmuch on their Jewishness, in particular their possession of the Mosaic law: "For it is not the hearers of the law who are righteous before God, but the doers of the law who will be justified [declared righteous]" (Rom 2:13). It is crucial to understand that Paul is *not* saying that justification comes from doing the law; this way lies the works righteousness that his letters to the Romans and Galatians refute. It is not enough merely to hear the law or to try and keep it according to the flesh, for all have sinned and fallen short of the glory of God and the requirements of the law (Rom 3:23). The "doers" in this case are those who believe in Jesus, meet "the righteous requirement of the law" (Rom 8:4) through justification by faith, and *as a result* do the law because of the law of the Spirit of life that has been given them in Christ (Rom 8:2). Hearers must indeed be doers, but the doing is a free obedience, a living out of the truth of what they have heard, trusted, and believed. The second text makes this even clearer.

In James 1:22–25 we see a close parallel to Jesus' parable about building on rock or sand. One who hears the word but does not do it is foolish because he succumbs to self-deception (Jas 1:22). For the word, says James, is a mirror in which we see our true faces. To hear this word but not do it is to forget your face, that is, your true identity. What's the connection between God's word and a mirror? Just this: those who look into the word of God—the two-Testament story of God bringing his people out of bondage—see themselves as they actually are "in Christ." James calls the mirror of Scripture "the perfect law, the law of liberty" (Jas 1:25) because the gospel is a story of liberation. Those who understand themselves in front of the biblical text know themselves to be people who have health (*salus*) and freedom only in Christ. As Jesus said, "And you will know the truth, and the truth will set you free" (John 8:32).

Those who hear that they have been liberated but fail to *act in* freedom are simply fooling themselves. Belief without behavior is empty. Genuine discipleship, in contrast, is the sustainable practice of hearing and doing freedom in Christ. This was the heart of Paul's gospel, as he reminded the Galatians (Gal 5:1). Peter says something similar: "Live as people who are free ... as servants of God" (1 Pet 2:16). What is striking about James's way of putting it, however, is his emphasis on *seeing* oneself in a *word*. This is precisely the way the social imaginary works: by lodging a control story in us that enraptures the "eyes of your heart" (Eph 1:18), the wellspring of everyday life (Prov 4:23).

Hearing and doing the gospel story, the law of life, is altogether different from hearing and doing a moral law: "For the law of the Spirit of life has set you free in Christ Jesus from the law of sin and death" (Rom 8:2). There is no freedom in moral striving when it is done in the strength of the flesh for the sake of making oneself right enough to merit God's approval. The word James asks us to hear and do is a liberating word, even if it requires doing on our part. How can this be? The answer, in brief, is that the disciple's doing is not a work of the flesh but of the Holy Spirit: "Now the Lord is the Spirit, and where the Spirit of the Lord is, there is freedom" (2 Cor 3:17). Again, the mirror of the word, the gospel, shows us that we have been set free in Christ: "Freedom is ... the capacity to realize what one is."[6] *Christian* freedom is the capacity to realize what one is *in Christ*: "Evangelical freedom is a form of life which acts out the fact that I have been set free from 'the law of sin and death' (Rom. 8:2)."[7] Discipleship is essentially a matter of hearing

---

6. Webster, "Evangelical Freedom," in *Essays in Christian Dogmatics*, vol. 2, *Confessing God*, 2nd ed. (London: Bloomsbury T&T Clark, 2016), 223.

7. Webster, "Evangelical Freedom," 225.

(authority), believing (trust), and doing the truth (freedom) that is in Jesus Christ.

Tragically, many people are either hearkening to other words that promise to ensure their identity or failing to attend sufficiently to the word of the gospel. James describes one who hears and does as "like a man who looks intently at his natural face in a mirror" (Jas 1:23). What is required is not a casual glance but careful consideration and constant attention (*katanoeō*) to Scripture's depiction of the new self in Christ. What we see in the mirror of the biblical text is Jesus, the image of the invisible God in human form. It was this same Jesus who stood before Pilate, a living mirror as it were. Jesus tells Pilate, "Everyone who is of the truth listens to my voice" (John 18:37). But Pilate was only half-listening, asking, "What is truth?" (John 18:38).

Jesus bears true witness to the truth. Indeed, Jesus himself *is* God's truth claim about God and humanity alike. Similarly, the gospel bears true witness to new life in Christ and tells the truth about existence in Christ. It is not an *obvious* truth, however, which is why, in making disciples, the church must persist in attending to it. Pilate's inability to attend to and subsequent dismissal of the truth standing before him was an epic failure of hearing and doing. Pilate does not follow Jesus but walks out on him. In doing so, he condemns himself, for he has failed to acknowledge the authority of truth, namely, the God who is the source of all truth. In failing to judge Jesus rightly, Pilate also fails at his primary vocation as governor. There is special irony in Pilate getting word from his wife declaring Jesus righteous, and ignoring it, "while he was sitting on the judgment seat" (Matt 27:19).

Pilate judged wrongly. The Roman social imaginary prevented him from seeing the truth standing before him. In mistaking truth, he abused his authority. In a real sense, discipleship is a response to truth and authority alike. Today we are confronted with more claims than ever before about which way leads to eternal youth, wellness, or flourishing. The problem of authority, in Pilate's day and ours, "is the problem of establishing criteria for the discernment and prosecution of truth: for 'hearing' the truth and 'doing' it."[8] In contrast to Pilate, who left the question of truth hanging midair, disciples respond rightly to Jesus by hearing and doing the truth that is in him, the truth (about God and humanity and their relationship) that Jesus *is*.

A true disciple of Jesus must be both a hearer and doer of Jesus' authoritative words. To hear and obey the word of Jesus is to respond to the truth in freedom. These are big ideas—authority, truth, obedience, freedom—and it is important to parse them correctly. The eminently biblical idea of "doing the truth" helps to unpack the grammar of these concepts. Pastors need to speak in grammatically correct ways (that is, in accordance with the Scriptures) in order to free their congregations from a secular social imaginary in which the words "authority" and "obedience" suggest a way of living that is either outmoded or oppressive. What we need to communicate is that, in following Jesus, disciples leave their bondage to the flesh and enter into a freedom of the Spirit in which obedience leads not to frustration, but flourishing.

Today people discover, declare, or dispute the truth, but few people speak of *doing* it like the Bible does: "But whoever *does* what is true comes to the light" (John 3:21). Truth is something to be not only believed but also *obeyed* (Rom 2:8; Gal 5:7). Furthermore, "If we say we have fellowship with [God] while we walk in darkness, we lie and do not *practice* [*do*] the truth" (1 John 1:6). In particular, disciples are to do or live out the truth

---

8. Nicholas Lash, *Voices of Authority* (London: Sheed and Ward, 1976), 24.

of the gospel (recall the face in James's mirror). The *doing* in question is not busywork, moral striving, or even works of love. The doing is from first to last a matter of *corresponding* to what is in Christ, that is, living in accord with the truth of the gospel.

We know what it is to proclaim the gospel, but how does one "do" the truth of the gospel? On the one hand, the gospel announces a one-time, never-to-be-repeated event: the good news that the Father raised the Son in the power of the Spirit, together with the people of God (adopted children) whom God adopts as his treasured possession. Strictly speaking, we don't "do" the gospel but proclaim it. Yet in another sense we do: "For as often as you eat this bread and drink the cup, you *proclaim* the Lord's death until he comes" (1 Cor 11:26). Arguably, everything we do that puts to death what is earthly (the old self) and puts on the new self is a way of proclaiming Jesus' death and resurrection, and thus of living in the light of the gospel (Col 3:1–10).

Disciples do the truth when they follow Jesus' new reality-depicting words (about the kingdom of God) and, ultimately, the risen Christ himself, the instantiation of this new reality. Disciples are called to follow neither a philosophy, nor a moral code, nor justice, nor inclusiveness, nor even orthodoxy, but the person of Jesus Christ: God's word made flesh, the image of true God and thus the exemplar of what it is to be truly human. Accept no substitutes! As Dietrich Bonhoeffer put it: in discipleship, "Jesus is the only content."[9] Disciples do the truth, then, by following his way and living out his life: "It is no longer I who live, but Christ who lives in me" (Gal 2:20). This is the truth the disciple sees when peering intently into the mirror of the gospel:

---

9. Dietrich Bonhoeffer, *Discipleship*, ed. Geffrey B. Kelly and John D. Godsey, trans. Barbara Green and Reinhard Krauss, Dietrich Bonhoeffer Works 4 (Minneapolis: Fortress, 2001), 59.

the reality of a new self, renewed in the image of Jesus Christ (2 Cor 3:18). It is this new reality of freedom in the kingdom of God's beloved Son (Col 1:13) that is the catalyst of the Christian *royal* imaginary. To be a disciple is to hear, do, and adore what we see there, in the mirror of Scripture: the lordship of Jesus Christ.

WAKING AND WALKING: STARTING AND STAYING THE COURSE OF DISCIPLESHIP

The Bible describes discipleship in terms not only of hearing and doing but also of waking and walking. All four terms are familiar to people of all classes and cultures—all the more reason to reclaim these powerful biblical metaphors as we seek also to reform the social imaginary of the society of Jesus, that is, the church.

Waking

A disciple is a follower. We speak of following directions, arguments, and stories as well as people. Literal interpretation of texts is a matter of "following the way the words go." But whose words—whose stories, whose social imaginary—are we following?

My strong conviction is that many people today, including many Christians, are following stories—which is to say, living them out—that enslave rather than free them. We have taken someone's word for it without testing the spirit behind that word to see whether it is from God or a false prophet (1 John 4:1). All we, like culturally conditioned sheep, have gone astray; we have turned to follow popular wisdom and political correctness; we have bowed the knee to Oprah or Chopra (or both). I worry that we are sleepwalking our way through life, asleep at the wheel of our own existence, going through the motions but not really

paying attention to whose story we inhabit. We may think we're
engaged in the real world—of salaries, taxes, home repairs, and
politics—but in fact we're caught in what C. S. Lewis calls the
shadowlands. If consciousness were a cinema, what film would
be playing most of the time? What is probably going through our
minds at any given moment is either the world news, a family
crisis, what's immediately in front of us, a long-term plan, or
a YouTube video.

Lewis describes his conversion to Christ as an awakening.
We might describe discipleship as the project of helping people
to become fully awake and to stay awake, by which I mean alert
to the opportunities and the dangers of the Christian life. Jesus'
disciples had a hard time staying awake, even when they were
living through the most dramatic scenes of Jesus' story. Just
before his arrest in the garden of Gethsemane, Jesus took Peter
and two others to pray. They fell asleep. Jesus tells them: "Watch
and pray that you may not enter into temptation" (Matt 26:41).
He again goes off to pray—which is to say, to focus with all his
being on what is most real: God's will—but upon his return he
finds them once again asleep.

True disciples are awake and alert to what is going on in the
world, to what is really real, namely, the "real presence" of Jesus
Christ. The true story of the world, narrated in Scripture, concerns God's presence and activity. However, the social imaginary
bewitches us with other accounts of what is really going on. Lewis
brilliantly illustrates the importance of waking to reality in a
scene from *The Silver Chair*. The queen of Underland is holding
Jill, Eustace, and Puddleglum captive in her subterranean lair
and tries to convince them that there is no other world outside
her cavern. (Recall the myth of the cave from Plato's *Republic*.)
She creates conditions conducive to sleepiness—soft music, dim
lights, a pleasant smell—and then lies, weaving a false story of

the world: "There is no land called Narnia. ... There never was any world but mine." Suddenly Puddleglum does something that ought to make Christian disciples proud: he stamps his feet in a fire, which rouses him and clears his head. He is awake, and alert to the witch's subterfuge.

Disciples of Jesus Christ have similarly been jolted awake, not by in-fired feet but by the tongues of fire, from above, that accompany the new birth and the gift of the Spirit (Acts 2:3; cf. Mt 3:11). The Spirit awakens us to life in the new reality in Christ, to the story of what the Triune God has done, is doing, and will do in Jesus Christ. It is this story that singes not our feet but our hearts, like those of the two disciples on the Emmaus road: "Did not our hearts burn within us while he talked to us on the road, while he [the risen Christ] opened to us the Scriptures?" (Luke 24:32).

This burning is the difference between merely hearing—a passive receiving of information—and the kind of hearing that leads to doing. Theology involves more than sifting through and settling on the right doctrinal position. Simply telling people what to think in order to be orthodox, and then expecting them to become disciples, is like telling people what they should eat in order to be healthy and then expecting them to lose weight. The Mayo Clinic Diet is more realistic: "To be successful at losing weight you need to figure out what will give you an *ongoing, burning desire* to succeed."[10] Desire is the operative term, as James K. A. Smith makes clear by putting it in the title of the first volume in his Cultural Liturgies series: *Desiring the Kingdom: Worship, Worldview, and Cultural Formation*. Following Augustine in particular, Smith calls the church (and Christian colleges) to

---

10. *The Mayo Clinic Diet* (Intercourse, PA: Good Books, 2012), 13 (emphasis original).

stop focusing on the intellect in discipleship, and to pay more attention to the heart—and to what makes it burn with desire.

Smith knows all about Taylor's social imaginary, and so, he argues, does Augustine: "Our ultimate love is oriented by and to a picture of what we think it looks like for us to live well."[11] Smith rightly sees that one cannot make disciples (or lose weight) simply by changing minds and worldviews. He wants to change patterns of behavior by socializing people into the bodily life of the church, and into an alternative social imaginary. I do too. We agree that the imagination is a key factor in making disciples. Yet we become disciples not simply by participating in Christian liturgical practices but by participating in—living into and acting out—Scripture's canonical practices and, yes, Christian doctrine (see 1 Tim 4:16).

The imagination is a cognitive faculty—a kind of thinking—which is precisely why Jesus *taught* by *telling stories*. Learning Scripture and theology similarly require imagination, by which I mean the ability to grasp patterns and relate parts to the whole that gives them meaning.[12] The imagination is what enables us to experience stories as both meaningful and powerful. What disciples need to learn is not simply discrete liturgical practices but the canonical habits that enable us to read Scripture as a unified story, a story that captures our imaginations—both our large-scale thinking and the desires of our hearts—and therefore a story we want to indwell.[13] It is by reading Scripture theologically

---

11. James K. A. Smith, *Desiring the Kingdom: Worship, Worldview, and Cultural Formation* (Grand Rapids: Baker Academic, 2009), 53.

12. For more on the imagination and discipleship, see my "In Bright Shadow: C. S. Lewis on the Imagination for Theology and Discipleship," in *The Romantic Rationalist: God, Life, and the Imagination in the Work of C. S. Lewis*, ed. John Piper and David Mathis (Wheaton, IL: Crossway, 2014), 81–104.

13. For helpful engagement with Smith's Cultural Liturgies project, see Ryan Jackson, "A Pauline Strategy for Challenging Cultural Liturgies: Making

and with imagination as a story of what God is doing in Christ through the Spirit that we come to see, and *feel*, our true selves in its mirror. It is seeing who we really are—those who by grace have been adopted into God's family in Christ, fellow heirs with Christ (Rom 8:17)—that forms the burning desire to become what we are: children of God; little Christs.

Walking

It takes imagination to see that God "has delivered us from the domain of darkness and transferred us to the kingdom of his beloved Son" (Col 1:13). The kingdom came with Jesus, and all who are in Christ are part of his realm and rule. Disciples must awake to the reality of this kingdom, stay awake, and then begin walking about in it. In the first instance, this means waking up to the reality of their union with Christ, their being "in Christ." In a real sense, Jesus is the substance of his call. In Jesus, the disciples encountered the in-breaking of the kingdom of God: God's rule as it was coming to be in Christ. To be called or elected by God is to be chosen for a kingdom purpose: "It is appointment to movement, movement in relation to a greater divine movement which is already underway in Jesus himself, the movement of the coming of God."[14]

To be a disciple, one has to get moving. It is important not to forget that the movement disciples make is enabled by the prior call and waking. John Webster explains: to follow Jesus "is not to start a fresh movement but to enter into one which precedes us

---

Corinthian Disciples," *Bulletin of Ecclesial Theology* 3, no. 1 (2016): 65–85; and David S. Morlan, "A Review of James K. A. Smith's Cultural Liturgies Series," *Bulletin of Ecclesial Theology* 3, no. 1 (2016): 1–13.

14. John Webster, "Discipleship and Calling," *Scottish Bulletin of Evangelical Theology* 23 (2005): 140.

and catches us up into itself."[15] This "movement" is the coursing of Jesus' life through ours. It involves faith and action, bodily movement. It involves, in a word, *walking*. Walking follows waking as doing follows hearing. Jesus calls disciples not to take up their bed and walk (John 5:8) but to get out of bed and walk. Paul tells the Ephesians that they are God's workmanship, "created in Christ Jesus for good works, which God prepared beforehand, that we should *walk* in them" (Eph 2:10). A disciple is a learner who spends his or her life walking after Jesus.

One of the names for the Christian community, used six times in the book of Acts, is "the Way" (Acts 9:2, 19:9, 23; 22:4; 24:14, 22). The background is probably the Old Testament contrast between two paths: the foolish "way of the wicked" and the wise "way of the righteous" (Ps 1:6). In the New Testament, Paul too depicts the Christian life in terms of contrasting ways: life versus death (Rom 6:4), wise versus foolish (1 Cor 1:18–31), light versus darkness (Eph 5:8), faith versus sight (2 Cor 5:7), good works versus sins (Eph 2:1–2, 10). To follow Jesus Christ is to belong to the Way of the one who is the righteousness of God (Rom 3:21). Of course, one cannot belong to the Way without walking in it. Walking is a transcultural human experience and is one of the Bible's key images for both personal lifestyle (think life trajectory) and interpersonal interaction (think companionship on a path or pilgrimage). One's "walk" refers to the way one lives. God requires that his people "walk before me, and be blameless" (Gen 17:1; cf. Ps 119:1). The tragedy of Israel was that, in spite of having God's way written, the law, most of her kings "walked in the ways" of previous kings, doing evil (see, for example, 1 Kgs 15:3).

---

15. Webster, "Discipleship and Obedience," 6.

Jesus encourages his followers to walk in the light rather than in darkness (John 8:12). Jesus is the light (John 9:5), so "whoever says he abides in him ought to walk in the same way in which he walked" (1 John 2:6). Jesus is the answer to the psalmist's petition, "Send out your light and your truth; let them lead me" (Ps 43:3), for Jesus is "the way, and the truth, and the life" (John 14:6). In a striking turn of phrase, the apostle John, addressing "the elect lady and her children" (2 John 1)—the local church and her members—twice expresses his joy at hearing that these church members are "walking in the truth" (2 John 4; 3 John 4). To walk in the truth is to live in accordance with the truth of the gospel, that is, the truth of the new reality that has come into being in and through Christ's person and work. This truth is that all church members are children of God who have been given the Spirit of adoption (Rom 8:15), the Spirit of Christ (Rom 8:9), so that there is no longer any ethnic or class divisions that separate members of the body of Christ (Gal 3:28). "If we live by the Spirit, let us also keep in step with the Spirit" (Gal 5:25). To walk in the truth is to live in the light of this knowledge of this truth in the power of the Spirit.

According to the US Department of Health and Human Services, physical activity "is key to improving the health of the Nation."[16] In 2008, the department released its "Physical Activity Guidelines for Americans," recommending at least 150 minutes a week of moderate-intensity activity, such as brisk walking. It does not endorse the trendy ten-thousand-steps-a-day rule, but it is consistent with it. As with physical walking, one's "walk" consists of the hundreds and thousands of choices we make: "Choose this day whom you will serve" (Josh 24:15).

---

16. "Physical Activity," Health.gov, https://health.gov/paguidelines/default.aspx (accessed July 11, 2018).

Every step we take is the result of a decision, either to follow our own way or the Way of Jesus Christ. Christian discipleship is companionship with Christ. The Christian Way is that of the long-distance walker, a long obedience in the same direction, where day in and day out, with each step we take, we choose to live in a way that follows Jesus and corresponds to the truth—our new life in him.

Making disciples is a step-by-step process of helping men and women to walk the Way of Jesus Christ. It involves waking up to the Way, then setting out on it. Scripture and doctrine are precious road signs and guardrails for staying on the Way. They help form what we might call the evangelical imaginary—a way of thinking about reality generated and governed by the gospel. When disciples lose sight of the evangelical imaginary, they risk making missteps. One egregious example of such a misstep is Peter's failure to stay "in step with the truth of the gospel" (Gal 2:14) by refusing to eat with gentiles when the "circumcision party"—Judaizers from Jerusalem—showed up in Antioch. The truth of the gospel is that there is "neither Jew nor Greek" (Gal 3:28), but Peter denied this truth by his actions. He failed to do the truth because, at least for a moment, his imagination was taken captive by a story about God and the world *not* governed by the gospel. It is no small thing to live in such a way that you deny the new reality that Jesus died to bring about. Peter's misstep led to hypocrisy, which is the profession without the practice of discipleship. Paul opposed Peter to his face and then corrected him through Scripture and doctrine (Gal 2:15–21).

We are now in a better position to appreciate the title and cover of the present book. The emphasis is on the ampersand—hearers *and* doers—and the ascent. The doing involves walking, and the walking involves climbing. For eight years, I walked to work when teaching at the University of Edinburgh. It was my policy never to be passed by another pedestrian, especially when going up a long incline called Middle Meadow Walk. I've never been as fit since. Edinburgh is a hilly city, but I now inhabit Midwestern plains.

For me and all the other inhabitants of Flatland, there is StairMaster, a fitness equipment company that has been making "stepping machines" since 1983. With the StairMaster, one does not simply walk, but climbs. The company features a number of products, including my favorite, the Gauntlet 8G, a machine that features a revolving eight-step staircase, a kind of "upwardly mobile" motorized treadmill. It comes complete with an LCD console that is loaded with the Landmark Challenge program, allowing users to climb their way to the tops of famous structures from around the world like the Statue of Liberty, Eiffel Tower, and Taj Mahal.

In addition to being the sort of movement we must make to follow a particular way, then, walking is a form of exercise. The apostle Paul agreed: "I press on toward the goal for the prize of the upward call of God in Christ Jesus" (Phil 3:14). This is the "one thing" for which Paul has a burning desire, the one thing that motivates his movement: "the surpassing worth of knowing Christ Jesus" (Phil 3:8). The movement of discipleship is "upward" because God "has blessed us in Christ with every spiritual blessing in the heavenly places" (Eph 1:3).

Discipleship is a walk "upward" to a higher place of existence, but not higher than the earth. After all, Jesus walked the earth, and taught his disciples to pray that God's will would be done "*on earth* as it is in heaven" (Matt 6:10). To do God's will on earth as it is in heaven is to walk around earth as if it were heaven, that is, the place of God's presence and the sphere of God's rule. We are to "walk by the Spirit" (Gal 5:16), and where the Spirit is, there is freedom. Jesus is less our moral exemplar (as in the once-popular WWJD bracelets) than the first of his kind, a new humanity (Eph 2:15) in which we discover a new self (Eph 4:24; Col 3:10). The upward steps represent a visual attempt to say something about the eschatological nature of discipleship, a topic to which we'll return in the next chapter. Suffice it to say that to walk in the truth is to live on a higher plane, for we "share in a heavenly calling" (Heb 3:1). I like to think of the church's corporate life as itself a parable of the kingdom. It is because we are *seated* with Christ in the heavenly places (Eph 2:6) that we can *walk* like him on earth.

The church is a body, and disciples are to walk, but disciples are after something more than physical fitness, something more even than the holistic fitness associated with wellness programs. As we have seen, a picture of wellness holds our fitness culture captive. The irony is that our preoccupation with physical fitness, health, and wellness has led us to overlook the fact that the church, as a body, lacks fitness. When physical bodies lack discipline, they fall out of shape. The same is true of the church, the body of Christ. When the church lacks discipline, the body of Christ becomes profane: *unfit* for purpose, unable to accomplish its mission.

Hearers and Doers calls church members, individually and corporately, to shape up.

4

DOCTRINE FOR DISCIPLESHIP

*From Bodybuilding to Building
Up the Body of Christ*

Spiritual formation is happening all the time. Culture and society are in the full-time business of making disciples, not to life in Christ but to a variety of *lifestyles*, all informed by culturally conditioned pictures of health, wellness, and fitness. As we have seen, however, it is notoriously difficult to define fitness by itself, which is why the US Armed Forces speak of *fit for purpose*. In a military context, the purpose was warfare, and though the concept of Total Force Fitness is more holistic, the basic idea behind basic training is that soldiers are being equipped on a variety of levels to be the kind of persons who will be able to carry out their mission efficiently and as safely as possible.

Theology serves the church by helping make disciples *fit for purpose*, but the purpose is not, strictly speaking, military.

Peter showed good fighting instincts when the Roman soldiers came to arrest Jesus, but Jesus told him, "Put your sword into its sheath" (John 18:11), and he later tells Pilate, "If my kingdom were of this world, my servants would have been fighting"—but it is not (John 18:36). Make no mistake: Jesus *did* think about discipleship in terms of fit for purpose. In Luke 9, a chapter that is all about discipleship, Jesus meets three people who say they want to become followers. Fittingly enough, the conversation takes place as they are *walking*, the operative concept in discipleship. Jesus gives each of them a brief lesson in discipleship, but it is the third that is most relevant for present purposes: "No one who puts his hand to the plow and looks back is *fit* for the kingdom of God" (Luke 9:62). To put your hand to the plow is to begin the work of a farmer, but looking back indicates distraction from the work, likely resulting in a crooked furrow.

And there you have it. Disciples of Jesus are *fit for purpose* when they are able to act as heralds and representatives of the kingdom of God. Humans were originally created in the image of God to be his vice-regents and representatives on earth, charged with cultivating creation. Similarly, disciples are re-created (regenerated) in the image of the one who is the image of God, namely, Jesus Christ. To be fit for the purpose of advancing the kingdom of God, disciples have to be like their king. To be fit for the purpose of representing the kingdom of God means becoming Christlike, which, as we have seen, means being able to embody the new creation that is in Christ, who is seated in the heavenly realms, on earth. Disciples are fit for their kingdom purpose not when they can fight for its coming, but rather when they can witness, with every fiber of their being, to its arrival.

CULTIVATING FITNESS, CIVILIZING CITIZENS

Discipleship is a call, a vocation, to follow Jesus everywhere, before everyone, at every time. Every step we take is part of our walk, and the way we walk defines who we are. Theology serves the church by helping make disciples fit for the purpose of walking after Jesus, representing him and his kingdom. There is an individual and corporate dimension to discipleship. Disciples must be fit for purpose: for godliness, for citizenship in the gospel, and for building up the church, the body of Christ. "You yourselves like living stones are being built up as a spiritual house" (1 Pet 2:5). Augustine famously compares this spiritual house to a city of God, a heavenly city marked by love of God rather than the self-love that characterizes citizens of the earthly city.

Paul says, "our citizenship is in heaven" (Phil 3:20), and this leads to the main claim of the present section: disciple-making is ultimately a matter of preparing persons to live as citizens of the gospel (Phil 1:27; cf. Eph 2:19). In ancient Greece, "the official purpose of the gymnasium was to create citizens and soldiers fit for the purpose of the *polis* [city]."[1] Aristotle saw the obligations of citizenship, to work for the common good, to encompass everyday life so that one could not separate private from public life.[2] Today we understand citizens to be members not simply of a *polis* (city) but of a nation in which one enjoys rights and assumes responsibilities.

Good citizenship involves actively assuming one's responsibilities for the common good, like keeping the law. In ancient Greece and Rome, citizenship was for an elite, in contrast

---

1. Eric Chaline, *The Temple of Perfection* (London: Reaktion, 2015), 13.
2. See the discussion in Aristotle, *Politics*, bk. 3.

with modern democracies, where almost anyone can be a citizen. A few years ago, E. D. Hirsch wrote *Cultural Literacy: What Every American Needs to Know*. The title prompts the question: need to know *for what*? Hirsch's answer: "To be culturally literate is to possess the basic information needed to thrive in the modern world."[3] Cultural literacy is about learning what one needs to know in order to become a competent participant in the American experiment, that is, the social experiment that is American democracy. Hirsch argues that there are certain things Americans need to know—"core knowledge"—in order to function in American society.

I propose that we combine Aristotle's and Hirsch's insights and apply them to the task of making disciples. In reading Scripture and formulating doctrine, the pastor-theologian forms competent citizens of the gospel and, in a sense, thereby "civilizes" them (from Latin *civilis* = "relating to a citizen"). What we're after is canonical and theological literacy—in a word, *catechesis*. Theologians are catechists, and a catechism is a training manual that sums up and spells out the biblical story, from creation and fall to cross and consummation. In doing so, the catechism informs disciples of what they need to know—core Christian knowledge—in order to be effective citizens of the gospel. Stated differently: we help disciples learn how to follow Jesus by teaching them Scripture and doctrine. The true disciple learns in order to become fit for purpose: fit for *polis*; fit for good gospel citizenship; fit to embody the values and proclaim the excellencies of the *holy* nation to which they belong (1 Pet 2:9).

Other theologians have recovered the key catechetical insight that doctrine serves the project of making disciples. One

---

3. E. D. Hirsch Jr., *Cultural Literacy: What Every American Needs to Know* (New York: Vintage, 1988), xiii.

book that does this is Keith Johnson's aptly named *Theology as Discipleship*, in which he argues that learning core Christian doctrines is "one of the ways we participate in the life of the triune God."[4] The book examines several doctrines, in each case showing how learning theology enriches discipleship and how faithful obedience to Christ enables the learning of theology. On this view, theology is itself a mode of following Jesus, a form of discipleship. Though he does not use the term *social imaginary*, he is aware of the importance of the big picture, and of capturing the disciple's imagination: "Scripture enables us to see the true nature of created reality and history, and one of our key tasks is to figure out how to participate in reality rightly by finding our place in the history narrated by the text."[5] In chapter 6, I will suggest something similar, describing doctrine as direction for participating in the drama of redemption. Finally, Johnson rightly insists that theology is valuable only to the extent that it helps disciples *learn Christ*: "One of the key tasks of a disciple is to seek to understand everything—from the nature of God's eternal being to the entire created order to our own lives—in the light of Jesus, because he is the one 'in whom are hidden all the treasures of wisdom and knowledge' (Col 2:3)."[6]

Trevin K. Wax's book *Eschatological Discipleship* also views theology as a means of disciple-making, but his focus is on one doctrine in particular: last things. Eschatology deals with end times, and if one of the challenges of discipleship is figuring out what it means to follow Jesus Christ *today*, then it becomes

---

4. Keith L. Johnson, *Theology as Discipleship* (Downers Grove, IL: IVP Academic, 2015), 12. See also Johnson's colleague Beth Felker Jones's book *Practicing Christian Doctrine: An Introduction to Thinking and Living Theologically* (Grand Rapids: Baker Academic, 2014), in which she states: "Doctrine and discipleship always go together" (4).

5. Johnson, *Theology as Discipleship*, 13.

6. Johnson, *Theology as Discipleship*, 15.

important to know *what time it is*: "Discipleship is grounded in the larger story of the world and where the world is going, as articulated in Scripture."[7] In a real sense, the end of history—the coming kingdom of God—has already broken into history in Jesus' resurrection. Accordingly, Christians are "a people belonging to that future."[8] Jesus reprimands the Pharisees for not knowing what time it was: "The kingdom of God *is* in the midst of you" (Luke 17:21).

Eschatological discipleship uses one particular doctrine to help draw a thick description of what it means to follow Jesus Christ today. When we seek to understand the times in which we live, we attend to the biblical account in contrast to rival stories and conceptions of time, history, and progress. Make no mistake: every social imaginary—the myth of progress, neo-Darwinism, Marxism, transhumanism, consumerism (their name is Legion)—has an eschatology, a sense of how the human story will end and where we are in relation to the end.[9] Accordingly, followers of Christ must have a sense of what history the church is a part, and where we are in that history. Toward the end of his closing exhortations to the church in Rome, Paul writes what could well be the magna carta for eschatological discipleship: "Besides this you know the time, that the hour has come for you to wake from sleep. For salvation is nearer to us now than when we first believed" (Rom 13:11). Disciples who have learned where they are in the biblical story will have a sense of urgency, but not anxiety, about the future.

---

7. Trevin K. Wax, *Eschatological Discipleship: Leading Christians to Understand Their Historical and Cultural Context* (Nashville: B&H Academic, 2018), 28.

8. Wax, *Eschatological Discipleship*, 34.

9. Wax examines three rival eschatologies: Enlightenment naturalism, the sexual revolution, and consumerism (*Eschatological Discipleship*, 99–187).

I welcome all attempts to show how theology serves the church by making disciples who can read Scripture well and live into the new reality—being in Christ—that doctrine describes. In addition to appreciating their being in Christ, disciples need to have the mind of Christ (1 Cor 2:16; cf. Phil 2:5): "If we know God through Christ ... then we should live like Christ by performing acts of humility and self-sacrificial love for others."[10] In other words, we should live out our citizenship of the gospel, and this requires living differently from those who do not know God, who are "darkened in their understanding, alienated from the life of God because of the ignorance that is in them" (Eph 4:18). There is more: these citizens of darkness "have given themselves up to sensuality, greedy to practice every kind of impurity" (Eph 4:19). But this, says Paul, "is not the way you learned Christ!" (Eph 4:20).

A disciple is a person who is learning Christ. It's a more ambitious subject than astronomy, history, physics, and philosophy combined, for Christ is the culmination of God's plan and the summation of God's wisdom as the gathering place of all things in heaven and earth (Eph 1:10). To learn Christ, then, we need to know how the Scriptures fit together and focus on him. Discipleship requires biblical interpretation, and biblical interpretation is a form of discipleship (that is, following the way the words are about the Word). To learn Christ is to learn to read the Scriptures as testimony to his person and work. To read rightly involves learning doctrine, the treasury of apostolic tradition, as well (2 Thess 2:15). To read rightly, we must also learn what it means to follow him in our contemporary context. Making disciples through Scripture and doctrine is a matter of following

---

10. Johnson, *Theology as Discipleship*, 147.

the words that lead to Christ in order to live lives worthy of our
citizenship of the gospel of Jesus Christ.[11]

THEOLOGICAL CORE EXERCISES FOR THE YOUNG AND OLD: BIBLICAL LITERACY FOR GOSPEL CITIZENSHIP

Jesus used a number of parables to describe the kingdom of God.
I am merely following in his steps by drawing on a number of
contemporary metaphors to describe the process of making disciples: physical (bodybuilding), medical (health and fitness), and
political (citizenship). All three images can claim biblical roots.
This continuity shows the importance of transforming the imagination in making disciples. To make hearers into doers, we need
to appeal not only to the intellect but also to the imagination.
To make disciples, pastor-theologians must take "every thought
captive to obey Christ" (2 Cor 10:5), a campaign that necessarily
includes capturing the social imaginary of our congregations.

I'll continue to use metaphors throughout the rest of the
book. This is one way of inciting hearers to become doers. In particular, I'll be using different metaphors to discuss the task and
contribution of theology, so often reviled as having nothing to
offer to the Christian life (hence the tired pun about seminaries/
cemeteries). The primary focus in part 2 is the role of reading
the Bible theologically in making disciples. After all, the Bible
is not only the story that ought to capture the church's imaginations but also the authoritative constitution that rules the

---

11. See further my "From Bible to Theology: Learning Christ," in *Theology,
Church, and Ministry: A Handbook for Theological Education*, ed. David Dockery
(Nashville: B&H Academic, 2017), 233–56.

freedom of the Christian. To make disciples is to teach people how to become biblically literate so they can be effective inhabitants and representatives of the city of God, for the purpose of gospel citizenship. *Accordingly, this book is a guide for hearing and reading the Bible rightly, as well as a training manual for doing the Bible rightly. The goal is to train disciples to walk around in the strange new world of the Bible even as they live in the familiar old world of the present. It is a pastor's guide for training hearers and doers, faithful followers of Jesus Christ and faithful interpreters of the Word that directs us in his Way.*

Biblical Literacy: What Every Christian Citizen Needs to Know

To read the Bible rightly is to read it as the word of God with and for the people of God, yesterday and today. This is more radical than it sounds. For more than two hundred years or so, the Bible has been treated in the academy as a document of the university, that is, a document that can be studied just like any other historical text. In other words, the church's Scripture has died, and what has risen in its place is the academy's Bible, to use Michael Legaspi's provocative turn of phrase.[12]

In the modern academy, the study of Scripture has become a largely secular science, known as "biblical studies." Biblical scholars take a critical rather than a confessional approach to the study of the Bible, taking great care not to impose later theological ideas onto the texts. The aim is to ascertain the meaning for the original historical authors and readers, and at least as concerns the Old Testament, this means keeping Jesus Christ out of the picture. Of course, individual scholars engaged in

---

12. Michael Legaspi, *The Death of Scripture and the Rise of Biblical Studies* (Oxford: Oxford University Press, 2010).

biblical studies may be Christians. By and large, however, they have to argue for their conservative positions with the same critical tools as their secular counterparts.

This situation has prompted a reaction, a "Let my people go read the Bible in an edifying way" kind of movement, if you will—an "exodus" from modern critical studies. Reading the Bible theologically, with and for the people of God, means reading it not with the scholar's interest of discovering what the historical authors behind the text thought about God but rather with the saint's interest in coming to hear God, to believe God, to do what God says, and thereby to grow more like God. In a word: reading the Bible theologically is less an academic discipline than a course in church discipleship. The aim of reading Scripture theologically is to train citizens of the gospel, disciples *fit for purpose*, having the core knowledge they need to function effectively as those who can follow Christ, embodying his mind everywhere, always, and to everyone. Here, then, are seven initial theses on reading the Bible theologically.[13]

1. *The nature and function of the Bible are insufficiently grasped unless and until we see it as having both human and divine authors, and therefore as no less than the living and active word of God.* Those who approach the Bible as Scripture must not abstract it from the Father who ultimately authors it, the Son to whom it witnesses, and the Spirit who inspired and illumines it. Reading Scripture theologically acknowledges the priority of God's communicative activity as well as the integrity of human authorship. That the Bible is (a) a word of God that (b) speaks to readers in

---

13. I have borrowed and modified these seven theses from a longer list, first published in "Interpreting Scripture between the Rock of Biblical Studies and the Hard Place of Systematic Theology: The State of the Evangelical (Dis)Union," in *Renewing the Evangelical Mission*, ed. Richard Lints (Grand Rapids: Eerdmans, 2013), 211–14.

their own day captures the two most important assumptions that all early Christians implicitly adopted.

2. An appreciation of the theological nature of the Bible entails a rejection of a methodological atheism that treats the texts as having a "natural history" only. The Bible is like and unlike other books: like other books, the Bible has authors; unlike other books, its primary author is God. As people who want to read the Bible for what it really is, the Word of God in human words, we must take care not to separate the biblical texts from the communicative action of the Triune God. Reading the Bible is part of our creaturely and covenantal relationship to God, hence the doctrines that speak to that relationship (such as sin, regeneration, sanctification, ecclesiology) also have a bearing on the act of reading.

3. Theological interpreters view the historical events recounted in Scripture as ingredients in a unified story ordered by an economy of Triune providence. The biblical authors are inspired witnesses to a coherent series of events ultimately authored by God. There is no square inch of human history that is extrinsic to the mission fields of Son and Spirit.

4. Because the Old Testament and New Testament testify to the one true God and the same story of redemption, to read the Bible theologically means reading it in canonical context. The Bible has a "natural history," but it also constitutes its own context as the "complete works" of its divine author. It is especially at the level of the canon that the divine intentions that unify the Old and New Testaments come into focus. It is at the canonical level that we see how the subject matter of the Bible is the history of God's covenant faithfulness. It is the story of how God keeps his word: to Adam, Noah, Abraham, Moses, David, and so on.

5. Because Jesus promised his disciples that the Spirit would lead the church into all truth, those who read Scripture today should do so with a healthy respect for the catholic tradition of reading. To read

the Bible theologically is to read in the communion of the saints.
For example, we owe the insight into the unity of the Old and
New Testaments to precritical readers—fathers and Reformers—
who developed and maintained the rule of faith that generated
in turn a typological rule for reading, in which earlier events
and persons prefigured later aspects of the person and work of
Christ. We shall return to this point in chapter 7.

6. *The end of biblical interpretation is not simply communication—the sharing of information—but communion, a sharing in
the light, life, and love of God.* The word of God is not mocked: we
may think we can master it, but it is "living and active," turning
the spotlight on us, "discerning the thoughts and intentions of
[our] heart" (Heb 4:12). It can also circumcise our hearts, renew
our minds, and transform us (Rom 12:2). We need to recover
the practice of reading Scripture in order to renew our mission and reform our habits. Reading the Bible theologically is
as much if not more a matter of spiritual formation as it is a
procedure readers work on the text: "God's employment of the
words of Scripture to be an instrument of his own communicative presence, by which process they [viz., the words] are made
holy, has its goal and essential counterpart in God's formation
of a holy people."[14]

7. *The church is that community where good habits of theological
interpretation are best formed and where the fruit of these habits are
best exhibited.* The Bible's communicative aim is to foster communion with God and one another. God calls the church into
being to be the community that facilitates this happening. The
church is not one more interpretive community with its own
set of idiosyncratic interests, but the divinely appointed context

14. Murray Rae, "On Reading Scripture Theologically," *Princeton Theological
Review* 14, no. 1 (2008): 23.

wherein God ministers new life via his word and Spirit. Strictly speaking, "Scripture" makes no sense apart from the community whose life, thought, and practice it exists to rule and shape.

These seven theses have set out what pastors need to know in order to help disciples to read the Bible theologically, that is, in ways that allow God's word to be the training manual in righteousness (2 Tim 3:16) God intends for it to be. Let the exercises begin!

Becoming Cross-Fit

On a Saturday morning in 2006, David Redding and Tim Whitmire held their first boot-camp workout for men, marking the beginning of what is now a nationwide organization: F3—Fitness, Fellowship, and Faith. You might say that F3 puts the *cross* into CrossFit, though both groups are known for their religious-like fervor. F3's mission is "to plant, grow and serve small workout groups for men for the invigoration of male community leadership."[15] The early-morning workouts are free, open to all, fairly intense, held outdoors, and led by participants in a rotating fashion. Each group becomes a Circle of Trust (their website has a Lexicon), each member a Man of Action, and together they constitute F3 Nation.

We saw in chapter 2 how many Americans are in thrall to a fitness culture that projects body images and promises health and wellness in return for buying into a particular diet or training program. We also saw how a concern for fitness prompts the important follow-up question, Fit for what purpose? The way one answers that question speaks volumes about the social imaginary that governs one's picture of the meaning of life and

---

15. "Introduction to F3," F3, https://f3nation.com/new-to-f3/ (accessed July 14, 2018).

fundamental desires. Finally, we saw a double irony: on the one hand, many of those whose imaginations are captive to images of physical fitness are themselves unfit; on the other hand, many Christians have neglected even to care about, much less make efforts toward, the fitness of the body of Christ—local churches. The way forward is to recognize what is good in the desire to be fit but to redirect it to a properly Christian end: making disciples fit for purpose, a purpose that includes building up the body of Christ. This is one way disciples live out their citizenship of the gospel.

To be doers and not mere hearers only means that our bodies must be able to move. Passive, sedentary, or lazy bodies risk being moved by some external force, perhaps the prevailing winds of the doctrines of popular culture. The church is the body of Christ, and its core—the community of disciples, the faith corps—enables its characteristic bodily movements: witnessing to the gospel, worshiping the God of the gospel, maintaining the health of the body, performing works of love. To perform these movements, and to have the strength to work and keep on moving, the church needs to attend to its core. In a word, the church needs theological exercises: training in godliness. I describe the pastor-theologian in various ways, but here the metaphor I want to develop is that of a *spiritual fitness trainer*. To make disciples is to train men and women to perform the characteristic bodily movements that enable the local church to perform its roles as an embassy of the kingdom of God, a Christ corps.

To make or train disciples fit for purpose involves certain kinds of exercise. I have in mind not simply bodily exertions for the sake of physical fitness, but all sorts of actions intended to improve a specific skill, like finger exercises for the piano, a military exercise, and exercises at the end of every textbook chapter. The particular skill in question in this book is reading Scripture theologically in order to take every thought, and imagination, captive to Christ in order to walk the Way of Christ and become more Christlike.

Seeing the Christian life as a series of exercises is, of course, nothing new. The most famous example is the sixteenth-century classic *Spiritual Exercises* by Ignatius of Loyola, a collection of prayers and meditations on what it means to live in relationship to God as a follower of Jesus. The exercises are not bodily but interior: they are designed to strengthen not muscle but the heart, what the apostle Paul calls our "inner being" (Rom 7:22; Eph 3:16). They are recommendations for maintaining and improving the health of one's soul: "We call Spiritual Exercises every way of preparing and disposing the soul to rid itself of all inordinate attachments, and … of seeking and finding the will of God in the disposition of our life."[16] The ultimate aim: to orient the heart to God, and to find God in all things.

An important part of the exercises is learning to discern one's own "spirit," that is, the inner motivation for our actions. Hans Urs von Balthasar, a Roman Catholic theologian, believes that this emphasis on *choice* lies at the center of the Ignatian exercises: they're all about helping persons to discern the heart of God, and the orientation of their own hearts, so that they choose God's choice for them in joyful obedience.[17]

C. S. Lewis, though no Ignatian, had a similar concern for the centrality of "the choice" in the life of the disciple, as Joe Rigney explains: "Every moment of every day, you are confronted with a choice—either place God at the center of your

---

16. Ignatius, *The Spiritual Exercises of St. Ignatius*, trans. Louis J. Puhl (Chicago: Loyola Press, 1968), 1.1 (1).

17. Hans Urs von Balthasar, *Theo-Drama, Volume 2: Dramatis Personae: Man in God*, trans. Graham Harrison, vol. 2 (San Francisco: Ignatius Press, 1990), 167–68.

life, or place something else there."[18] Reality—the world we live in, the only world there is, the world created by God—always and everywhere presents everyone with a choice, an unavoidable "either-or": "Choose this day whom you will serve" (Josh 24:15), either the one true God (the Father of Jesus Christ) or some false god, be it money, sex, fame, power, or something else—their name is Legion. Discipleship involves waking up to the realization that there is a choice, and we must stay awake to the lordship of Jesus Christ long enough to make the right one: to obey, and thereby to exercise, like Jesus, genuine freedom.[19]

Ignatius's exercises eventually became a core component of the training of Jesuit priests. Yet it would be a mistake to infer that spiritual fitness is for the clergy alone, says Tim Muldoon, in *The Ignatian Workout: Daily Exercises for a Healthy Faith*. This is a book for twenty-first-century Roman Catholics who want to begin a program of "spiritual workouts." As the author explains in his introduction: "This book takes a look at the practice of spirituality in a way similar to getting in physical shape. We can learn a great deal about 'spiritual fitness' from understanding physical fitness."[20] His four foundational principles are: (1) build your life on praise, reverence, and service; (2) focus on your eternal well-being; (3) put aside concern for the externals; and (4) want to become what you were created for. One of the workouts is "following the leader," and it is all about understanding one's vocation as servant-image of Christ the King. Another workout involves "walking with Christ" and

---

18. Joe Rigney, *Lewis on the Christian Life: Becoming Truly Human in the Presence of God* (Wheaton, IL: Crossway, 2018), 29.

19. It's worth noting that Luther published his *On the Freedom of a Christian* at about the same time (the 1520s) as Ignatius's *Spiritual Exercises*.

20. Tim Muldoon, *The Ignatian Workout: Daily Exercises for a Healthy Faith* (Chicago: Loyola Press, 2004), xii.

is all about following the way of the cross. I don't know enough about F3 to say whether the end result is making disciples into a holy nation.[21] I do like the vision of making cross-fit (that is, cruciform) disciples, but the fitness the church should care about matters not for aesthetic or therapeutic or military reasons, but for making disciples. Physical fitness is part of the disciple's total fitness, but only if oriented toward the purpose of exercising one's gospel citizenship. I don't think that Jesus was speaking of whether people could actually deadlift a heavy piece of wood when he encouraged his disciples to take up their cross daily and follow him (Matt 16:24; Luke 9:23). I think Jesus was rather exhorting disciples to act out his story in their own lives. Doing *that* is what I call a theological exercise in reading the Bible as formative Christian Scripture.

A Diet of Hearing and Doing

This book argues that one of the most important ways to make disciples is to train them to read the Bible rightly, as hearers and doers who live not by bread alone but "by every word that comes from the mouth of God" (Matt 4:4). Jesus was probably talking about discipleship when he instructed Peter, "Feed my sheep" (John 21:17). The word of God is indeed nourishing: "Your words were found, and I ate them, and your words became to me a joy and the delight of my heart" (Jer 15:16; cf. Ezek 3:1–3). Feeding on God's word involves more than tasting or taking a bite; it means making a meal of it, *digesting* it. Eugene Peterson calls Christians to absorb and imbibe the Bible so that it seeps into all our pores. If we want to make it the story we live by, we have to immerse ourselves in it. Peterson's concern is with

---

21. See further Bob Smietana, "Mending Men's Ministry: How to Disciple in an Era of Male Floundering," *Christianity Today*, June 2018, 26–32.

spiritual reading: "This is the kind of reading ... that enters our souls as food enters our stomachs, spreads through our blood, and becomes holiness and love and wisdom."[22] I mean something similar but prefer to call it theological reading to keep it God-centered. Theological exercises in right reading are all about the people of God learning to read the word of God as hearers and doers. Reading Scripture theologically enables disciples both to build up (individually) and to become (corporately) the city of God.

As Peterson notes, the most striking biblical metaphor for reading is John the Seer eating a book: "And I took the little scroll from the hand of the angel and ate it" (Rev 10:10). This is the passage from which Peterson derives his title, *Eat This Book*. It is a gripping picture not only of reading but also of eschatological discipleship, for what John the Seer eats/reads is Scripture, which, when digested, gets metabolized into the book of Revelation, the apocalyptic vision of the Son of God filling all in all (cf. 1 Cor 15:28).

Of course, pastors would be advised not to give disciples the book of Revelation right away. Those recently born again require milk, not meat: "Like newborn infants, long for the pure spiritual milk, that by it you may grow up into salvation" (1 Pet 2:2). There is a place for milk, for learning one's theological ABCs, yet Paul was anxious to move on to further lessons with the Corinthians: "I fed you with milk, not solid food, for you were not ready for it" (1 Cor 3:2). The normal expectation for disciples was that they would become more advanced readers. However, the author of Hebrews says his readers have become "dull of hearing" (Heb 5:11). He goes on: "For though by this time you

---

22. Eugene Peterson, *Eat This Book: A Conversation in the Art of Spiritual Reading* (Grand Rapids: Eerdmans, 2006), 4.

ought to be teachers, you need someone to teach you again the basic principles of the oracles of God. You need milk, not solid food, for everyone who lives on milk is unskilled in the word of righteousness, since he is a child. But solid food is for the mature, for those who have their powers of discernment trained by constant practice to distinguish good from evil" (Heb 5:12–14).

The context of this rebuke is the author's lesson about Jesus being a high priest "after the order of Melchizedek" (Heb 5:10). He fears his readers are not sufficiently literate in Scripture to make the necessary (typological) connections. It's as if they had to go back to McGuffey Readers (the graded primers popular from the mid-nineteenth to mid-twentieth centuries) so that they could work their way back up to reading Dostoevsky. Building up one's reading strength to discern the connection between Melchizedek and Jesus means flexing the muscles of our imaginations to the limit. Those who read the Bible well are also able to employ metaphors that connect ordinary life to the gospel.

Eat this book. Unlike other diets, there is no restriction on how much of the Bible people can ingest each day. *People of faith require theological exercise in order to make the biblical story the story they live by—their social imaginary and plausibility structure.* The exercises in reading Scripture theologically I here propose build on and integrate what others have said. Let me mention three recent books in particular.

The Institute for Bible Reading (IBR) was formed as a response to polls indicating that people are abandoning Bible reading in unprecedented numbers and to the perception that those who continue to read the Bible struggle to engage it meaningfully. According to the IBR, 87 percent of churchgoers say "what they need most from their church is help understanding the Bible in depth."[23] Glenn Paauw, the IBR's senior director, summarizes the problem, and the way forward, in his book *Saving the Bible from Ourselves: Learning to Read and Live the Bible Well*. Alluding to the versification of the Bible—its division into chapters, verses, headings, and notes—he worries that for most people most of the time, "small readings prevail over big readings."[24] A "small reading" is a diluted sampling of a fragmentary bit taken out of the bigger narrative context—a sip of milk, not a slab of meat: "For far too many folks there is a hoped-for-but-as-yet-undiscovered spiritual meal in the Bible."[25] It is no wonder, then, that the Bible no longer functions as a culture-shaping force. Paauw especially regrets that many Bible readers "have been sold the mistaken notion that the Bible is a look-it-up-and-find-the-answer handy guide to life."[26]

According to Paauw, the way forward is to acknowledge that reading the Bible is challenging. It is easier to swallow a proof-text than to imbibe a library, but that's what the Bible is: a unified collection of different kinds of books. What we need are reading practices that correspond to what the Bible really is, and that means eating it organically—in its natural (literary) forms—rather than as the processed McNuggets of individual verses. The "big reading" that Paauw calls for involves reading and living the Bible well, and this turns out to involve understanding the stories of our own lives in light of the story of Jesus Christ, an exercise I shall return to in part 2.

---

23. Institute for Bible Reading website, https://instituteforbiblereading.org (accessed July 17, 2018).

24. Glenn Paauw, *Saving the Bible from Ourselves: Learning to Read and Live the Bible Well* (Downers Grove, IL: InterVarsity Press, 2015), 11.

25. Paauw, *Saving the Bible*, 15.

26. Paauw, *Saving the Bible*, 15.

Many people read the Bible in private, on their own. Paauw suggests that this practice encourages the (false) assumption that right reading involves individual application: "By reading individualistically, I neglect the overriding concern of the Bible throughout its many pages to form the lives of a new community."[27] We should be asking, "What does this Bible passage mean for our life together?"[28] And this leads me to the second book I want to mention, Brian J. Wright's *Communal Reading in the Time of Jesus*, a groundbreaking investigation into early Christian reading practices.

Communal reading was apparently much more common in the ancient world than scholars previously realized: "Communal reading events were a widespread phenomenon in the Roman Empire during the first century CE."[29] People from all walks of life, social classes, and educational levels experienced and engaged texts by *hearing* them read. The Bible itself provides key evidence: "Until I come, devote yourself to the public reading of Scripture, to exhortation, to teaching" (1 Tim 4:13); "And when this letter has been read among you, have it also read in the church of the Laodiceans; and see that you also read the letter from Laodicea" (Col 4:16); "I put you under oath before the Lord to have this letter read to all the brothers" (1 Thess 5:27). Even if 99 percent of the people in a church were illiterate, all they needed was one person who knew how to read to do so, out loud, for the rest. In the words of the church father Tertullian: "We meet to read the books of God."[30] Wright argues that it was

27. Paauw, *Saving the Bible*, 168.

28. Paauw, *Saving the Bible*, 180.

29. Brian J. Wright, *Communal Reading in the Time of Jesus: A Window into Early Christian Reading Practices* (Minneapolis: Fortress, 2017), 207.

30. Tertullian, *Apology*, trans. T. R. Glover, Loeb Classical Library (Cambridge, MA: Harvard University Press, 1931), 39.3 (175).

largely through such communal reading events that the Way grew and multiplied: "Communal reading was a powerful discipleship tool because it aided understanding."[31]

According to Wright, Christians read communally "so they and others would become more like Christ."[32] This, after all, is the end of discipleship, to become like the master, and is why Paul exhorts the Philippians, "Have this mind among yourselves, which is yours in Christ Jesus" (Phil 2:5). To have the mind of Christ is to have the same convictions and dispositions, the same willingness to take part in the story of what God is doing to renew the world. In a word, it is to have Christian wisdom.

This brings me to the third book I want to mention, J. de Waal Dryden's *A Hermeneutic of Wisdom: Recovering the Formative Agency of Scripture*. If to read the Bible well we have to know what the Bible is, Dryden wants us to know that the Bible is a wisdom text, written "to shape the people of God in particular ways—to cultivate certain devotions, beliefs, desires, and actions"—or in the terms of the present work, *to make disciples.*[33]

If the Bible is indeed a book intended to make disciples wise unto salvation, able to live as citizens of the gospel, then it is dismaying—nay, alarming—to hear that "our current reading strategies and critical methodologies, while very good at historical reconstructions, ignore and usually deconstruct this wisdom intentionality."[34] The wisdom-forming way forward is not to read the Proverbs piecemeal, a strategy that persists in fragmenting the text, but rather to appreciate the Bible's big picture—the vision of creation, fall, redemption, and consummation—which

---

31. Brian Wright, interview with *Christianity Today*, May 2018, 64.

32. Wright, interview, 64.

33. J. de Waal Dryden, *A Hermeneutic of Wisdom: Recovering the Formative Agency of Scripture* (Grand Rapids: Baker Academic, 2018), xvi.

34. Dryden, *A Hermeneutic of Wisdom*, xvii.

functions as the disciple's biblical imaginary and which generates a way of life spent in wonder, love, and praise. Everything
begins with biblical interpretation, however, and the modern
picture of knower and known has long held biblical hermeneutics captive too.[35] The way forward for disciple-makers is to
pursue reading strategies that conform to what the Bible is and
recognize its formative agenda, namely, a divine address bent
on remaking our deepest convictions, desires, and practices to
conform to the gospel.

Every person is someone else's disciple. We're all following
somebody's words, everything from Plato (Greek philosophy)
to platitudes (like the ones we find in fortune cookies). We have
all imbibed somebody's vision of wellness, somebody's ideal of
health, or somebody's idea of fitness. Reading the Bible theologically, as teaching by God, of God, and leading to God, is our
best hope for breaking free of the pictures that hold us captive:
consumerism, humanism, transhumanism, nihilism, existen-
tialism, moralism, scientism, and so on—idols all, of heart and
mind. Reading Scripture theologically means reading it together,
in the church, in ways that lead to its readers' moral, spiritual,
and sapiential formation.

Reading Scripture theologically means being willing to go
against the cultural grain where and when it is necessary to do
so. It is a demanding, upward path, but there is joy in the climb.
To this point, I have cast a vision for discipleship: a picture of
what it involves and why it matters. Hopefully I have persuaded
you that spiritual formation is already happening to your church

---

35. Dryden, *A Hermeneutic of Wisdom*, 4.

members, and that it is working to conform them to some other image than Christ. In part 2 I therefore lay out a plan of counterattack: a plan to retake the disciple's imagination for Christ.

The following chapters explore further how to make disciples by casting a vision of what the Bible is and is for, complete with concrete proposals designed to improve the church's spiritual fitness, especially by strengthening its God-centered social imaginary. These concrete proposals I have called "core exercises," for developing disciples who are fit for purpose. In physical fitness, core exercises are all-important. So too with local church bodies. The exercises all have to do with some aspect of reading Scripture theologically or with "core" doctrine: what disciples have to know to be competent citizens of the gospel. Specifically, the exercises are intended to strengthen both the "core" of the disciple and the "core" of the church, the body of Christ.

A "core" designates the inmost part of something, like an apple or a pear. The English term probably derives from the Latin *cor* or French *coeur*, which mean "heart." In the context of nuclear physics, it refers to that inner part of a reactor that contains the fuel and where the reactions take place. In the context of computer hardware, the core is where processors are linked together to form one integrated center of operations. In the context of physical fitness, the "core" refers to what lies at the foundation of bodily movement. The core, of a disciple or church body, similarly, is the most important inmost part, the place containing the basic dispositions and desires whence comes all action.

The core is a key part of the body's support structure and, as such, is crucial for carrying out the everyday activities that make up the bulk of our waking hours: standing, sitting, turning, walking, lifting, carrying—as well as all the basic movements ingredient in more complex activities like playing the piano, cooking a meal, performing surgery, or fixing a broken furnace.

Sedentary lifestyles make for inactive cores, and a weak core makes it harder to perform everyday tasks. The core is what enables the pelvic, abdominal, and back muscles to provide support for the spine, the axis for moving one's legs and arms. One telltale sign of a compromised core is poor posture. Paul knew about the importance of good posture and of being fit for purpose: "Put on the full armor of God, so that when the day of evil comes, you may be able to stand your ground, and after you have done everything, to stand" (Eph 6:13 NIV).

As the apostle Paul knew, the church body is made up of many parts, and we need them all: "We, though many, are one body in Christ, and individually members of one another" (Rom 12:5; cf. Eph 3:6; 4:25; 5:30; Col 3:15). What Paul may not have known, however, is how important the core is for *coordinating movement*, for making sure that muscles, joints, and neurons work together to enable bodily movement. Without the ability to move, we lose the ability to act. The core, then, is essential to human (and ecclesial) agency.

The core exercises I propose in the following chapters, then, are not punitive but regenerative (and restorative). They are the kind of exercises that do not simply spend but renew energy. A theological exercise hears and does biblical truth in order to make disciples more like Christ, able to live as citizens of the gospel, fit for the purpose of representing, and building up, the city of God.

PART TWO

*Working Out:
How Discipleship Happens*

5

CREATURES OF THE WORD

The Pastor as Eye Doctor (and General Practitioner) of the Church

Hearers and Doers aims to encourage pastors to recover their vocation as ministers of the word and to reclaim Scripture and doctrine as a means for making disciples. Unlike the other chapters in part 2, however, this one is primarily about the way pastors see themselves and their vocation. Today, there are many pictures from which to choose, including manager, therapist, celebrity, fund-raiser, and community organizer, to name but a few. The image pastors see when they look in the mirror affects their sense of identity, view of mission, and concept of authority. What does one say to a pastor who asks, "Who do you say that I am?"

I have written elsewhere on the pastor as public theologian, one charged with the task of doing theology with *people* (the assembly gathered to hear and do the gospel) rather than arguments and textbooks.[1] People are the medium of church theology, the word is the means, and making disciples is the goal. What I want to add here is that the pastor ministers the word to people to make them *fit for purpose*. This is the image that was dominant among pastor-theologians during the Protestant Reformation, who were keenly aware that the risen and ascended Christ did not abandon his church, but sent the Spirit and gave pastors to be "shepherds and teachers, to equip the saints for the work of ministry, for building up the body of Christ" (Eph 4:11–12).

Previously we saw how easy it is for a holy nation to become like the other nations through living by the same pictures that secular nations live by. Accordingly, one way that pastors build up the body of Christ is by correcting its vision. However, the Reformation image of the pastor-theologian as a doctor of the church who ministers health to the body of Christ precisely by teaching God's word has been eclipsed by other images. Accordingly, before we can provide a guide to disciple-making, we need to recover the centrality of the ministry of the word, and the pastor's vocation as an eye doctor who fits congregations with what Calvin calls the "spectacles of faith," namely, the corrective lenses of Scripture.

We need to reclaim certain Reformation insights for the health of today's church. In particular, I shall propose that we retrieve *sola Scriptura*, often described as the Protestant's Achilles' heel (because Protestants cannot agree on what it means). Retrieving *sola Scriptura* is a way to reclaim the pastor's birthright, namely, making disciples, little creatures of the word. So, what is the church, how should it be reformed,

---

1. Kevin J. Vanhoozer and Owen Strachan, *The Pastor as Public Theologian: Reclaiming a Lost Vision* (Grand Rapids: Baker Academic, 2015).

and how is the pastor a doctor of the church, the disciples' ophthalmologist?

BRINGING THE CHURCH INTO FOCUS

"I believe in ... the holy catholic church, the communion of saints." Of all the lines in the Apostles' Creed, this may be one of the most difficult for many twenty-first-century Christians to confess. We believe that the Father raised Jesus from the dead, and we even believe in the Trinity (insofar as we can understand it), but to say we believe in the holy catholic church is hard, precisely because it is one of the few items in the creed that we're asked to believe *and that we can see.* That's the problem: we see the divisions, we hear the drivel that sometimes comes from the pulpit, we feel the pain of needs not met, and we witness the spectacle of congregations whose life together too often mirrors the same kinds of brokenness we see in broader society: broken marriages, personal traumas, feuds and factions. Wretched layman that I am! Who will deliver me from this body of death and disappointment (see Rom 7:24)?

Why does the church exist? Jesus in Matthew 5:13–16 describes the church as the salt of the earth, the light of the world, and a city set on a hill whose purpose is to witness to and thus glorify the Father in heaven.[2] Another right answer, and the one that I want to emphasize here, is that the church exists as a place to make disciples. The two answers are related, of course, for disciples are people who know how to bear witness in word and speech to the gospel, and in so doing glorify God. The church, like the pastor, has both a Godward and a

---

2. See further Graham Hill, *Salt, Light, and a City: Ecclesiology for the Global Missional Community*, 2nd ed., Western Voices 1 (Eugene, OR: Cascade, 2017).

humanward orientation: it exists to build up the people of God to the glory of God. Both of these orientations involve theology writ large: *orthodoxy* (rightly ordered minds), *orthopraxis* (rightly ordered embodied practices), and *orthokardia* (rightly ordered hearts and desires).

The church is the primary location for transforming minds, hearts, and practices, primarily by ministering understanding of Scripture. It is for this reason that *sola Scriptura* is intimately tied up with the pastor's vocation. Pastors must do everything they can to ensure that Scripture alone, and not some other story, serves as their congregation's essential social imaginary.

The Protestant church has now been in existence for five hundred years. Some say that it was an accident of history: the Reformers never intended to start a new church, only to reform the church to which they belonged. Today, some people suggest that the Reformation instead created a monster, a Frankenchurch, because, half a millennium later, Protestant churches continue to divide, even if denominationalism, another alleged offshoot of the Reformation, now appears to be dying.[3]

In recent years we have witnessed many experimental movements having to do with church, often with exciting qualifiers like "emerging," "missional," "incarnational," "total," "connected," "ancient-evangelical," "center," even "slow." Conspicuous by its absence is "Protestant." Surely this was an experiment that went terribly wrong, judging by the thirty thousand denominations it inadvertently spawned? Yet I view the Reformation not as an experiment that failed, but one that has been left unfinished.

---

3. For the claim, see Brad S. Gregory, *The Unintended Reformation: How a Religious Revolution Secularized Society* (Cambridge, MA: Belknap Press of Harvard University Press, 2012). For a rebuttal, see my *Biblical Authority after Babel: Retrieving the Solas in the Spirit of Mere Protestant Christianity* (Grand Rapids: Brazos, 2016).

What might it mean to keep reforming? Let me suggest two possibilities: first, there will always be a need to keep reforming individuals in the church. Conversion is a radical reformation, a re-forming of the defaced image of God; sanctification is a continuing reformation, a polishing of the image of God in imperfect human sculptures. Second, the church ought *always* to be reforming, for we are not there yet. By "there," I mean our destination: correspondence with the Word of God. This has always been God's project for his people: to remake and reform them until they conform to the written and living Word, even Jesus Christ, the image of the invisible God (Col 1:15). The church must always be reforming until it attains to "the measure of the stature of the fullness of Christ" (Eph 4:13).

In an important sense, the Reformation was a revolution in biblical interpretation, a return to the sources rather than man-made traditions, with an aim to correcting the church. In another sense, it was a retrieval of the idea that the church, the gathering of disciples, is a creature of the word. And in still another sense (and now I'm thinking primarily about justification by faith), the Reformation was a clarification of the implications of the doctrine of the church. It's not that doctrine had achieved such a pure form in the Reformation that it stopped developing. It's rather that the Reformation church had certain theological insights that are permanently valid, as did the early church at Nicaea. One such insight is that the church must always be "reforming" its thought and life in accordance with the Scriptures. In particular, the church must always be reforming in order to imagine the world that the Bible imagines. One way to do this is to practice the twelve core exercises I discuss in part 2.

THE FOUR PRINCIPLES OF THE PROTESTANT REFORMATION

In one sense, the Reformation was a call to order Christian doctrine and church life under the supreme authority of Scripture. In my book *Biblical Authority after Babel*, I argue that the Reformation *solas* of grace alone, faith alone, and Scripture alone represent the "spirit" of Protestantism, a phrase I take from the still-helpful book by Robert McAfee Brown.[4] Here, however, I want to focus briefly not on the three *solas* but on four principles that capture what the Reformation was really about and, together, inform not simply the spirit but, more importantly, the *social imaginary* of Protestantism.

1. **The material principle: justification by faith (*sola gratia, sola fide, solus Christus*).** Luther famously contended that justification is the article by which the church stands or falls. This material principle of Reformation theology is essentially "a deeper plunge into the meaning of the gospel."[5] It is a recovery of the grace of God, who gives us light and life through faith by uniting us to Jesus Christ through the Spirit. It is necessarily Trinitarian, and it accords priority to the speech and act of God over the response and experiences of human beings. It helps the church be focused on God in both its reading of Scripture and its worship.

---

4. Robert McAfee Brown, *The Spirit of Protestantism* (Oxford: Oxford University Press, 1965).

5. So Philip Schaff in *The Creeds of Christendom*, as cited by Brown, *Spirit of Protestantism*, 15.

2. **The formal principle: "according to the Scriptures" (*sola Scriptura*).** We only know this content of the gospel, however, because of the witness of the prophets and apostles. The formal principle of Protestant theology, the standard to which sound doctrine must measure up, is "the Holy Spirit speaking in the Scripture."[6] Protestants agree with Jaroslav Pelikan's definition of doctrine as "what the church of Jesus Christ believes, teaches, and confesses on the basis of the word of God,"[7] but we go further in according supreme authority to Scripture alone.

3. **The dynamic principle: the Spirit who ministers, illumines, enlivens, and unites.** Justification focuses on the fact that we are in Christ, but the good news is also that Christ is in us. He is so by his indwelling Spirit. It is the Spirit who has transferred us into the kingdom of light and now progressively imparts the life of Christ to us, especially by ministering the word and illumining our hearts and minds more fully to receive it. In particular, Protestants believe the Spirit uses the early ecumenical church councils, as well as other means, like biblical commentaries, to deepen the church's understanding of the word.

4. **The final principle: a citizenship of the gospel.** The fourth or final principle of the Protestant

---

6. Westminster Confession of Faith 1.10.

7. Jaroslav Pelikan, *The Christian Tradition: A History of the Development of Doctrine*, vol. 1, *The Emergence of the Catholic Tradition, 100–600* (Chicago: University of Chicago Press, 1971), 1.

Reformation is its telos: not a system of orthodoxy but a city of God populated with citizens of the gospel—in a word, disciples who together constitute a kingdom of priests, a holy nation (1 Pet 2:9). The true end of theology is not a systematics textbook but grown-up children of God. The church is like a nursery, in which tender plants grafted onto Christ receive spiritual nurture. C. S. Lewis's words bear repeated reflection: "The Church exists for nothing else but to draw men [and women] into Christ, to make them little Christs. If they are not doing that, all the cathedrals, clergy, missions, sermons, even the Bible itself, are simply a waste of time."[8] This is the Great (Pastoral) Commission: "Make disciples of all nations ... teaching them to observe all that I have commanded you" (Matt 28:20–21). Dallas Willard calls the church to get serious about this task in his book *The Great Omission*. The great issue facing the church today, he says, "is whether those who, by profession or culture, are identified as 'Christians' will become disciples—students, apprentices, practitioners—of Jesus Christ."[9] Willard believes that, for many churches, discipleship has become optional. N. T. Wright raises a similar concern when he criticizes understandings of the gospel as the news that saved individuals can go to heaven whereas in fact Jesus' good news was about heaven coming to earth to form a new humanity.

8. C. S. Lewis, *Mere Christianity* (New York: Touchstone, 1996), 199.

9. Dallas Willard, *The Great Omission: Reclaiming Jesus' Essential Teachings on Discipleship* (San Francisco: HarperSanFrancisco, 2006), xv.

The burning issue, perhaps the preeminent challenge facing heirs of the Reformers today, is to practice *sola Scriptura* in a way that makes disciples—and glorifies God—in accordance with the other Reformation *sola, soli Deo gloria.* Pastors need to recover anew a confidence and competence in the ministry of the word of God. It has been thirty years now since John Leith wrote *The Reformed Imperative: What the Church Has to Say that No One Else Can Say.*[10] Other institutions pursue justice, heal the sick, and entertain us, but only the church proclaims the gospel, and it does so in sermon, sacrament, and saintly living.

We need to retrieve the Reformers' doctrine (and practice) of the church, focusing in particular on the project of making disciples. The church is a place to make disciples because the people are the place where the word gets ministered. In particular, I want to examine the significance of *sola Scriptura* in making disciples by stressing its role in fostering the Christocentric social imaginary that makes the church a creature of the word. Though it was forged in the sixteenth century, *sola Scriptura* has the potential to cure what ails us in the twenty-first, namely, our captivity to a sub-evangelical account of human flourishing. Ultimately, Scripture alone makes disciples fit for purpose.

ECCLESIOLOGY AND FIRST PROTESTANT THEOLOGY: THE CHURCH AS CREATURE OF THE WORD

Before I turn to consider *sola Scriptura* and the formation of the Christian imagination, let me spend a few moments reviewing the Protestant understanding of church vis-à-vis Scripture.

---

10. John Leith, *The Reformed Imperative: What the Church Has to Say that No One Else Can Say* (Louisville: Westminster John Knox, 1988).

I begin with a question: Does the church belong in Protestant first theology? First theology pertains to what is of first importance. For years, I have insisted that what is of first importance is God's speech and God's action. These come together in the gospel: God's word about God's work of salvation in Jesus Christ. My book *First Theology* argues that theology starts with the interplay between the doctrine of God and the doctrine of Scripture, for the simple reason that we could not fully know the one without the other. Most Protestant confessions of faith begin either with the doctrine of God or with Scripture.

Protestants resist the Roman Catholic tendency to see the Bible as a product of the church, effectively making ecclesiology first theology. On the contrary, the Reformers insisted that the church is a "creature of the Word."[11] The ministers at Bern, Switzerland, summarized the Protestant understanding of the church in the first two of their Ten Theses of Bern (1528):

- Thesis 1: "The holy Christian church, whose only head is Christ, is born of the Word of God, abides in the same, and does not listen to the voice of a stranger." Nor, we might add, does it attend to the *imaginaries* of a stranger.

- Thesis 2: "The church of Christ makes no laws or commandments without God's word; hence, all human traditions ... are binding on us only insofar as they are based on and commanded by God's word." *Sola scriptura* means that Scripture alone is the rule for the church's belief and behavior.

---

11. See Christoph Schwöbel, "The Creature of the Word: Recovering the Ecclesiology of the Reformers," in *On Being the Church: Essays on the Christian Community*, ed. Colin E. Gunton and Daniel W. Hardy (Edinburgh: T&T Clark, 1989), 110–55.

The church is not about humans going through religious motions (this gets us only as far as sociology, not theology). It is rather about the word gathering hearers into its domain through the Spirit's gift of faith. The church is beholden to the word of God for its existence, nature, proper function, and destiny. To understand the church as it really is we must therefore describe it as a creature of the word. This is what Philipp Melanchthon does when he says in his *Loci communes* that the church is the people gathered around the voice of the gospel. There is church not where there are towers or altars or clerical robes, but where the gospel is rightly preached and the sacraments rightly administered, and there only. This was the thrust of the so-called marks of the church that enabled the Reformers to discern true from false churches.

The late theologian John Webster has helped to specify the dogmatic location of the church in the work of the Trinity and the structure of the gospel. Here are his two fundamental principles for an evangelical ecclesiology: First, "there can be no doctrine of God without a doctrine of the church, for according to the Christian confession God is the one who manifests who he is in the economy of his saving work in which he assembles a people for himself." Second, "there can be no doctrine of the church which is not wholly referred to the doctrine of God, in whose being and action alone the church has its being and action." The church belongs in first theology because of its interrelationship with God and Scripture.[12]

When I first began to teach theology, I asked my head of department to be excused from teaching Theology III

---

12. See John Webster, "The Self-Organizing Power of the Gospel of Christ: Episcopacy and Community Formation," *International Journal of Systematic Theology* 3, no. 1 (2001): 69–82.

(ecclesiology and eschatology). At the time (the 1980s), the syllabus looked like a hit parade of controversial topics, and I preferred to stick with things that were of first importance: first theology. I have now repented of that error, and the doctrine of the church is one of my favorite topics to teach. As the realization of the new humanity that is now in Christ, the church is part of the content of the gospel itself. In this sense (and perhaps in this sense only), the church is one of the doctrines "of first importance." It is also part of the pattern of theological authority inasmuch as God has given the Spirit to the church to lead it (and not individuals only) into all truth. Indeed, we could even go as far as to say there can be no complete doctrine of God without mention of the church, inasmuch as God has as his eternal purpose the formation of a people for his own treasured possession.

The church is the place where people read the Bible as the word of God in order to proclaim, teach, celebrate, and live out the gospel and to cultivate godliness. The church, a new human social order, is intrinsic to the gospel, an implication of what God was doing in Christ through the Spirit.

SOLA SCRIPTURA AND THE SOCIAL IMAGINARY

We can now return to the task at hand, namely, explaining what the Reformation, and *sola Scriptura* in particular, could possibly have to do with the need of the hour, which is to free disciples from a secular social imaginary. *Sola Scriptura* is rarely mentioned in the same breath as imagination. Yet the supreme authority of Scripture includes the imagination in its domain. We must take captive not only every thought, but every imagination, to obey Christ and to make disciples (2 Cor 10:5).

That the word of God should rule the pictures by which we live is not new; the Reformers themselves had to challenge the medieval picture of what it meant to "do church." In medieval Roman Catholicism, preaching had been overshadowed by the Eucharist, and practices not authorized by Scripture, like indulgences, had become part of the fabric of the church's life. The Reformation in Switzerland began in 1522 when Huldrych Zwingli, pastor at the Grossmünster in Zurich, protested the tradition of fasting during Lent by cutting and distributing two sausages during a Sunday morning service. That's one way to capture a congregation's imagination.

The best way to take captive the imagination of Christians in any age is through the church's proclamation of the gospel in word and deed: in sermon, sacrament, and shapes of everyday living. That's the big idea. Let me now explain why it matters.

The Incredible Shrinking Evangelical Imagination

Like the Reformers, we're still wondering what it means to gather as disciples to do church in the twenty-first century. Even more challenging is knowing how to communicate orthodox Christianity to the next generation, inside and outside the church. Robert Louis Wilken, a church historian at the University of Virginia, said in 2004: "Nothing is more needful today than the survival of Christian culture."[13] A culture is a way of community life that involves belief, behavior, and belonging. A genuinely Christian culture is the way Christ followers follow his Way in their own place and time, and it's largely pastors who have the privilege, and shoulder the responsibility, of growing

---

13. Robert Louis Wilken, "The Church as Culture," *First Things*, April 2004, https://www.firstthings.com/article/2004/04/the-church-as-culture.

Christian cultures. This is not civil religion but a radically evangelical social project, by which I mean the local church.

The United States had its origins in Judeo-Christianity, but
the influence of Christianity has waned remarkably in recent
years. You may have heard about the "nones," those who mark
"none" when asked about their religious affiliation. What happened? Why are there so many? I think one of the most important causes of the decline in Christianity, Christian culture, and
the notion of the pastor-theologian, is the loss of the evangelical imagination, an imagination nurtured—by which I mean
discipled and disciplined—by the Bible.

It's not simply that people in the church no longer believe the
Bible. If we want to understand what happened, we need to draw
on C. S. Lewis's statement: "I believe in Christianity as I believe
that the Sun has risen, not only because I see it but because by
it, I see everything else."[14] It is one thing to believe in the sun,
quite another to see by its light. So too with Scripture. Many
Bible-believing Christians profess the authority of Scripture
but no longer take their existential bearings from its pages.
They no longer walk by its light, perhaps because they have
forgotten how to do so. Scripture's images—its metaphors and
stories—are no longer the ones by which people actually live.
This is the heart of the problem I'm trying to address: how to
get hearers of the word (nominal Christians) to become doers
(genuine disciples).

Other pictures now hold the imagination captive. As we saw
in chapter 2, even many confessing Christians have had their
imaginations taken captive by other pictures, other stories, of
what it is to be well, healthy, and fit. They may profess faith, but

---

14. C. S. Lewis, "Is Theology Poetry?," in *The Weight of Glory* (1949; repr., San
Francisco: HarperOne, 2001), 140.

they live like everyone else, according to the prevailing "plausibility structures" of the day. For example, certain segments of the church have succumbed to cultural conditioning about the good life or about what counts as success. Pictures of success disseminated by business schools and television shows have not trickled but slammed into our collective Christian unconscious.

What is behind the pictures that we now take for granted? Charles Taylor says that our secular age is characterized by a "disenchanted" view of the world as a closed system of nature, with no room for grace. We may hold doctrines to be true, but if we cannot imagine the world the way these doctrines say it is then they will not be compelling. Theory alone is not enough; it must be lived, put into practice. Indeed, Taylor says "the way ordinary people 'imagine' their social surroundings ... is often not expressed in theoretical terms, but is carried in images [and] stories."[15] As we have seen, Taylor defines the "social imaginary" as "what enables, through making sense of, the practices of a society."[16] The loss of belief in God was the result not of some scientific discovery or logical argument but of a tectonic shift in those taken-for-granted assumptions that frame our everyday beliefs and practices. One of the main theses of the present work is that church members are today at risk of exchanging one social imaginary for another, an exchange that would set disciples walking in some other way than the Way of Jesus Christ.

On the one hand, then, contemporary Christians profess "the faith once proclaimed"; yet many take part in cultural practices that, at least implicitly, proclaim a very different gospel. If the fundamental problem is the disconnect between what

---

15. Charles Taylor, *Modern Social Imaginaries* (Durham, NC: Duke University Press, 2004), 23.

16. Taylor, *Modern Social Imaginaries*, 2. See also his *A Secular Age* (Cambridge, MA: Belknap Press of Harvard University Press, 2007), esp. ch. 4.

evangelicals confess and the cultural practices in which they engage, then the solution is not merely to believe *harder*. We must address the problem at its source: the captive imagination.

For over a hundred years now, modern culture has been secularizing the social imagination. The so-called masters of suspicion—Marx, Freud, Nietzsche—have explained away Christianity in terms of ideology, wish-fulfillment, and the will to power, all terms that modern people readily understand. Modern and postmodern culture has cultivated ways of living and seeing the world that simply left God out of the picture. Yet even a secular culture's pictures are powerful means of spiritual formation. One trivial example: awhile back I became convinced that my glasses were growing bigger. I'd look at myself in the mirror in the morning, sure that someone had substituted larger frames during the night. What was going on? I eventually came to understand: it wasn't that my glasses had changed, but my perception of them had. I was meeting more and more people with smaller frames and that trained me (you could say *discipled* me) to *feel* as if there was something wrong with my glasses. If you can do it with glasses, you can certainly do it with other things, like gender. And that's exactly what's happening.

A (Brief) Theology of the Imagination

What can we do about this? The short answer is that we need to recover the Bible as our control story, and that means making *sola Scriptura* the ruler of the congregational imagination. I understand that this suggestion may make many pastors nervous. What does *sola Scriptura*, and its cousins *authority* and *truth*, have to do with the imagination? The very question shows how a culturally conditioned picture of the imagination holds us captive. The imagination has been the whipping boy of Western philosophy and theology alike. The imagination has been seen as *unfaithful* representation, the faculty for creating images of things that are not there. That sounds a lot like lying: saying of what is *not* that it *is*.

In response to this objection I would say that yes, there are such things as "vain imaginings" (see Rom 1:21). But this no more disqualifies the imagination from serving theology than the existence of logical fallacies disqualifies reason. It is a false picture of the imagination—as the power of conjuring up the unreal—that has held us captive.

I take the imagination to be not primarily a picture-making factory but rather, and more importantly, a faculty for making connections and discerning meaningful patterns. Analytic reason typically takes things apart: analysis breaks things down into their smallest components. By way of contrast, the imagination—"synthetic" reason—puts things together and forms wholes. Think of the imagination as the ability to perceive coherent patterns and meaningful forms. The imagination is a vital aid in discerning fittingness: the way parts belong to a whole. As such, the imagination is an essential ingredient in achieving biblical literacy, namely, the ability to see the various parts of the Bible as part of a single, unified, and meaningful whole. George MacDonald defines the imagination as "that faculty which gives form to thought."[17] Scripture, by presenting God's thoughts in a variety of *literary* forms, addresses both reason and imagination.

Unlike analytic reason, however, the imagination engages the mind, will, and emotions alike. It is an integrative faculty that involves human beings in their entirety. It is precisely for this reason that some posit a connection between

---

17. George MacDonald, "The Imagination," in *A Dish of Orts* (London: Sampson Low Marston & Company, 1893), 2.

the imagination and what the Bible calls the "heart" (*leb* in Hebrew). First Chronicles 29:18 speaks of the "thoughts" of the heart, and the apostle Paul speaks of "having the eyes of your hearts enlightened" (Eph 1:18). This suggests that taking every thought captive involves capturing the imagination, the "eyes of the heart." This is why pastors are eye doctors, charged with correcting our (secular) near-sightedness.

In spite of the presence of "image" in the word, the imagination is primarily *verbal* (don't confuse etymology with definition). In the imagination's beginning is the *word*, not the image. Christians of all people should be able to affirm this. Genesis depicts God's own creativity in terms of his speech act that brings things into existence and then orders and relates them. Similarly, the Bible's literary compositions do more than convey information; they display the world in ways that we might not be able to see without just those words used in just those ways. Jesus' parables teach us about the kingdom of God by telling stories.

The imagination, precisely in its verbal dimension, is a valuable cognitive tool. "To imagine something is to *think of* it as possibly being so."[18] The imagination is a "seeing as" in the mind's eye and, as such, is an essential ingredient in theology's search for understanding: "Seeing so-and-so *as* such-and-such combines seeing and thinking."[19] Faith—the imaginative seeing that enables us to perceive God at work in the world—comes by *hearing*, and hearing through the word of Christ (Rom 10:17). Scripture sets the imagination free to see, and more importantly to *inhabit*, the world we live in *as* the world that was made through Christ and to which he came, and will come again.

---

18. Alan R. White, *The Language of Imagination* (Oxford: Blackwell, 1990), 184.
19. White, *Language of Imagination*, 190.

The evangelical imagination is the power of indwelling a reality we cannot empirically see. This is why I associate the imagination with faith, "the conviction of things not seen" (Heb 11:1).

Sola Scriptura and the Disciple's Imagination

As I mentioned above, many churches are suffering from malnourished imaginations, captive to culturally conditioned pictures of the good life. Chapter 2 focused on wellness, health, and fitness, but these are only symptomatic of other things that have dominated the social imaginary, like celebrity, wealth, and social power. Christians *want* to believe the Bible—they *do* believe it and are prepared to defend doctrinal truth—but they nevertheless find themselves unable to see or feel their world in biblical terms ("I believe; help my unbelief!" Mark 9:24). Consequently, they experience a disconnect between the world they actually inhabit and the world of the biblical text whose truth they confess. Their professions of faith are out of whack with their lived practices. If faith's influence is waning, then it is largely because of a failure of the evangelical imagination to connect the biblical and cultural dots. Pastors can help, especially by reminding their congregations again and again what the Bible is and what it is for. *Sola Scriptura* is a shorthand way of doing this insofar as it reminds us that *Scripture alone* should exercise supreme authority over Christian faith and life, including the imagination.

In his essay "The Demise of Biblical Civilization," historian Grant Wacker claims that during the twentieth century, the average American did not renounce the Bible but simply stopped using it as the primary plausibility structure with which to make sense of the world.[20] People began to understand the meaning of

---

20. Grant Wacker, "The Demise of Biblical Civilization," in *The Bible in America: Essays in Cultural History*, ed. Nathan O. Hatch and Mark A. Noll (Oxford:

events in terms of this-worldly historical processes rather than in terms of divine providence. The demise of biblical civilization was a failure of the imagination to read our world in terms of God's word. The demise of biblical civilization is related to the replacement of *sola Scriptura* in the social imaginary of the West by other stories.

Christian imaginations are captive to nonbiblical stories that do not lead us to Christ and thus fail to nourish our souls. We need to call these stories out and expose their shortcomings, for there is no other gospel (Gal 1:7). We cannot hide behind orthodox theology and pretend that we are invulnerable to the cultural programming that is happening to us 24/7. We need to know that the church is in competition with the powers and principalities that are trying to capture our imagination, and from thence our body, heart, and soul.

The gospel, especially the dramatic announcement that God has raised Jesus from the dead, sets the captive imagination free. What we might call the "evangelical" imagination—an imagination ruled by the story of the gospel—frees us to see, judge, and act in faith, in accordance with the way things really are rather than the way secular science or Madison Avenue say they are. It is all those other words and all that noise in contemporary culture that disorient and deserve to be called vain imaginings. The evangelical imagination alone opens up the real possibility of living along the grain of reality: according to what is really the case "in Christ."

If the church is to fulfill her remit as a holy nation and live out her citizenship of the gospel, she must pit her evangelical imagination against every counterfeit. To see the world and oneself with evangelical imagination is to live not in fantasyland

Oxford University Press, 1982), 125.

but in the only real world there is: the world created by God's word; the world into which God's word has entered and will return. The ten plagues of Egypt played this role in the minds of the ancient Israelites: they freed the imagination of the Israelites from thinking that the power of Egypt was sovereign. They deconstructed Pharaoh's claim to power. It takes imagination to see that what God is doing with a small tribe of slaves is greater than the might of Egypt—or that what God is doing in the early church is greater than the grandeur that is Rome.

Having an imagination shaped by *sola Scriptura* necessarily involves engaging in the making of metaphors, or "placing our community's life imaginatively within the world articulated by the texts."[21] Metaphors structure our way of thinking about things. In an influential book titled *Metaphors We Live By*, George Lakoff and Mark Johnson argued that images do not simply show up in our language but in our thinking, as *conceptual* metaphors that govern the way we think and act.[22] At the heart of metaphor is understanding one thing in terms of another. "Time is money," for example, is only one of many metaphors by which our modern culture lives. The church should be that place where people learn to live by biblical metaphors—like taking up your cross (Matt 16:24)—everywhere, before everyone, at all times.

Metaphors with staying power, such as the world as "creation" or the church as "the body of Christ" (1 Cor 12:27), are models that structure our thinking and experience. One of my favorite metaphors for the church is "holy nation" (1 Pet 2:9). As a holy nation of "elect exiles" (1 Pet 1:1), the church is charged

---

21. Richard B. Hays, *The Moral Vision of the New Testament: A Contemporary Introduction to New Testament Ethics* (San Francisco: HarperSanFrancisco, 1996), 299.

22. George Lakoff and Mark Johnson, *Metaphors We Live By* (Chicago: University of Chicago Press, 1980).

with demonstrating the reality of God's reign on earth as it is in heaven. The church, as a holy nation, marches to the beat of a different social imaginary. Its worship, witness, and wisdom is distinct inasmuch as each takes its bearing from what God was doing in Jesus Christ. It is in this people, this holy nation, that God reigns. The church is a local embassy and living parable of the kingdom of God.

It is not enough to affirm the truth of the Bible's teaching, or even to live by biblical metaphors. The Bible is more than a collection of wisdom sayings from which we take our bearing. It is a unified narrative that encompasses the whole of reality. Disciples need to learn to inhabit the story of the Bible. They need to hear and to do—to indwell as whole, embodied persons— the strange new graced world of the Bible. For this we need to understand how it all fits together and culminates in what the Father was doing in the Son through the Spirit to renew and reconcile humanity and all things (2 Cor 4:16; 5:17–19). This is the strength of biblical theology and figural interpretation, which is really the biblical imagination at work, discerning the unity that ties the various events, people, and symbols together. Too often when we study the Bible we try to figure out how its history fits into our world when in fact we should be doing the opposite: we should be trying to read our world in light of the story of the Bible. If we know the Bible well, we will begin to see large patterns—for example, "salvation through judgment"—that ultimately direct our attention to Jesus Christ. We begin to see how the church is the new Israel, the new Jerusalem, and the temple at the center: the place where God dwells with humanity and heaven comes to earth.

This is the unseen truth about the church: not what historians and sociologists tell us, but what the biblical authors tell us. The church really is a holy nation made up of people from all tribes, classes, and countries, but it takes the faith summoned by the word in the power of the Spirit to see it. The biblically disciplined imagination sees reality as it truly is: not a mechanical universe in perpetual motion but rather a divine creation in the midst of labor pains, where the new in Christ struggles to come forth from the old in Adam. Pastors make disciples by helping congregations recover *sola Scriptura*. Scripture alone should rule the Christian social imagination. Scripture alone should be our supreme plausibility structure. Scripture alone should provide the images and metaphors by which God's people live.

IMAGINING THE PASTOR: METAPHORS TO MINISTER BY

I have a pet theory that every significant cultural or academic trend eventually shows up in the way people write biblical commentaries. Recently I've wondered if there is a similar dynamic when it comes to pastors—that our pictures of leadership in society come to define leadership in the church. As William Willimon observes, the past fifty years or so has seen a bewildering variety of images describing what pastors are and what they do: "Contemporary ministry has been the victim ... of images of leadership that are borrowed not from scripture, but from the surrounding culture—the pastor as CEO, as psychotherapeutic guru, or as political agitator."[23]

Eugene Peterson has been especially critical of the managerial metaphor: "The vocation of pastor has been replaced by the strategies of religious entrepreneurs with business plans. ... I love being an American ... [but] I don't love the rampant

---

23. William H. Willimon, *Pastor: The Theology and Practice of Ordained Ministry* (Nashville: Abingdon, 2002), 55.

consumerism that treats God as a product to be marketed."[24]
He is particularly critical of the understanding of the pastoral
vocation in terms of career: "American pastors, without really
noticing what was happening, got our vocations redefined in
terms of American careerism. We quit thinking of the parish
as a location for pastoral spirituality and started thinking of it
as an opportunity for advancement."[25]

A misleading picture of what it means to succeed as a pastor
contributes to the secularization of the church. The problem is
with the hidden curriculum, the pictures we live by, and hence
the captive imagination. If living by biblical metaphors is vital
for disciples, how much more vital is it that pastors learn to
minister by biblical metaphors? This is simply a way of saying
that pastors too may need to reform their self-conceptions by
adhering to *sola Scriptura*. Put differently: *Scripture alone* ought
to rule our thinking about what a pastor is and does. Here I will
offer three metaphors that pastors would do well to allow to
reshape their vocational imaginations.

The first metaphor the Bible offers us is the *shepherd*. It's not
quite as exciting as fireman or policeman—that is, at least not
until you read about young David, who had to fight off lions and
Goliaths and bears, oh my (1 Sam 17:34–37)! Most people today,
including pastors themselves, probably don't think of gospel
ministry in terms of waging a shepherd's heroic war. But that's
exactly what it is, as we will see if we can reinvigorate the biblical imagination that should be at the forefront of the congregation's consciousness.

---

24. Eugene Peterson, *The Pastor: A Memoir* (New York: HarperOne, 2011), 4.
25. Eugene Peterson, *Under the Unpredictable Plant: An Exploration in Vocational Holiness* (Grand Rapids: Eerdmans, 1992), 20.

The second metaphor is of a *minister of the word*. The idea of "ministering" the word appears in Acts 6:4, where the twelve apostles decide to let others serve tables while they devote themselves to serving up God's word. After all, "One does not live by bread alone, but by every word that comes from the mouth of God" (Matt 4:4 NRSV).

There are many ways to minister the word, but interpreting the Bible theologically has a special role in educating the imagination, especially when it is done from the pulpit. Preachers should worry less about entertaining and more about paying attention to what Scripture says and to expositing it as faithfully as possible. This is the special remit of the preaching pastor. John Leith says, "The Reformation can best be understood as a revival of preaching, the principal means by which God's grace was mediated to human beings."[26] The Second Helvetic Confession (1566) went so far as to say: "The preaching of the Word of God is the Word of God." It is in hearing the word of God that we are remade into creatures of the word. Through hearing the word of God, the Spirit can break us, humble us, and make us more like Christ.

It is important to remember that it is God at work in his word, which will not fail to accomplish the purpose for which he has sent it (Isa 55:11). As Ephraim Radner says, preaching "is a way of putting us back where we belong: into the text itself ... where God's word, in all his creative omnipotence, does *its* work of self-giving and conformation."[27]

The final metaphor is of a *doctor of the church*. We get our English term "doctor" from the Latin *docere* (to teach).

---

26. John Leith, *The Reformed Imperative: What the Church Has to Say that No One Else Can Say* (Philadelphia: Westminster, 1988), 24.

27. Ephraim Radner, *Time and the Word: Figural Reading of the Christian Scriptures* (Grand Rapids: Eerdmans, 2016), 263.

In medieval times a doctor was a learned person. Theologians were called "Doctors of the Church" because they taught doctrine. Other learned persons learned the science of healing. These are medical doctors. I like to think of pastor-theologians as doctors in both senses of the term: people who know how to restore and maintain the health of the body of Christ precisely by teaching.

In one sense, pastor-theologians are the general practitioners of the body of Christ—the church's primary-care physicians. In another sense, though, the special vocation of the pastor is to be the *eye doctor* of the body of Christ. Jesus himself taught his disciples about the importance of the eye: "Your eye is the lamp of your body. When your eye is healthy, your whole body is full of light, but when it is bad, your body is full of darkness" (Luke 11:34–35). Jesus was referring, I believe, to what Paul calls the "eyes of the heart" (Eph 1:18), which we could paraphrase as "the mind's eye," namely, the imagination.[28] This eye has to do with the most important way we see things, our inmost vision, our perception of what is most real—what I have in this book been calling the social imaginary, our story-shaped plausibility framework.

The church, the body of Christ, has a vision problem. This could be diagnosed as a culturally induced myopia that allows us to see only what is in the material world immediately in front of us. Or perhaps the problem is an astigmatism that prevents the light of what can be known of God in creation from shining through. In either case, the pastor-theologian can help by giving

---

28. For the relation of "eyes of the heart" to the imagination, see Alison Searle, *"The Eyes of Your Heart": Literary and Theological Trajectories of Imagining Biblically* (Milton Keynes, UK: Paternoster, 2008).

congregations the corrective lenses of Scripture, which Calvin calls the "spectacles" that allow us to read the world rightly.[29]

As we have seen already, the Protestant Reformers put a high value on the office of the teacher, largely on the basis of Ephesians 4:11–12, which speaks of the risen and ascended Christ giving "pastors and teachers" to equip the saints for building up the body of Christ. Helping people understand who they are, why they're here, and where they should be going on the journey that is life is perhaps the most important ministry there is. It is hard to make progress or to flourish when you are existentially disoriented. Pastors minister this needed understanding by helping people make connections in three areas: between the parts of the Bible and the overarching story; between the Bible and the world in which they live; and between who they are at the moment and who God calls them to be in Christ.

When it comes to understanding the Bible, disciples need *canon sense*: the ability to interpret particular passages of Scripture in light of the flow of redemptive history. To summarize the plot of redemptive history as simply as possible: God meets (creates) world; God loses world; God gets world back; God and world live happily ever after.

Luther said that the Bible presents Christ. Understanding how each passage does this is also the goal of theological Bible reading. Doctors of the church help disciples to read the Bible to see Christ, and what is in Christ: true deity, true humanity—"all the treasures of wisdom and knowledge" (Col 2:3). If we look hard enough, we see the truth about ourselves, buried and raised in Christ (Rom 6:4), adopted into the family of God,

---

29. John Calvin, *Institutes of the Christian Religion*, ed. John T. McNeill, trans. Ford Lewis Battles, Library of Christian Classics (1960; repr., Louisville: Westminster John Knox, 2011), 1.6.1.

members of the reconciled people of God made one in Christ: Israel and the church, Jew and Greek, male and female, slave and free (Gal 3:28).

Doctors of the church also help people to read their own world—their own particular cultural context—in light of the overarching drama of redemption. The institutions of society are its hardware, but culture is society's software, its "program" for cultivating humanity and shaping its freedom. Pastor-theologians must educate their people about culture, for culture is in the full-time business of educating people, cultivating their humanity. Culture ultimately educates not minds but hearts when it provides its own lenses for the imagination.

To minister the gospel is not just to minister understanding, but also to minister reality: a clear-eyed vision of our new humanity in Christ. To say *what is* in Christ is to set captive imaginations free from the false pictures that rule so many lives. In preaching the word of God, preachers hold up a mirror in which we see ourselves as we truly are. There is no more basic reality than what is in Christ.

In ministering the word of God, the pastor helps disciples get real. The sermon is not a secondhand description of what is happening in a historical galaxy far, far away. No, gospel preaching proclaims the true story of the world, acknowledging that all things are "from him and through him and to him" (Rom 11:36). The sermon is the heavy artillery in the pastor-theologian's arsenal, and the best frontal assault on imaginations held captive by other stories promising other ways to the good life. A sermon must not only say *what is in Christ* but also communicate its *excellence*.

CORE EXERCISES FOR THE EYES OF THE HEART

It is the pastor's privilege and responsibility to serve the church, the principal place to make disciples. I have been talking about the importance of images and vision, and the aim of this chapter was to get the church, and the pastor, into better focus by recovering the Reformation ideas of the church as "creature of the word" and the formal principle of *sola Scriptura*.

Sola Scriptura is not simply a doctrine about the relationship of Scripture and tradition. It is also a rule that applies to the Christian imagination: *Scripture alone is the ultimate story from which disciples must take their existential bearings*. Scripture alone provides the metaphors, images, and narratives that are the authoritative guides for both thinking about and *doing* life together as Christ's church. Scripture alone defines the kind of wellness, health, and fitness that disciples should be striving for.

I presented the pastor as an eye doctor, charged especially with maintaining, correcting, and improving the church's corporate vision, largely, but not exclusively, by preaching. There are, however, many ways to minister the word, to help people both read Scripture theologically and to participate in the story at its heart, and thereby make *sola Scriptura* their social imaginary. Let me now suggest some exercises in lived theology intended to strengthen our grip on the material we have covered in this chapter.

As with any other form of exercise, what I propose here needs to be practiced on a regular basis in order to reap the benefit. A person cannot become physically fit by climbing a flight of stairs one time only. Similarly, pastors cannot change a social imaginary with a single sermon. Keep in mind that the ministry of the word extends beyond preaching. Spiritual formation happens whenever words are ministered: in counseling sessions, Sunday school classes, prayers, pastoral visitations, even everyday conversation. Paul encourages his readers to perform something very much like what I am calling a core exercise when he asks them to remind each other that the story in whose light they live ends with Jesus' triumphant return: "Therefore encourage one another with these words" (1 Thess 4:18). Similarly, each of the core exercises is a way of helping one another to inhabit the new reality in Christ—what Karl Barth called "the strange new world of the Bible"—indicated by Christian doctrine.

Exercise 1: Read Scripture to Correct Our Pictures of Church Leadership

How would you describe the kind of leader people follow today? What images of leadership hold sway in contemporary culture? To what extent have cultural pictures of leaders infiltrated the church—in particular, our thinking about pastors? The Bible provides corrective lenses that allow us to align the eyes of our heart with the way God wants us to see things. It is vital that church elder boards and congregations become aware of the influence of secular pictures of leadership on their thinking about pastors.

Encourage your elders and congregation to think biblically about leadership. For example, think about the leaders God gave Israel and the church: How are pastors like prophets, priests, and kings? Think in particular of the role the word of God played in each of these offices. Think of leaders in the early church and how they decided to devote themselves to the ministry of the word (Acts 6:1–6). Use Scripture to reform your church's notions of what church leadership should look like. Hopefully your congregants will come to appreciate the pastor not only as a preacher, program manager, and people helper but also as a theologian: one who casts biblical visions of new life in Christ, individual and corporate. These are the pictures pastors can lead by and local churches can live by.[30]

Exercise 2: Read Scripture to Open Your Congregation's Eyes to the Way in Which a Culture's Social Imaginary Is a Means of Spiritual Formation

Pastors cannot know everything about everything, but they should be able to know one big thing about everything: whether or not it fosters life in Christ. Pastors need to practice reading the signs of the times, and that means learning to read cultural texts and cultural trends. By *culture* I mean everything in our world that is man-made, especially the things that embody and give visible expression to the meaning of life.

Whether we are aware of it or not, everyone who is part of culture receives cultural messages, some of which are explicit but most of which are implicit—messages that work their way into our subconscious, there to construct a plausibility structure, brick by brick. Chapter 2 above is an example of using the Bible to expose certain cultural messages (about wellness in that case), and the convictions that undergird them, as false gospels. Pastors do disciples a great service by opening their eyes to the social imaginaries that so often hold us in their grip. Use Scripture to expose the idols and ideologies of our time, perhaps by preaching on the forms contemporary idolatry takes.[31]

---

30. See further Todd Wilson and Gerald L. Hiestand, eds., *Becoming a Pastor Theologian: New Possibilities for Church Leadership* (Downers Grove, IL: IVP Academic, 2016).

31. See further my introduction to *Everyday Theology: How to Read Cultural Texts and Interpret Trends* (Grand Rapids: Baker Academic, 2007), 15–60.

*Exercise 3: Read Scripture to Exercise the Eschatological
Imagination and Strengthen the Eyes of the Heart*

We read the Bible in order to discern the Way of truth and life
that leads to fellowship with God and human flourishing from
ways of falsehood and illusion that lead only to the dead end of
idolatry and human frustration. The Bible orients us to what is
real and will endure forever: the word of God, which is to say all
the promises that find their "Yes" in Christ (2 Cor 1:20). One of
the great promises is that God has made believers "alive together
with him" (Col 2:13). Another is that God has broken down the
dividing wall of hostility in Christ (Eph 2:14), with the result
that "there is neither Jew nor Greek ... neither slave nor free ...
for you are all one in Christ Jesus" (Gal 3:28).

These statements of *what is* in Christ require eschatological
imagination to see their truth, by which I mean the ability to
see what is *not yet* complete as *already* finished, in Christ. We
have to practice seeing others not after the flesh, according to
their backgrounds, jobs, or social class, but rather in terms of
their being in Christ, according to the eschatological imagination. Jesus' parables cultivate this eschatological imagination
when they help us perceive the kingdom of God in the ordinary. So, I suggest, does the Lord's Supper—sharing in "one
loaf" (1 Cor 10:17 NIV)—an enacted parable of our union with
one another in Christ. In many and various ways, pastors can
strengthen the eyes of the heart by helping church members
to view themselves and their fellow believers through biblical
spectacles, as new creatures in Christ.

CONCLUSION:
THE PASTOR-THEOLOGIAN
AS GENERAL PRACTITIONER

Pastors are theologians charged with proclaiming the gospel, ministering its understanding, and facilitating practices that correspond to what is in Christ. What pastors know, and have to contribute, is something quite particular (what God was doing in Christ), though it has enormous, even universal, implications. What God is doing in Christ through the Spirit is to create a people for his treasured possession (Exod 19:5; Deut 7:6; 14:2; 26:8; Mal 3:17; Titus 2:14; 1 Pet 2:9). Think of the pastor-theologian as a general practitioner, a doctor who ministers health to the body of Christ in multiple ways, not least by recommending core exercises for spiritual fitness. Most of these core exercises are forms of the ministry of the word and have to do with verbalizing the meaning of our life hidden in Christ (Col 3:3). Pastor-theologians know something particular and definite, but strictly speaking it is not "specialized" knowledge. The pastor-theologian is a special kind of generalist, *a generalist who "specializes" in relating all things to the gospel of Jesus Christ* in order to make disciples, especially by disciplining their imaginations to conform to the unified biblical narrative with Christ at its center. To minister the word is thus to speak not your own mind but the *mind of Christ*, and to do so in order to animate and guide the *body of Christ*.

The church is the place to have our imaginations reshaped, and in that sense pastors are also eye doctors. Even to confess "I believe in the church" is to begin to have your imagination reshaped from seeing the church as a fault-filled human institution to the holy nation, the temple. This reshaping of the imagination makes all the difference for how pastors see their own vocations in the church.

Two stonemasons were hard at work. When asked what they were doing, the first said, "I am cutting this stone in a perfectly square shape." The other answered, "I am building a cathedral." Both answers are correct, but it takes imagination to see that you are building a cathedral, not simply making blocks of granite.

Likewise, two pastors were hard at work. When asked what they were doing, the first said, "I am planning programs, preparing sermons, and managing conflict." The other answered, "I am building a temple." It takes an imagination shaped by the Bible to see one's congregation as a living temple, with each member a living stone (1 Pet 2:5). These stones are being worked—chiseled, fitted, and polished—in order to be joined together with Christ, the cornerstone (Eph 2:20). It takes a biblically formed eschatological imagination to look at a sinner and see a saint.

It is one thing to build a cathedral, quite another to assemble a holy temple with Jesus Christ as the chief cornerstone, a dwelling place for God, out of human beings (Eph 2:21–22). How then can we form men and women fit for the purpose of representing the new humanity in Christ, a fit temple for the Spirit of Christ? My hope and prayer is that pastors will have David's burning desire to build a house for the Lord (1 Chr 21:6–10), but this time with living stones (1 Pet 2:5).

I believe in the church, the new humanity in Christ—and in the importance of eye doctors who, in teaching disciples to read the Bible theologically, help us to see it.

6

COMPANY OF
THE GOSPEL

The Disciple as Member of the Church

We are living in an age dominated by suspicion of institutions, the church included. The suspicion is so ensconced, and so extreme, that some young Christians may prefer to be discipled by individuals they know and trust rather than by institutions that may seem to be interested in their own growth only. In this chapter, then, I want to argue that the church is the biblically mandated place to make disciples.

Many have difficulty confessing belief in the one, holy, catholic, and apostolic church. Institutions are organized and have authority structures—that's two strikes against them already. What makes it even more difficult is that there are so many institutions, including churches, to choose from. People who have been spiritually formed to be consumers may have a harder time choosing one way only.

In his book *The Future of Faith*, Harvey Cox argues that we are entering a third stage of church history: not the apostolic

Age of Faith, concerned with adhering to Jesus' moral teaching, nor the Age of Belief, concerned with right doctrine, but an Age of the Spirit, marked by a cynicism toward authoritative institutions and a concern for spirituality rather than doctrine. Cox cites Aldous Huxley's variation on the Lord's Prayer: "Give us this day our daily faith, but deliver us from *beliefs.*"[1] Can there be discipleship without doctrine?

WHICH GOSPEL?
WHOSE CHURCH?

Not every assembly that gathers Sunday morning for fellowship is convened by God's word. Take, for example, the Humanist Community at Harvard University, which holds Sunday morning meetings geared toward that part of the population that responds to surveys of religious affiliation by choosing "none." These new humanist communities are coming increasingly to resemble Christian churches, except they are trying to do community without God and without Christ. The Houston Oasis, for another example, bills itself as "a community of compassion and reason that seeks to create a safe and welcoming environment for freethinkers to celebrate the human experience in a positive way."[2] It meets Sunday mornings at 10:30 to provide fellowship and support. Their web page proudly states, "People are more important than beliefs," yet the community still has something like a confession of faith, even if it begins not with "I believe" but "we think." As I have insisted throughout this work, we are *all* disciples; the only question is whose words we are following. Like it or not, we've all been filled with teaching of one kind or

---

1. Harvey Cox, *The Future of Faith* (New York: HarperCollins, 2009), 213.

2. "Code of Conduct," Houston Oasis, www.houstonoasis.org/code-of-conduct (accessed August 23, 2018).

another. The only question is whether the doctrines we live by lead us to flourish or perish—and that eternally!

These nonreligious communities force the church to think more carefully about its distinct nature, identity, and mission. They also force us, like the Reformers, to formulate criteria that will help us discern the spirits. For not every spirit is the spirit of Jesus Christ: "Anyone who does not have the Spirit of Christ does not belong to him" (Rom 8:9). Jesus himself says, "Not everyone who says to me, 'Lord, Lord,' will enter the kingdom of heaven, but the one who does the will of my Father who is in heaven" (Matt 7:21). Jesus here makes a distinction between insiders and outsiders.

The Reformers also wrestled with the problem of how to recognize the true church, and developed three criteria: the right preaching of the word, the right administration of the sacraments, and the proper exercise of discipline. In these you might say there was actually only one mark: the right administration of God's gospel—through preaching, the sacraments, and the life of the church.[3] The key assumption was that word and Spirit belong together. We test the spirits by measuring whether they correspond to what God has said in Scripture.

God's word gathers God's people to "do" the word—to hear, sing, study, confess, celebrate, obey, and generally to live into it and act it out. Disciples are members of this company of the gospel. The church, as the gathering of the word, is that peopled place where Christians are built up by the written and proclaimed word into the living Word of God, Jesus Christ. The true end of theology, its final purpose, is not an orthodox

---

3. So Herman Bavinck, *Reformed Dogmatics*, vol. 4, *Holy Spirit, Church, and New Creation*, ed. John Bolt, trans. John Vriend (Grand Rapids: Baker Academic, 2006), 312.

compendium of doctrine but an orthodox community of disciples who embody the mind of Jesus Christ everywhere, to everyone, at all times. The church, says Bonhoeffer, is "God's new will and purpose for humanity."[4]

The church gathers to hear and do the word or, in a word, to *worship*. The Reformers acknowledged worship as the final end of the human creature, who exists "to glorify God, and to enjoy him forever."[5] Worship is a verb, but what the church does is a response to a prior initiative from God. This initiative, this word, is God's self-communication. It is something that God both says and does. God's performance—his mighty acts whereby he communicates his light and life in love (grace)—is the proper framework for human performance (gratitude). The church is a place to make disciples primarily because it is a place where God's people learn right worship, in spirit and in truth (John 4:24). Just before I make good on that claim, let me first set the stage by showing you how biblical interpretation is like theatrical performance.

HISTORY AS THE THEATER OF THE GOSPEL: THE DRAMA OF REDEMPTION

Everyday life is theatrical: each time one person meets another person, there is a hint of dramatic suspense. Picking up on this, in 1959 sociologist Erving Goffman wrote a book titled *The Presentation of the Self in Everyday Life*.[6] The essence of theater

---

4. Dietrich Bonhoeffer, *Sanctorum Communio: A Theological Study of the Sociology of the Church*, ed. Clifford J. Green, trans. Reinhard Krauss and Nancy Lukens, Dietrich Bonhoeffer Works 1 (Minneapolis: Fortress, 2009), 141.

5. Westminster Shorter Catechism 1.

6. Erving Goffman, *The Presentation of Self in Everyday Life* (New York: Doubleday, 1959).

is not a static thing or abstract truths but happenings. And the medium of theater is not disembodied thinking but physical and personal, involving bodily action and interaction, like the gospel itself. Theater speaks the language of action.

Salvation history is also theatrical. In it, God acts out. The essence of Christianity is not a system of ideas or morality but God presenting or communicating himself in everyday life: to Adam, Abraham, Israel, Mary, Paul, and others. It is the story of light entering the world in the person of Jesus Christ to cast away darkness.

What pastors have to say that no one else can say is not simply that there is a God but that God has acted. The gospel is a report of something that has been done. We have news—breaking news that the kingdom of God has *broken into* our world in the person and work of Jesus Christ. God has acted (creating news to report) and God has spoken (the news is reliable because those who reported it were inspired by God).

I have taken to calling God's historical self-presentation in word and deed *theodrama*. *Drao* means "doing"; *theos* means "God"—hence "God doing." The Bible recounts the mighty acts of God from the beginning of creation to its final consummation. This is the big story of the Bible, and it requires big reading. This drama is the story that ought to rule the Christian imaginary, and it entails a particular way of viewing church, pastors, disciples, and the world itself. For example, Calvin calls the world the "theater of God's glory"; this is a lovely description, for what God does on the stage of world history is to display his perfections. In particular, God out of free love communicates his light and life with those whom he has chosen to be his people.

The drama of redemption begins, fittingly enough, with a word from God. In particular, it begins with God's promise to Adam to crush the serpent (Gen 3:15) and to Abraham to bless through his seed all the families of the earth (Gen 12:3). The way God fulfills his promise, and overcomes resistance, constitutes the story of the Bible, a drama of the redemption God works in history through his Son and Spirit. This drama is a story *made flesh*: first by Jesus Christ, in whom the story reaches its climax, then by disciples who continue to embody and enact the story in the power of Christ's Spirit.

It requires imagination to see world history as a drama of redemption. Yet this is precisely what reading Scripture theologically requires. Think of the drama as a five-act play. Each act of the play is set in motion by a speech act of God. The first act is creation and its subsequent corruption (Gen 1–11), the setting for everything else that follows. Act II, beginning from Genesis 12 and running through the rest of the Old Testament, concerns God's election, rejection, and restoration of Israel that begins with his promise to make of Abraham a great nation and by him to bless all the families of the earth. The pivotal and climactic third act is Jesus: God's definitive saving Word. Act IV begins with the risen Christ sending his Spirit to create the church. The fifth and final act is the last judgment and the consummation of all things. To understand this drama rightly you need to know where you are, in order to determine your position in the overarching plot. Christians today are living between the first and second comings of Jesus, in the closing scenes of Act IV, poised between memory and hope. To make disciples is to teach them where they are in this drama, and then to encourage them to take up their parts and walk.

The incarnation is the climax of a whole series of divine entrances. It is also what makes the world a theater of the gospel: "And the Word became flesh and dwelt among us, and we have seen his glory" (John 1:14). The life and work of Jesus is the self-presentation of God's eternal being on the stage of world history. Now there's an entrance! There are also some dramatic *exits*. The exodus—God's delivery of Israel from their oppression in Egypt—is the great saving event of the Old Testament. It is also the singular act that, more than any other, identifies the God of Israel: "I am the LORD your God, who brought you out of the land of Egypt" (Exod 20:2). Jesus refers in Luke 9:31 to his own death as the "departure" (*exodos*) that he would accomplish in Jerusalem. This, along with the resurrection, is arguably the climax of the New Testament drama. Both the Old and New Testaments, then, highlight "exits": of Israel from Egypt and bondage; of Jesus from Jerusalem and ultimately from the grave. Note, too, that Jesus' resurrection makes possible an entrance— that of the Holy Spirit: "It is to your advantage that I go away [exit, die], for if I do not go away, the Helper will not come to you" (John 16:7).

These comings and goings that make up the dramatic action are actually sendings or missions. God makes good on his *promissio* to Abraham by the *missio* of Son and Spirit. God indeed moves in mysterious—missionary!—ways. The whole theodrama is essentially missional and Trinitarian. Jesus sends the Spirit to incorporate believers into one body and then sends them out to make disciples. The gospel is the good news that, because of the missions of Son and Spirit, we have a share in the very light and life of God: "In [Christ] we have obtained an inheritance" (Eph 1:11). Theodrama is the story of God, the true story of the world, made flesh.

As disciples seek to live in and live out the drama of salvation history, Scripture alone is their divinely authorized transcript, a trustworthy record of what God has said and done in the past. It is the written record of God's loving self-presentation in history "for us." It is also a living and active word (Heb 4:12), a character in the drama of redemption. It is the means by which the God who is offstage (so to speak) speaks into it.

The Bible also provides stage lighting. "Thy word is a lamp to my feet and a light to my path" (Ps 119:105 RSV; cf. 2 Pet 1:19). The Scriptures serve as *footlights*: the means by which we see the stage clearly and make our way across it. Perhaps the best way to view Scripture is as a divinely appointed ingredient in what we could call the economy of light, the divinely ordered way (the plan, or *oikonomia*—Eph 1:10) in which God shines his light (his will, his self-knowledge) into the world.

The Bible is both a theatrical and a pharmaceutical script, providing written instruction for the church's bodily performance and for the health of the church body. The point is that the Bible's words provide direction (light) for disciples' right participation in the theodrama. So does doctrine.

DOCTRINE AS DIRECTION
FOR DISCIPLES

Philosopher Alasdair MacIntyre says that stories so shape our self-understandings that we can't answer the question, "What ought we to do?" until we have answered the prior question, "Of which story are we a part?"[7] We are part of a story made flesh, and our flesh—our embodied action—participates in that story too. To be a disciple is to be able to take up one's God-appointed role, follow Christ, and speak-act to the glory of God. This may sound abstract, but the disciple is in the details. How exactly do we participate in the drama of redemption in the twenty-first

---

7. Alasdair MacIntyre, *After Virtue: A Study in Moral Theory*, 2nd ed. (Notre Dame: University of Notre Dame Press, 1984), 216.

century, when the church faces new challenges and is forced to play new scenes in new cultural contexts?

Scripture is the story that disciples live by, but *doctrines are summaries and explorations of the story that disciples live by*. This is why pastors need to make disciples through Scripture *and* doctrine. Doctrine does not add content to Scripture, but it does add understanding. Doctrine develops only because the church's understanding of the biblical story and its implications has developed, just as Jesus promised it would: "When the Spirit of truth comes, he will guide you into all the truth" (John 16:13).[8]

In addition to seeing the gospel as news of something done and the Bible as a transcript of what God has done, doctrine helps the church see what it needs to do in response to keep the action going. In C. S. Lewis's words: "The 'doctrines' we get *out of* the true myth are of course *less* true: they are translations into our *concepts* and *ideas* of that which God has already expressed in a language more adequate, namely the actual incarnation, crucifixion, and resurrection."[9] The goal of doctrine is to help people understand the story of which they are a part—the drama of redemption—so well that they know what to say and do to correspond and continue it, even though the cultural scenery has changed. Doctrine is a special kind of instruction that offers directions for both theoretical and practical understanding, for *doing* faith: it is theatrical direction for discipleship.

---

8. Evangelicals are sometimes suspicious of the development of doctrine. When I speak of doctrine here, I am thinking of the doctrines that lead us further into what Scripture is saying, not away from it. For a defense of how doctrine serves rather than subverts Scripture, see my "Improvising Theology according to the Scriptures: An Evangelical Account of the Development of Doctrine," in *Building on the Foundations of Evangelical Theology*, ed. Gregg Allison and Stephen Wellum (Wheaton, IL: Crossway, 2015), 15–50; and Rhyne R. Putnam, *In Defense of Doctrine: Evangelicalism, Theology, and Scripture* (Minneapolis: Fortress, 2015).

9. Letter to Arthur Greeves in *Yours, Jack: Spiritual Direction from C. S. Lewis* (Grand Rapids: Zondervan, 2008), 28–29.

As we have seen, one of the acts of the risen Christ was to appoint "pastors and teachers" to equip the saints for the work of ministry (Eph 4:11–12). In the theatrical model I am here commending, pastors and theologians are first and foremost agents and ministers of understanding who equip disciples for active participation in the drama of the Christ, through reading Scripture and teaching doctrine.

Doctrine makes disciples when it yields not merely propositional knowledge (though this is part of it) but practical reason: the knowledge of what to say and do in particular situations. It does this, as we have seen, by explaining the main action of the story, but also by helping us to understand ourselves and why we are here: to display the new life in Christ in the freedom of the Spirit and, in so doing, to glorify the Father.

At its best, doctrine serves not only the theoretical purpose of providing a comprehensive account of what a Christian believes but also the more practical project of forming disciples: people who are ready, willing, and able to display the mind and wisdom of Christ in every situation by doing the kind of thing Christ commanded, the kind of thing that corresponds to the new reality "in Christ." The doctrines of creation, incarnation, Trinity, and atonement are not theoretical abstractions—things primarily to be thought—but meaningful patterns that provide orientation for everyday existence, and hence things primarily to be *lived*. Doctrine is not a distraction but the church's main business: living each day, all day, to the glory of God. We can only do this when we understand the story in which we are caught up.

Doctrine educates what we might call the theodramatic imagination: the ability to see redemptive history and our own historical situation as a unified drama centered on Jesus Christ. Doctrine shapes our imagination in ways that help the church to appreciate the goodness of the good news of Jesus Christ, and thereby to create in believers not only understanding but also a desire to be part of the story. After all, this is the goal of making disciples: forming people who are fit for theodramatic participation—living as children of light and walking in the truth of the gospel.

Doctrine provides theatrical direction for discipleship, direction for embodying and enacting the way, the truth, and the life of Jesus Christ faithfully in new situations. The "fit" disciple will do the "fitting" thing. "Fittingness" is the key term. *Pastor-theologians train people to be spiritually fit (ready, willing, and able) to say and do what is fitting for citizens of the gospel to say and do.* Fittingness is a matter of corresponding in our speech, thought, and life today to what God has done, is doing, and will do to sum up all things in Christ. Making disciples ultimately concerns forming people to be fit for the purpose of gospel fittingness.

Doctrine is "sound" (Titus 2:1) when it says *what is* in Christ. To follow the direction of doctrine is to take a dose of reality. Doctrine helps us understand how all things were created through Christ and for Christ, and how in Christ all things hold together (Col 1:16–17). The job of pastor-theologians is not only to describe but also to direct disciples to conform to *what is in Christ*. As we saw in the previous chapter, pastors have a particular role to play as ministers of understanding, and they play this role in large part by both offering and encouraging big, theological readings of Scripture—readings that are less theoretical than theatrical, by which I mean a reading where one's interpretation is an embodied performance.

In the previous chapter I mentioned the idea that pastors are teachers of doctrine and hence doctors of the church. (Remember that the Latin for doctrine, *doctrina*, means "teaching.") Paul could describe doctrine as "sound" because it is vital to the life of the church, and not only true but also "healthy" or "health-giving." Sound doctrine stands in contrast to false doctrine, which is *toxic* or *noxious*—inimical to the community's well-being inasmuch as it directs disciples to participate in unholy dramas.

Pastors are doctor-directors who prescribe "scripts" (and now I'm using the term in its pharmaceutical rather than theatrical sense) to be followed. Prescription medicine that remains in the bottle is of no use to anyone. Its healing power is released only when the body ingests or absorbs it. Similarly, doctrine is a prescription for the health of the body of Christ, yet many churchgoers refuse to take their medicine, preferring to swill the low-intellectual-calorie, sickly sweet soft drinks of popular culture. It is largely thanks to the doctoral work of pastor-theologians that sound doctrine—heavenly medicine from above—gets into the bloodstream of the body of Christ.

The pastor-theologian is also a theatrical director who offers health-giving direction to disciples and congregations. Sound doctrine gives theological description of the kind of wellness, health, and fitness disciples should be pursuing. To be well, theologically speaking, is to be "in Christ." To Jesus' idea that man does not live by bread alone but from every word of God, we can add, and by a diet of doctrine.

I want you to think of the pastor as a theatrical director of the company of the gospel, a gathering of people who assemble to proclaim, celebrate, reflect on, and act out the truth of the gospel. In preaching and teaching the Bible, the pastor becomes midwife of the holy script's performance by the gospel company, the mediator between the word written and the word enacted by the community for its own edification and as a witness to the world. The first commandment of the theatrical director is faithfulness to the script. This accords with the Reformers' emphasis on *sola Scriptura*, and with the argument of the present book that Scripture alone ought to rule the social imaginary of the company of the gospel.

True, Jesus Christ alone is Lord of the church, but he has given the church pastor-teachers as assistant directors. While divine providence oversees the global production, pastors bear the primary responsibility for overseeing local performances. The pastor's work is largely about communicating: to the actors about the meaning of the script and then, indirectly through the actors, to the audience outside about the meaning of the play. In particular, the pastor-director disciples the congregation's imagination so that the theodrama becomes the governing framework of the community's speech and action (see 2 Cor 10:5). But in our anti-institutional age, some may ask, Why must we do this together? Isn't there a place in theater for the one-man show? Isn't the pastor a solo performer? Some pastors might prefer it if they were the stars of the show, but to suggest this is to short-circuit the process of disciple-making. The pastor's task is to make sure that everyone has a speaking and acting part that corresponds to his or her spiritual gift: "As each has received a gift, use it to serve one another, as good stewards of God's varied grace" (1 Pet 4:10; compare 1 Cor 12:4–11).

THE CHURCH AS THEATER OF THE GOSPEL: WHY A GATHERED COMPANY?

God's mighty acts whereby he communicates his light and life in love form the church's plausibility structure and the proper framework for evaluating the church's live performances. God's word is powerful, and God can do what he likes, so why do we need the church? I have found no better answer to this question than Calvin's. Calvin begins book 4 of the *Institutes* with a section on the church as "the external means ... by which God invites us into the society of Christ and holds us therein."[10] The basic idea is that God in his wisdom has created the church and declared it "very good," at least when it is functioning as God intended it to function—as a place where God's people, the community of gathered disciples, could grow in their faith and in godliness by feeding on God's word. This involves hearing *and* doing it.

But we can say even more, for the church is not simply a place where the gospel is proclaimed. The church is an element in the good news itself. The final purpose of God's communicative action is to form a people for his treasured possession: not simply a group of holy individuals but a "holy nation" (1 Pet 2:9). God acts out grace in Jesus Christ. The church is the place where disciples gratefully act out, individually and corporately, their life in Christ. I'll first explain why theater is such an appropriate image, then I'll present the six marks of the theatrical church.

Let me first say what kind of theater the church is *not*. First, it is *not* a place for pastors to perform to further their own careers (2 Cor 2:17). This is a danger, to be sure. Those who have been entrusted with the gospel have a responsibility to please God, not human audiences (1 Thess 2:4).

Second, the church is not a place for congregants to become passive observers of the pastor who becomes the sole performer, as if doing church were something pastors do alone. This picture encourages congregants to be hearers only. Unfortunately, many churches have succumbed to this temptation. This distortion of church ultimately produces a worship space that caters to an entertainment model, as Jeanne Halgren Kilde points out

---

10. John Calvin, *Institutes of the Christian Religion,* ed. John T. McNeill, trans. Ford Lewis Battles, Library of Christian Classics (1960; repr., Louisville: Westminster John Knox, 2011), 1011.

in her book *When Church Became Theater: The Transformation of Evangelical Architecture and Worship in Nineteenth-Century America.*[11] This is what may be called a "bad faith performance." It is worship in bad faith insofar as it requires only passive hearing, not active doing. On the contrary, Paul makes clear that the purpose of pastors is "to equip the saints for the work of ministry, for building up the body of Christ" (Eph 4:12).

Third, the church is not a theater in which people "play act" the Christian faith. Mark my words: not all "doing" is fit for the purpose of gospel citizenship. Some doing is simply busywork (compare Col 2:23). Mistaking this kind of doer for a genuine disciple is a mortal danger for which the New Testament has a special word: hypocrisy. The danger is real, but the whole point of being a creature of the word is that the disciples are not to pretend to be something they are not, but to become the role to which they have been cast, or rather, the vocation to which they have been called. Followers of Jesus are more than moralists or busybodies.

More positively, the church is a theater in which we see stories acted out. Indeed, the church is the enacted story of forgiven and transformed sinners. We need a company of the gospel because it is impossible for a one-man show to act out love for others. The church is both the area where the action is and the company that acts there. The church is a place where people gather to be and to do theater of the gospel, a place to enact, with likeminded others, the drama of the Christ made flesh. There are six marks of the church as a theater of the gospel:

---

11. Jeanne Halgren Kilde, *When Church Became Theater: The Transformation of Evangelical Architecture and Worship in Nineteenth-Century America* (New York: Oxford University Press, 2002).

1. **Amateur theater.** Unlike professionals, amateurs
   do things for the love of it ("amateur" comes from
   Latin *amator* = "lover"). The church performs the
   gospel not for the love of performance itself, but
   rather for the love of the truth, goodness, and
   beauty made known in and by Jesus Christ. Each
   one of us has a part to play, lines to say. Each of us
   has a gift we can exercise that will somehow contribute to the main theme of the play: the glorious reign of God. In particular, we're to "perform"
   resurrection—to "put on" our new humanity in
   Christ—and we're to do it for the love of it, or rather,
   for the love of him.

2. **Royal theater.** The church is Jesus' *command performance*, his royal theater, a theater of kingdom operations: "Do this in remembrance of me" (Luke 22:19).
   Jesus spoke in parables, and the church that
   obeys him becomes a parable of the kingdom, an
   embodied manifestation of his will on earth as it
   is in heaven.

3. **Martyrological theater.** The way Christians live
   together or *do church* ought to be doctrine's primary exhibit. Lesslie Newbigin says that congregations are the "only hermeneutic of the gospel."[12]
   Paul explains the aim of his apostolic ministry is
   "to make all men *see*" the plan of salvation, the mystery of Christ, so that "through the church the man-
   ifold wisdom of God might now be made known to

---

12. Lesslie Newbigin, *The Gospel in a Pluralist Society* (Grand Rapids: Eerdmans, 1989), 227.

the rulers and authorities in the heavenly places" (Eph 3:10). The author of Hebrews asks his readers to remember their previous endurance of sufferings, which included "being publicly exposed [*theatrizō*] to reproach and affliction" (10:32–33). What is shown in the theater of faith is the truth that endures everything: critical testing, suffering, ridicule, and death. This is the martyrdom of Christian life, a show of faith and reason alike. The chief martyr is, of course, Jesus Christ: "Christ also suffered for you, leaving you an example, so that you might follow in his steps" (1 Pet 2:21).

4. **Doxological theater.** While doctrine sets forth in speech the truth of what is in Christ, worship sets forth this truth in forms of song, service, and sacrificial action. This too is theatrical: "Present your bodies as a living sacrifice, holy and acceptable to God, which is your spiritual worship" (Rom 12:1).

5. **Interactive theater.** Elsewhere I have compared the church to an interactive theater, a company of "costumed interpreters" whose task is to draw the audience ("guests") into the action.[13] This is the kind of theater the company of the gospel ought to create in order to evangelize the world. Paul tells his readers to "put on"—clothe themselves with— Christ, that is, the new, Christlike self (Rom 13:14; Gal 3:27; Eph 4:24). Those who put on Christ also stage mini-parables of his kingdom, often creating

---

13. See my *Faith Speaking Understanding: Performing the Drama of Doctrine* (Louisville: Westminster John Knox, 2014), 182–85.

scenes, just as Jesus did when he taught and did things that astonished the crowds. Similarly, the company of the gospel puts on spectacles of faith that should grab the world's attention. The church is the theater in which to display God's extraordinary love for sinners. It is the privilege and responsibility of the company of the gospel to embody a form of communal life that invites others in because it is so attractive. As one expert in interactive theater says, "Creating relationships with the guests, thereby involving them in the story, is the primary focus of the interactive genre."[14] If this is the case with secular interactive theater, how much more should it be the case in the church!

6. **Local theater.** Theaters of the gospel are "placed" gatherings. This is because theater has to do with embodied personal relationships. Pastors have the privilege of directing these local theaters of the gospel. The challenge is to know how to act out new life in Christ in our particular time and place.

Charles Taylor has a very helpful discussion of gnostic or disembodied views of humanity in *A Secular Age*. He calls it "excarnation," which he defines as "the steady disembodying of spiritual life, so that it is less and less carried in deeply meaningful bodily forms, and lies more and more in the head. ... Christianity, as the faith of the Incarnate, is denying something essential to itself as long as it remains wedded to forms which

---

14. Gary Izzo, *The Art of Play: The New Genre of Interactive Theatre* (Portsmouth, NH: Heinemann, 1997), 188.

excarnate."[15] The truth of the gospel is intrinsically incarnate. It is not abstract, but concrete, and it takes a physical company of the gospel to communicate it. It is hard to act out love for one's enemies in a one-man show. It takes a company.

This picture of church as theater corrects two false pictures of the church. First, with Luther, we must discard the dualism that reserved the role of ministers of the word to the ordained clergy. In his view, all believers are in one sense ministers of the word—called to speak and enact it—even if not all are called to exercise the special office of the pastor. This means that all disciples are called not to preach but to perform the story at the heart of the Scriptures. Second, we must no longer think of the church merely as an antechamber to heaven, a place to wait around. Rather, the church—the company of those in union with Christ—is the anticipation of heaven, a place to begin practicing it, because Christ is among us. It is a local embassy of God's coming kingdom, a parable of the kingdom of heaven localized on earth. Hence the church is the best place on earth to get real, and to exhibit reality. Pastors make disciples through Scripture and doctrine by helping them to be fit for the purpose of exhibiting reality, namely, the new reconciled creation that is in Christ (2 Cor 5:17).

LITURGY AS A THEATER OF THE GOSPEL: LEARNING BY HEART AND HABIT

"Get real." People usually say this when they think someone is living in a fantasy world and is overdue for a reality check. From the standpoint of Christian faith, the process of making

---

15. Charles Taylor, *A Secular Age* (Cambridge, MA: Belknap Press of Harvard University Press, 2007), 771.

disciples is the process of helping people to get real. We saw in chapter 3 that Jesus speaks of discipleship in terms of waking and walking, specifically, waking from the dream of our current social imaginary to the truth of the story of Jesus and then walking in the light that he is. So how do we learn to get real?

The answer I've been pursuing throughout this book is "by reading Scripture theologically," that is, with the help of doctrine's ministry of understanding, and with a view to participating in the story Scripture tells, the ongoing drama of redemption. Of course, it all starts by acknowledging that the secular picture that currently holds captive our thoughts and social imaginary does *not* picture ultimate reality. It is not wholly false, only partial, thin, and unnecessarily reductionist. As we saw in chapter 2, this was also the problem with contemporary descriptions of wellness, health, and fitness. They deal with only the physical aspect of human being, not with the whole person, who is an embodied soul or ensouled body.

Scripture alone is a description of the only ultimate reality that is—the reality created by Christ, that exists in Christ, and that is being redeemed for Christ. And a doctrinally informed reading of the Bible is the chief means by which readers come to understand this reality *and be conformed to it.* This reading of the Bible (1) keeps God's story at the center and (2) keeps godliness as the goal.

That's the long answer. The short answer—though not a shortcut—is that we learn to get real by living liturgically. By liturgy I have in mind both a church's order of worship (the regular activities that fill out a church service) and a church's forms of life (the regular common practices that fill out a church year). Both "high church" and "low church" liturgies are lived theological interpretations of Scripture, involving both literal reading (hearing) and lived interpretation (doing). For example, in their worship services many churches say the Lord's Prayer together, out loud. This is a way of reading Scripture that is quasi-dramatic. Other moments of the liturgy, such as the offering or the celebration of the Lord's Supper, are explicitly dramatic inasmuch as they involve embodied acting out the new humanity made possible by the blood of Christ's cross.

Each part of the church's worship service—spoken or sung word, bath, table, prayer—focuses on some aspect of Jesus' story.[16] Taken together, then, the liturgy is the church's spoken and enacted interpretation of the reality attested in and by Scripture. The liturgy is therefore theodramatic. It is all about rehearsing what the Triune God has done, is doing, and will do to renew creation and form a holy nation to be his treasured possession. Accordingly, the liturgy is a prime training ground for making disciples fit for theodramatic purpose.

Liturgy as Formation

One of my main motivations in developing the theatrical model of theology has been to overcome the theory/practice dichotomy characteristic of so many seminaries. This dichotomy is responsible for the misconception that systematic theology, and doctrine in general, is impractical. Presenting doctrine as direction for understanding is my attempt to present theology in terms of wisdom: *lived* knowledge. I'm keenly aware that it is not enough simply to tell people the truth. The question is how the ministry of the word can be transformative. To see the liturgy as itself a corporately enacted biblical interpretation already begins to

---

16. This is an important point, which allows us to find middle ground between liturgical and evangelical churches. See further Melanie C. Ross, *Evangelical versus Liturgical? Defying a Dichotomy* (Grand Rapids: Eerdmans, 2014).

form the disciple's notion of what it is to read the Bible as God's word. The liturgy is both a hearing and a doing of Scripture.

Before we look at church liturgy as a means of formation and transformation, we need to return to what James K. A. Smith has dubbed "cultural liturgies": everyday social practices that capture our imaginations and form habits by inserting us (bodily!) into stories that appear to make our lives meaningful.[17] Smith is alert to the fact that we can learn things, even theology, by doing things with our bodies. What we do habitually begins to shape how we imagine ourselves in the world. It is the imagined story of which we are a part that makes sense of what we do on an everyday basis. For example, there is an academic liturgy—a course of preparation followed by exams—intended to form you into an academic. Everything in which we habitually participate leaves a little mark on our soul, forms our spirits, and trains our loves.

What makes Christian discipleship so challenging is that churches are competing with a host of cultural liturgies, all of which are vying for the hearts of congregants. These rival liturgies want to capture people's attention, then their love, and ultimately their worship. Spiritual formation happens 24/7. The films and advertisements we see, the novels and newspapers we read, the clothes we wear, and the stuff we buy all produce an effect on us. For example, much of the mainstream culture in the modern and postmodern West contributes to the formation of individualist consumers who believe that certain things or experiences will complete their identity and satisfy their desire for happiness. And as we saw in part 1, pictures and practices of

---

17. Smith's Cultural Liturgies series, published by Baker Academic, consists of *Desiring the Kingdom* (2009), *Imagining the Kingdom* (2013), and *Awaiting the King* (2017).

wellness, diet, and fitness exert their own kind of influence over our bodies and our spirits. Health clubs have their own liturgies that exercise their own kind of spiritual formation.

These forms we inhabit eventually colonize our lives. Liturgy enculturates. When we gather together as believers to "do" church, we inhabit particular forms of corporate worship, whether we are "high church" or "low church" Christians. In this respect, learning a liturgy or form of worship is like learning a culture, and the thing about culture is that it cultivates particular forms of life. In the words of Stefan Schweyer, a Swiss practical theologian: "We form forms; and forms form us." One of the tasks of the pastor-theologian is to assess whether the forms of thinking, speaking, and living that characterize the local church correspond to or *fit* the forms and content of the Bible. We have to discern whether contemporary forms of life are indeed following the way of truth and life set out in the Scripture. The ministry of the word therefore involves not only informing people but reforming their habitual forms of speaking, thinking, and living together in light of the form of forms: the truth, goodness, and beauty of the crucified and risen one.

The Church as Theater of Liturgical Speech Acts and the Drama of Discipleship

Liturgy involves words and actions. So does drama—"Action!" is the language of the theater. But the point about liturgy is that, when done in faith, it involves much more than simply going through external motions. Indeed, unless our hearts are prompted by the love of God, external motions alone get us no further than hypocrisy. Yet the liturgy also teaches us how to worship in spirit and in truth, for, when enlivened by the Holy Spirit, participating in worship trains disciples to *become* the role they have been assigned to play: genuine, sincere, and joyful

witnesses to Jesus Christ. To participate in the liturgy is therefore to engage in what can by grace become a means of spiritual
formation. In Calvin's words: "Believers have no greater help
than public worship, for by it God raises his own folk upward
step by step."[18]

Worshiping involves doing things with our bodies, yes, and
this is why liturgical formation is so important: some things,
like learning to play the piano, are best learned through repeti-
tive movements. The liturgical actions I have in mind, precisely
by inserting us, bodily, into the story of Jesus Christ, teach us
how to get real.

Of course, what we mean by "reality" these days is often up
for political grabs. In 1990 Judith Butler, for example, argued
in her book *Gender Trouble* that masculinity and femininity are
culturally constructed through the repetition of stylized acts in
time.[19] She actually compares the way we do "male" and "female"
to performative speech acts. However, it is linguistic utopianism
to say, "If only we could change our language, we could change
the world." This way lies the performance tradition of social
constructivism, which is based on the idea that there is no such
thing as the "real" or the "natural," but only what we agree by
social convention to treat as "real." "I declare, therefore I am"
is a dubious truth. A biological male may identify as trans, but
it is harder for a white person to self-proclaim as black than it
is for a camel to go through the eye of a needle. (We know this
because Rachel Dolezal attempted it.[20])

---

18. Calvin, *Institutes* 4.1.5.

19. Judith Butler, *Gender Trouble: Feminism and the Subversion of Identity* (London: Routledge, 1990).

20. Kirk Johnson, Richard Pérez-Peña, and John Eligon, "Rachel Dolezal, in Center of Storm, Is Defiant: 'I Identify as Black,' " *New York Times*, June 16, 2015, https://www.nytimes.com/2015/06/17/us/rachel-dolezal-nbc-today-show.html.

I raise this issue to pose the question: What exactly are we doing with words in liturgical actions? Does saying something make it so? I submit that, far from playing at make-believe, when we perform a liturgical act we are in fact rehearsing reality: *eschatological* reality, namely, the new reality we have in Christ. The etymology of the Greek term from which we get our English word "liturgy" is instructive: *leitos* (public; people) + *ergos* (working) = public service. Liturgy acts out the theodramatic truth that the church is a "public work of God."

When Christians praise the Triune God, what is happening is not social construction. To think that God is the way the church says he is gets it the wrong way around. Rather, what happens in the liturgy is that disciples are taught to conform to a prior word, God's own word of self-revelation. Here I want to consider the sacraments of baptism and the Lord's Supper, two central disciple-making liturgical practices. If spiritual formation is the process of becoming who we truly are in Christ, then baptism and the Lord's Supper are key ingredients in the process that helps disciples to learn to become *real*. The pastor-theologian's job is to facilitate the people's work of participating in this divine drama. People are the medium with which pastors do theology.

Baptism

Baptism is an apt example of spiritual formation through liturgical practice because in the early church, baptism was the culmination of a disciple's year-long period of catechism. Catechism was the early church's method of teaching disciples what they needed to know in order to be competent citizens of the gospel. Baptism was the sign that a believer was ready to publicly affirm his or her willingness to walk the Way of Jesus Christ.

Yet baptism is also an object lesson, a visual dramatization of a doctrinal truth concerning union with Christ. Water baptism inserts the disciple, in a very visible and tangible manner, into the story of Jesus. Baptism marks a disciple's setting out on Jesus' way by ritually enacting the death of the old self and the birth of the new. Baptism is the actor-disciple's port of entry into the action. Baptism by water is a public declaration that an individual agrees to be an active participant. It is a communicative act that corresponds to the disciple's new reality in Christ. Moreover, the use of a material element, water, engages the disciple in a way that a verbal formula alone does not. Going through this watery motion now becomes part of the disciple's personal history.

We can go further. Baptism is a public performance of our union with Christ. Baptism is a participative act that dramatically depicts our dying with Jesus (Rom 6:4: "We were buried therefore with him by baptism"). Think also of Paul's "I have been crucified with Christ" (Gal 2:20). Liturgical speech acts proclaim our real participation in Christ. To be "in" Christ is to be in the sphere of his personal influence. The church is the domain of Christ, the place where Christ rules through his word and Spirit. In submitting to baptism, a person publicly and symbolically performs union with Christ and membership in the company of the gospel, for the baptized disciple has theatrically identified with the death and resurrection of Jesus.

Baptism is Christian doctrine taught by embodied symbolic action. It is integrated into the liturgy as one of the things God's word commands the church to do on a regular basis. Baptism not only presents before the congregation's eyes the death to the old self and resurrection of the new self in Christ, which is dramatic enough, but also shows, by baptizing a person in the name of the Father, Son, and Spirit, that those who have been united with Christ enjoy fellowship in him through the Spirit with God the Father. It is a rich theological lesson that also grips the church's imagination, particularly when congregants are exhorted to "remember your baptism" as they watch the baptism of someone else.

Lord's Supper

Believers gather together to hear the word of God and to perform liturgical acts that the Lord has commanded. Disciples are baptized once only, but celebrate the Lord's Supper on a regular basis: "Do this in remembrance of me" (Luke 22:19; cf. 1 Cor 11:24–25). In keeping the feast, the church rehearses a climactic scene of the New Testament, one that recalled earlier covenant meals in Israel, foreshadowed Jesus' impending death, and anticipates the future marriage supper of the Lamb of God (Rev 19:9): "Learning how to act shapes a person into a disciple."[21] How does celebrating the Lord's Supper contribute to disciple-making?

It is easy to lose sight of how radical a scene it must have been in New Testament times: people from different ethnicities and classes eating together. This meal is different from other meals because it faithfully represents the climax of the drama of redemption: Jesus' death for us.

The church gathers at the Lord's Table not as onlookers but as actors—active participants in the eating and drinking. The church is not *pretending* that the bread is Christ's body, nor is it simply going through the motions in an attempt to reenact a past event. No, the church is celebrating something that is in one sense already past (Christ's death) but in another sense not yet fully realized (the marriage supper of the Lamb).

---

21. Terrence W. Tilley, *The Disciples' Jesus: Christology as Reconciling Practice* (Maryknoll, NY: Orbis, 2008), 73.

Dietrich Bonhoeffer says in his book *Life Together*, "Christian community is not an ideal we have to realize, but rather a reality created by God in Christ in which we may participate."[22] In sharing the Lord's Supper, we remember the love of God poured out for us on the cross, we celebrate new life in Christ and fellowship with one another in the present, and we anticipate Christ's future return.

The Lord's Supper is a celebrative liturgical act that asserts and expresses, but not like ordinary assertions and expressions. To identify the bread and wine with the body and blood of Christ is to acknowledge a mode of his presence. The cup overflows with meaning. Celebrative speech acts make something nonempirical present. Eating and drinking is something we do with our bodies, but it is an action that exercises most of all the imagination. A celebrative speech act is an astonished indication of an *eschatological* reality, and so differs from mere historical assertions. To hear a celebrant say, "The body of Christ, broken for you," both informs and affects us at a deep level. In addition to reminding us of our union with Christ, and thus of our baptism, it also exhibits in a physical, tangible way our communion with one another. It's hard to bicker with someone with whom you have just broken bread.

In sum, participating in liturgical acts helps us learn with our bodies as well as our minds what it means to be the church of God, companions (literally, "those who share bread") of the Lord's Table. The Supper communicates what God has done for us in Christ and makes us communicants with one another. It is an "incorporative" liturgical act. By breaking the body of Christ,

---

22. Dietrich Bonhoeffer, *Life Together and Prayerbook of the Bible*, ed. Geffrey B. Kelly, trans. Daniel W. Bloesch and James H. Burtness, Dietrich Bonhoeffer Works 5 (Minneapolis: Fortress, 1996), 38.

we enact the body of Christ. This too is a practice that forms disciples to conform to reality.

CORE EXERCISES FOR IMPROVING MOBILITY

What follows are three core exercises for improving the spiritual fitness of one's congregants. Everything begins with disciples' ability to inhabit the biblical story and thus let Scripture serve as their primary imaginary. Each of the following exercises is designed to do precisely that. Note, too, that these are "take-home" exercises, for the simple reason that we need to inhabit the Bible's imaginary not only in church, on Sundays, but in all times, places, and circumstances. Think of these exercises as the cultural liturgies that ought to characterize gospel communities in their Monday-through-Saturday lives. These are not "one and done" exercises. Rather, these core exercises are the warp and woof of a disciple's life.[23]

The Bible provides a script the church can follow when it baptizes disciples and celebrates the Lord's Supper. However, most of the disciple's life is not scripted by Scripture, or the liturgy, if by "scripted" we mean a detailed blueprint for how to live every moment of every day. The Bible does give us some lines to speak, but these do not often fit the particular situation disciples happen to be in. Disciples today daily face opportunities, problems, and challenges that the Bible does not explicitly address. Are transgendered persons the contemporary equivalent of eunuchs? Should Christian couples make use of the latest

---

23. I am grateful to Ryan Fields for calling this point to my attention, and for its formulation.

medical technologies to deal with infertility and, if so, which ones? Is it appropriate for disciples to play the lottery? Is it right for Christians, particularly in our tolerant, pluralistic society, to tell sincere Jews and Muslims that they will spend eternity in hell if they do not trust Jesus Christ as their Lord and Savior? Should a Christian baker refuse to make a wedding cake for a same-sex couple? To respond to such questions, disciples must do more than repeat lines or perform scenes from the biblical script.

The point of liturgical performance is not to give disciples lines but rather to help shape their understanding of the story of Jesus of which they are a continuing part, and to prepare them to be the kind of people who want and are able to continue acting out new scenes of the same drama: "Stay dressed for action" (Luke 12:35). In short, the pastor's task is to train the company of the gospel to be a performing troupe of free and faithful improvisers: people who are ready, able, and willing to embody the mind of Christ always, everywhere, and to everyone.

Please don't confuse improvisation with innovation, or with clever ad-libbing. The true improviser does not simply go his or her own original way but rather contributes, with other like-minded improvisers, to the development of a prior premise. A typical improvisation begins with an idea that the improvisers work together to unpack, often in creative ways, but ways that are always true to, or *fit*, the initial idea. Here, too, the most important thing is *fittingness*: the true improviser says and does things that are neither prescripted nor cleverly original but fitting, things that may appear obvious, but only in retrospect.[24]

---

24. For more on discipleship and improvisation, see my *Faith Speaking Understanding*, 189–99.

Paul asked Philemon to improvise Christian discipleship by receiving his runaway slave Onesimus in a way that fit not with the Roman script, which involved punishing or perhaps even killing him, but rather with the gospel script, which involved welcoming him as a brother in Christ. Note that Paul does not give Philemon specific lines to say or a particular course of action to follow. On the contrary, Paul simply encourages Philemon to do the *fitting* thing, that is, what is required given the reality of the gospel (Phlm 8). Paul trusts in Philemon's maturity as a disciple, which is why he can ask him to act not "by compulsion but of your own accord" (Phlm 14). Philemon has to improvise a solution of what to do with a runaway slave and, because he is a Christian, he goes off Roman script. Paul fully expects Philemon to *freely* do the *fitting* thing, and thereby to refresh Paul's heart (Phlm 20).

Paul's request to Philemon is an example of what I'm calling a theological exercise in core mobility. Recall from chapter 4 that the core is the key part of the body's support structure, and that most of what we do with our bodies involves using the muscles associated with our trunk or torso. Core exercises are an important part of becoming fit for purpose. Core exercises strengthen core muscles, and thereby improve the body's stability, flexibility, and mobility. Without a strong core, the body's range of movement would be severely limited, for the core is where all bodily movement begins. The church, too, must have a sound core if it is to be able to move in the ways the body of Christ ought to move in order to do the kinds of things it is called to do. Core *knowledge* is not enough. In order to be a hearer and doer, the disciple must develop core mobility. To follow Jesus, we must engage our core and walk. Improving the body's core mobility is a prerequisite for fulfilling the body's mission.

The church's core is more than moral, and discipleship is about more than morality. The things that disciples say and do are right and Christlike not simply because they adhere to the law of God (Jesus often asks his disciples to do the *more* than moral) but because they fit with the drama of redemption. Disciples must do more than follow moral prescriptions; they must live out their citizenship of the gospel, embodying and enacting the mind of Christ.

Exercise 1: Searching for Samaritans

Read the parable of the good Samaritan (Luke 10:25–37) and discuss who might be the contemporary counterpart of the man robbed, stripped, beaten, and left for dead by the side of the road. In an age where most people stay in their own homes or frequent third places, who is our neighbor? The purpose of the exercise is to help disciples see themselves in the role of Samaritans.

Compassion is part of the church's core. Jesus' compassion on the crowds *moved* him to do things for them, like feeding, healing, and teaching (see Matt 9:36; 14:14; 15:32). The Greek term for Jesus' "having compassion" is the same as he uses for the good Samaritan's response to the victim in Jesus' parable. Disciples imitate their Lord when they are moved by, and respond to, people in the way Jesus did. It all starts with seeing our world today, and ourselves, as analogous to the stories and characters we read about in the New Testament.[25] So, after we find a contemporary equivalent to the beaten man in Jesus' story, we need

25. This is an exercise in making metaphorical connections between the world of the New Testament and today's world. See further Richard B. Hays, *The Moral Vision of the New Testament: A Contemporary Introduction to New Testament Ethics* (San Francisco: HarperSanFrancisco, 1996), 298–303.

to determine which character in the story most resembles *us*.[26] The purpose of this exercise is twofold: first, to help people learn the skill of reading our world as belonging to the world of the biblical text; second, to help us to see ourselves in the mirror of the text as we actually are, and to *want* with all our heart to be like the good Samaritan, an improviser who, like Philemon, spontaneously does what is fitting for a follower of Jesus Christ.

Exercise 2: Sharing Your Table

Read the biblical account of the Lord's Supper (preferably in conjunction with celebrating it) and relate it both to Israel's Passover meals and to the description in Acts 2:42–46 of the apostles breaking bread together in their homes. Encourage each person or family in the church to invite someone home they don't know well to share a meal, preferably someone as different from them as possible.

Jesus is singularly unimpressed by people who stay only with their own sort: "For if you love those who love you, what reward do you have? Do not even the tax collectors do the same? And if you greet only your brothers, what more are you doing than others? Do not even the Gentiles do the same?" (Matt 5:46–47). Jesus here adds an important amendment about discipleship that all hearers and doers do well to hear: Christian love exceeds social expectations. The reason: the improvisations that fit with the drama of redemption must be more than merely moral, for the drama of redemption explodes all moral conventions. The Lord Jesus Christ is under no obligation to offer hospitality to sinners, to invite unworthy rebels to share his table. It is an

---

26. This exercise is a variation on the celebrated Good Samaritan Experiment, devised by two psychologists in 1973. For a description of the experiment, and its results, see my *Faith Speaking Understanding*, 195.

act of pure grace that he invites those who cannot return his hospitality: "Invite the poor, the crippled, the lame, the blind" (Luke 14:13). This radical hospitality is fitting because it corresponds to God's grace extended to the company of the gospel in Jesus' incarnation and cross.

I submit that extending hospitality to neighbors is one of the best ways to embody the mind of Christ. As a help to this theological exercise, I suggest reading Rosaria Butterfield's *The Gospel Comes with a House Key: Practicing Radically Ordinary Hospitality in Our Post-Christian World.*[27] Furthermore, extending hospitality today to those who are unlike us continues a history of such improvisations: "Early Christian writers claimed that transcending social and ethnic differences by sharing meals, homes, and worship with persons of different backgrounds was a proof of the truth of the Christian faith."[28] In contrast, monochrome, racially homogenous churches reinforce the prejudice that 11:00 a.m. is the most segregated hour in North America, hardly a witness to the new humanity that is in Christ.[29]

Exercise 3: Shining as Lights

Read the account of Peter's denial of Jesus (Luke 22:54–61). Then read what Peter says in 1 Peter 2:9 about the company of the gospel being a holy nation fit to "proclaim the excellencies of him who called you out of darkness into his marvelous light" (1 Pet 2:9). Disciples should do as Peter says, not as he did (cf. Luke 12:8–9). Encourage each person in the company of the

---

27. Rosaria Butterfield, *The Gospel Comes with a House Key: Practicing Radically Ordinary Hospitality in Our Post-Christian World* (Wheaton, IL: Crossway, 2018).

28. Christine D. Pohl, *Making Room: Recovering Hospitality as a Christian Tradition* (Grand Rapids: Eerdmans, 2009), 5.

29. See further Michael O. Emerson and Christian Smith, *Divided by Faith: Evangelical Religion and the Problem of Race in America* (Oxford: Oxford University Press, 2000), 71, 150.

gospel to be a confessor, not a denier, to look for opportunities to proclaim the wonders of God's love poured out in Jesus Christ, and to be on the lookout for occasions when one is tempted, because it is easier, to say nothing.

The liturgy teaches disciples to say things, like the Lord's Prayer, during worship services. Some churches have times set aside for disciples to say together the Apostles' Creed. The point of that exercise is to prepare disciples to be ready to speak the truth of the gospel not only during the Sunday service but at all times, everywhere, and to everyone. This is a good example of how the liturgy forms disciples to be ready to confess Christ in new situations, when they are "away from the body," as it were. Worship services teach congregants the grammar of the faith through Scripture readings, sermons, prayers, and songs.[30] Yet the purpose of grammatical rules is to help competent speakers form *new* sentences. The *rules* of grammar are the enabling condition of *free* speech. Similarly, the liturgical formation of disciples, though rule-based, is the condition for their exercising their Christian freedom in the Spirit (2 Cor 3:17).

One purpose of regular Sunday worship is to practice *sola Scriptura*, that is, helping disciples to let Scripture alone rule their imagination so that they become skilled story-dwellers. Scripture helps form the ability to discern God's will in part by telling stories of people who either follow God's will or defy it. "Dare to be a Daniel!" This children's song has it exactly right.

The readings, prayers, songs, and sermons that make up our worship should lead us to identify with Scripture's saints. Dare to be a Daniel, but don't you dare be a denier of Jesus! In helping

---

30. Cf. David W. Fagerberg: "Liturgy Creates a Christian Grammar in the People of God Who Live through the Encounter with the Paschal Mystery," in *Theologia Prima: What Is Liturgical Theology?*, 2nd ed. (Chicago: Liturgy Training Publications, 2004), 3.

us to identify with true followers of Jesus, worship also helps us to get real—rooted in Christ. Of course, we have to *stay* real and not forget what we have seen in the mirror of Scripture—and the liturgical looking glass. The truth we hear in church worship must be the truth in which we walk day in and day out. Jesus says, "Let your light shine before others" (Matt 5:16), and Paul says to his Philippian readers that they "shine as lights in the world" (Phil 2:15). This exercise is all about learning to see oneself as a beam of gospel light (truth) by identifying with those, like Peter, who are charged to tell others about Jesus, the light of the world.

CONCLUSION: LEARNING CHRISTLY GESTURES

It is one thing to be suspicious of the institutional church, quite another to interact with a vital company of the gospel who are ready and able—fit for purpose—to embody the mind and enact the heart of Christ in new situations. It is easy to find fault with the slow, grinding movements of an institution. It is not so easy to be skeptical about communities that speak the truth in love and act out the truth they speak.

In this chapter, we have explored the way in which worship forms hearers into doers by encouraging imaginative and bodily participation in the drama of redemption. What I am calling liturgical formation is the process of helping disciples enter into the drama to the point of becoming story-dwellers, people whose imagination is fixed on the reality of what God is doing in Christ through the Spirit to renew humanity and all creation. After all, it is to these divine doings, this theodrama, that the doxology is a fitting response.

Participating in worship already inserts the believer into the action, at least for as long as the service lasts. The goal, however, is to live out the story of Christ the rest of the week. I argued that what we do on Sunday to conform ourselves to the new reality in Christ prepares us to conform to that new reality outside of church as well. The liturgy we rehearse and perform on Sunday trains disciples to be *fit for purpose*, that is, to live as citizens of the gospel the rest of the week. Similarly, the theological exercises I here propose are intended to train disciples to develop new reflexes, a readiness to act according to their new nature in Christ. In this way, disciples become fit for the purpose of embodying the mind of Christ in all situations, familiar and unfamiliar (cf. Luke 12:11-12).

Liturgy, like doctrine, sets forth the truth of what is in Christ, and it does so as a fragrant offering to God. The most important offering we can make is our whole self: "Present [theatrically!] your bodies as a living sacrifice, holy and acceptable to God, which is your spiritual worship" (Rom 12:1). In many militaries around the world, "Present arms!" is the command to stand at attention, with one's weapon, in salute. But Paul calls us to present not only our arms but also our legs, feet, head—the whole person—not in static salute but in active worship. This demands core mobility.

The Bible does not define but depicts worship, often in terms of "bending" or "prostrating" oneself as a sign of reverence. Liturgy trains us in these bodily motions, trains us to be worshipful witnesses to the key events in the drama of redemption. The "embodied" nature of our sacrifice means that it is not enough to "think good thoughts" about God. No, we must be Christlike in everything that we say, think, desire, and do. For the disciple, all of life is potentially liturgical, a forum for presenting our bodies as living sacrifices. Everything the church does as a body communicates something. Core mobility is its body language, a kind of gesture.

Gestures do not simply express thought or language but are part of language. Together, doctrine and doxology, theology and liturgy, nurture the body of Christ to make what we could call "Christly" gestures.

Participating in the traditional forms of worship prepares disciples to give new bodily forms to the drama of the Christ. There is a wonderful irony here. What some may consider old, even outdated, forms of worship become the means of equipping disciples freely to continue the same story of Jesus Christ in new settings. Ancient worship trains us for contemporary discipleship.

Liturgical acts nurture Christian identity, forming and reforming us by incorporating us through word and deed into the reality of our union with Christ and our communion with one another. Liturgy helps the body of Christ express the typical gestures of Christ in news ways that are as free as they are fitting. (Remember Philemon's "fresh" performance of Christian fellowship with his runaway slave.) Theology helps us acquire the mind of Christ; liturgy helps us to embody the mind of Christ. Liturgical acts are the body language of the church, and like other forms of regular exercise, the more we perform them, the stronger the body gets. We go through liturgical exercises to improve the church's core mobility, the free and fitting Christly gestures of the company of the gospel.

Who are we, for Jesus Christ, today? We have made some progress answering this question I posed in the introduction. We are a company of the gospel charged with embodying the mind of Christ. We have seen that there is good reason to think of this company as being more like improvisers than performers of a script, even though there is a place for the latter conception. However, we are not the first generation who has had to improvise discipleship with the aid of our holy script. Accordingly, in the next chapter I will argue that making disciples requires knowledge of the Spirit-led theological tradition, and not of the biblical text only. Who are we, for Jesus Christ, today? I hope that we will be able to answer, after reading the next chapter, "We are members of the communion of saints, catholic Christians."

7

COMMUNION OF SAINTS

The Disciple as Catholic Christian

We have been thinking about the church as a place to make disciples by ministering the word of God, reading Scripture theologically as the story of the Triune God's plan to create a people for himself. Disciples interpret this story especially by enacting it as individual members of and corporately as the body of Christ. The church is not an institution invested in maintaining or increasing its own power (though sadly it sometimes acts like it), but a company of the gospel intent on communicating the truth and love of God poured out in Jesus Christ, which is its service to God on behalf of the world.

There is a suspicion about the church, however, that if true would compromise the integrity of its witness. This suspicion is shared by those outside and, increasingly, inside the church as well. It amounts to a skepticism about *sola Scriptura*. Specifically, it is the charge that the Protestant Reformation led to interpretive pluralism, such that Scripture's hearers become all kinds of doers, with every disciple doing what was right (that is, biblical) in his own eyes (Judg 17:6). Protestant disciples seem to be faced not with the two diverging roads of Robert Frost's poem "The Road Not Taken" but with a crossroads where paths lead in many different directions. The suspicion is that the Bible alone is not sufficient for directing the disciple's walk, and that Protestant disciples use their freedom individualistically, veering off in different directions, formulating and then enacting conflicting doctrines: the Bible tells *me* so. It is a serious concern.[1]

DOCTRINAL FORKS IN THE DISCIPLE'S ROAD

Interpretive pluralism provokes a crisis in discipleship. We want to follow Christ, and the words of the prophets and apostles he commissioned, but it sometimes seems as if we are following only someone's *interpretation* of these words. What do we do when our interpretation differs from that of another Christian? If Jesus Christ is the same yesterday, today, and forever (Heb 13:8), then why are there so many ways to enact discipleship? To put it in terms of the present work: Why do hearers of the same word become different kinds of doers? Is the passage from hearing to doing arbitrary? Or are only some disciples hearing rightly?

From its inception, the church has been interpreting the Bible in imitation of Christ, who read the Old Testament as testimony about what God would do for Israel and the whole world

---

1. For a fuller explanation of the suspicion, see Christian Smith, *The Bible Made Impossible: Why Biblicism Is Not a Truly Evangelical Reading of Scripture* (Grand Rapids: Brazos, 2011); and Kathleen C. Boone, *The Bible Tells Them So: The Discourse of Protestant Fundamentalism* (Albany: State University of New York Press, 1989).

through his Messiah. The Protestant Reformation recovered this gospel-centered reading. Luther saw his own life and ministry as very much a part of the biblical narrative, for he, like Paul, had to combat those who relied overmuch on their own ability to secure righteousness by doing the law. However, while the Reformers agreed to view the Bible as their authoritative social imaginary, they appear to have disagreed as to what they saw there. Is recovering the Reformers' practice of *sola Scriptura* enough to make disciples given the doctrinal disagreements that led in different denominational directions?

In chapter 5 I argued that, if we want to follow the gospel of Jesus Christ rather than some other story, we need to have our *imaginations* reformed by Scripture too. Then in chapter 6 I suggested that if we want to become the kind of people with hearts and minds ready and willing to play our parts in God's drama of redemption, we need to have our habits and reflexes formed by regular worship. Pastors make disciples biblically and liturgically. Now, in the present chapter, I want to suggest that if we want to be truly *Protestant* in our approach to biblical interpretation, we must also be *catholic*—that is, in line with the doctrine of the whole (Greek *kata* + *holos* = "with respect to the whole") church that came into focus over time.

It is important to see that there is a genuinely Protestant way to affirm doctrinal development and church tradition. Calvin observes that God gave the church—the *universal* church as well as local churches—to be the disciples' "Mother," a means of spiritual nurture, not least when it comes to reading the Bible theologically. Calvin says that, for those to whom God is Father, the church may also be Mother, and then proceeds to cite Mark 10:9: "What therefore God has joined together, let not man separate," thereby strongly suggesting that Scripture and tradition belong together too.[2] This is why Calvin prefers the wording of the Apostles' Creed that reads, "I believe the church" (not *in* the church). Specifically, we believe the church's teaching: "Our weakness does not allow us to be dismissed from her school until we have been pupils all our lives."[3]

BREAKING THE BODY? THE REFORMATION AS TRAGIC NECESSITY

However, before we can fully appreciate the teaching role of the church and church tradition in the making of disciples, we first have to confront a deep and commonplace suspicion. This suspicion is that the Reformation was a net loss *to* the church, nay, a loss *of* the church, and of the possibility of consensus in biblical interpretation.

"Rightly handling" the word of truth (2 Tim 2:15) — "orthotemnology" for short (from *ortho* + *tomeō* = "to make a straight cut") — is a mark of genuine discipleship. Has the Reformation made right handling easier or harder? I believe that *sola Scriptura* is vital for disciple-making. Nevertheless, it is salutary to listen to the critics, at least for a few moments, because members of our congregations hear them too. Young people in particular may be especially susceptible to the concerns about interpretive pluralism expressed in a spate of recent books.

Alister McGrath calls "Christianity's dangerous idea" the combustion of two notions that, when combined, proved lethal to medieval society: the supreme authority of Scripture (*sola*

---

2. John Calvin, *Institutes of the Christian Religion*, ed. John T. McNeill, trans. Ford Lewis Battles, Library of Christian Classics (1960; repr., Louisville: Westminster John Knox, 2011), 4.1.1.

3. Calvin, *Institutes* 4.1.4.

Scriptura) and the supreme right of individuals to interpret it (the priesthood of every believer).[4] Now, five hundred years after the Reformation, many academics have been telling the story in a way that highlights its unintended consequences—secularism, skepticism, and schism—and lays the blame at the door of *sola Scriptura*.

Diarmaid MacCulloch says the Protestant Reformation "was a revolution in how to read" the Bible.[5] Instead of deferring to the authority of the institutional church, individuals were now encouraged to use their own judgment: "Here *I* stand." Brad Gregory claims that the unintended consequence of the Reformation's critique of church authority was interpretive anarchy.[6] The problem, you see, is that those who rejected Rome's authority disagreed about what the Bible said. Not only that: Carlos Eire describes the Reformation as a process of "desacralization" (otherwise known as secularization) because the Reformers reconceived the relationship between nature and grace, insisting that the grammar was sufficient for determining textual meaning. He also says that Protestants disrupted the communion of saints, both vertically (communion with saints in heaven) and horizontally (communion with saints on earth).[7] The Eastern Orthodox theologian Georges Florovsky

---

4. Alister McGrath, *Christianity's Dangerous Idea: The Protestant Revolution—A History from the Sixteenth Century to the Twenty-First* (San Francisco: HarperOne, 2007).

5. Diarmaid MacCulloch, *All Things Made New: The Reformation and Its Legacy* (Oxford: Oxford University Press, 2016), 8.

6. Brad S. Gregory, *The Unintended Reformation: How a Religious Revolution Secularized Society* (Cambridge, MA: Belknap Press of Harvard University Press, 2012).

7. Carlos M. N. Eire, *War against the Idols: The Reformation of Worship from Erasmus to Calvin* (Cambridge: Cambridge University Press, 1986).

has identified *sola Scriptura* as the "sin of the Reformation."[8] Reformation may have been necessary, but it is thought to be tragic insofar as it acted as a corrosive to the communion of saints and generated what Christian Smith calls "pervasive interpretive pluralism." Smith writes, "It becomes beside the point to assert a text to be solely authoritative ... when, lo and behold, it gives rise to a host of many divergent teachings on important matters."[9]

Wittenberg, we have a problem. The problem with biblicism, according to its critics, is that "everyone reads what is right in his own eyes." It's a serious problem, not least because Proverbs 12:15 says that "the way of a fool is right in his own eyes."

What does this have to do with the church as a place to make disciples? Quite a bit, because a disciple is one who follows biblical words in order to follow the way of the living Word, Jesus Christ. How do we know which way to go? Pastors and church members are increasingly aware of the challenge of determining *whose* interpretation of our authoritative text is legitimate, and why. I regularly have students in my seminary classes who either have not grown up in a confessional tradition or who did but are then shocked to discover there are other traditions, each of which may claim the mantle "Protestant" or "evangelical" or, simply, "biblical." Has Protestantism doomed disciples to be perennial consumers, always looking but never able to arrive at a knowledge of the true church (see 2 Tim 3:7)? As pastors, I'm sure you've heard some variation of this question: Why can't Protestants just get along?

---

8. Georges Florovsky, *Bible, Church, Tradition: An Eastern Orthodox View* (Belmont, MA: Nordland, 1972), 20.

9. Smith, *Bible Made Impossible*, xi.

Let me add one more critical voice into the mix before suggesting a constructive response. Peter Leithart has recently called for the "end" of Protestantism. Jesus wants unity for his church—he even prays for it (John 17:21)—but unified "is *not* what his church is."[10] What the church is is divided, just as it had become in ancient Corinth: "One of you says, 'I follow Paul,' or 'I follow Apollos,' or 'I follow Cephas,' or 'I follow Christ'" (1 Cor 1:12). Only the names have changed: "I follow Calvin," "I follow Luther," "I follow Wesley"—or perhaps "I follow Piper," "I follow MacArthur," "I follow Sproul." Leithart says the Reformation divided the Western church, Protestant denominationalism perpetuates this disunity, and, we might add, the cult of personality and the rise of megachurches seem to have multiplied disunity even further. Despite the intent of the Reformers themselves, says Leithart, from the looks of the present-day Protestant church "one might conclude that the Spirit never arrived to overcome the divisions of Babel."[11]

The issue concerns the kind of disciples we're making in our local churches. Are they following Jesus Christ, a denomination, a particular Bible teacher, or their own whims? How can we train disciples to be uniters rather than dividers of Christ's body? And what kind of unity ought to characterize Christ's church in the first place? Must every doctrinal or denominational difference result in division? These are important questions for churches that confess *sola Scriptura*, and we'll come back to them. For now let me round out this discussion by recalling our theme: the church as creature of the word and a place

---

10. Peter Leithart, *The End of Protestantism: Pursuing Unity in a Fragmented Church* (Grand Rapids: Brazos, 2016), 1.

11. Leithart, *End of Protestantism*, 76.

to make disciples, a place to train "little creatures of the word" and turn hearers into doers.

The way forward is to see one's own church or denomination as a local expression of the church universal. The local church is the place where disciples learn both to pray for and to exhibit the reality of the unity for which Jesus prayed before us: "That they may be one" (John 17:11). And, just as word and Spirit belong together, we will see that Scripture and church tradition do too. In Calvin's words: "Our opponents locate the authority of the church outside God's Word; but we insist that it be attached to the Word, and do not allow it to be separated from it."[12]

So, do *sola Scriptura* and the priesthood of believers (the Reformation idea that biblical interpretation is the privilege and responsibility of every believer) work *against* the unity for which Jesus prayed? Did Protestants teach the priesthood of *each individual* believer (as in every interpreter for him- or herself), or the priesthood of *all* believers, and what difference does that distinction make? These are important questions, especially in an age where more and more churchgoers are exposed to pluralism but don't know what to do about it. The temptation is either an authoritative absolutism (my tribe, right or wrong) or a cynical relativism (who can say, anyway?). Neither of these attitudes is conducive to the task of making disciples.

To get to the bottom of this matter, we need to return to the scene of the "crime." What did the Reformers really mean by *sola Scriptura* and the priesthood of all believers? The two questions are linked, for *sola Scriptura* names both a theory and a community practice.

---

12. Calvin, *Institutes* 4.8.13.

THE PROTESTANT PRINCIPLE OF AUTHORITY: SOLA SCRIPTURA

Let me be clear: I am not for a moment departing from the Reformation principle of the supreme authority of Scripture. Yet this Protestant principle is not itself alone, but part of a Protestant pattern of authority. We begin, however, with the principle.

The Bible's authority derives from its nature as holy: set apart by God for a divine purpose. Here I will set forth five premises of *sola Scriptura* and then clarify in what sense the Bible can be authoritative for making disciples according to *sola Scriptura*. Because disciples follow God's written word, it behooves them to know something about its nature, function, and purpose.

First, *the Bible is the word of God written in human words inspired by the Holy Spirit*. God elected, commissioned, and set apart certain human authors to be the instruments through whom God communicates his word.

Second, *God both authors and authorizes the Bible*. The special office of Scripture—to be the creaturely yet authoritative agent of God's special self-communication—derives from its divine authorship.

Third, *God's word is God's discourse: something God says about something to someone in some way*. The Bible is divine discourse fixed in writing: something God says about something (the drama of creation, redemption, and consummation) to someone (the company of the gospel) in some way (the forms of biblical literature) for some purpose (making disciples fit for gospel citizenship). Scripture is not simply a handbook of information, a record of God's action in history, but divine address, a medium of divine action in the present. God addresses the church in many ways, for God can do more than one thing with human words, including tell the truth, make promises, issue commands, and reveal the end of history. Each kind of speech act contributes to the formation of the disciple's faith, hope, and love.

Fourth, *different types of discourse exercise authority in different ways over different domains*. For example, the authority of "exalted prose" may work differently than that of law or history. What we read in Isaiah 55:11 is true—"[my word] shall not return to me empty, but it shall accomplish that which I purpose, and shall succeed in the thing for which I sent it"—yet we have to discern the intent and domain of particular biblical passages.

Finally, *all divinely authored discourse serves the same ultimate divine end*. The different forms of biblical discourse serve the end of communicating Christ to God's chosen people. In many and various ways, the Father commissions the human authors of Scripture, prophets and apostles, to communicate his light and life, his Son and Spirit. In the eloquent words of J. I. Packer: the Bible is "God the Father preaching God the Son in the power of God the Holy Spirit."[13] It is therefore important not to separate Scripture's communicative authority from its communal purpose. All of Scripture is profitable for training disciples, to make them fit for the purpose of leading lives worthy of their citizenship in the gospel.

Some critics of *sola Scriptura* contend that disciples ought to be following Jesus Christ, not a book. This is an unhelpful and misleading dichotomy, for Luther rightly describes the Scriptures as Christ's scepter. In other words, being biblical is not an idolatrous alternative to following Christ; it is rather the mark and means of genuine discipleship. "Scripture alone" does

---

13. J. I. Packer, *God Has Spoken: Revelation and the Bible*, 3rd ed. (Grand Rapids: Baker, 1994), 91.

not mean that the Bible functions as an authority *independently of Christ*!

In Luther's late medieval context, the *solas* were exclusionary. However, we need to exercise care in saying what exactly they excluded. For example, *sola gratia* and *sola fide* deny the meritorious nature of good works, though not the importance of human obedience. Similarly, *sola Scriptura* denies the equal authority of church traditions, as well as the claim that Rome has the authority to decide the rightness of biblical interpretations. Luther lost his temper when, in the heat of doctrinal disputation, Johann Eck could not give him biblical reasons for his position, only quotations from church fathers. Appeal to tradition, Luther believed, is no good unless it ultimately derives from Scripture. Yet, as we shall see, *sola Scriptura* does not exclude church tradition as a theological resource altogether, but rather seeks to put tradition in its rightful place in a broader pattern of authority.

Remember that everyone, Christian or not, is a disciple, a follower of some set of words or another. The disciple does not set the course but follows the instruction of another. Put differently, the disciple acknowledges the authority of the master: "A disciple is not above his teacher, nor a servant above his master" (Matt 10:24). It is impossible to discuss discipleship without invoking the concept of authority. Here we should note that some of the suspicions lodged against the church as an institution and the Reformation principle of *sola Scriptura* ultimately amount to a suspicion of authority, especially *interpretive* authority. Who are you to tell me what to do? Here we come to the crux of the problem of hearing and doing: Why should I listen to this voice, whether of a pastor or a theologian or a denomination, rather than my own voice? It is against such a suspicion of authority that the Reformation principle of *sola Scriptura* comes into its own. But first we have to take care to define authority.

Authority is rightful say-so, the power to commend belief and command obedience over a certain domain. For example, a medical doctor is an authority over the domain of physical health, which is why we follow a doctor's prescription. Now, who has more expert knowledge, and thus right to say-so, than the author of a domain? As Creator, God is the ultimate "expert," the all-knowing one, because he is the author of all domains (Pss 50:11; 139:2; 2 Tim 2:19). This gives him right of say-so: ultimate authority over all things. The crucial question is whether God has *expressed* his authority and, if so, where. Authority must be verbally expressed—*said*—because, apart from meaningful content, there is nothing else that holds persons accountable. Protestants confess that God expresses his authority verbally, and that the Old and New Testaments are God's last will and testament, as it were.

A picture of authority as an oppressive power that impinges on our freedom holds many modern and postmodern people captive. Yet God deploys his authority not to oppress but to release us (from sin, ignorance, and captivity), to reorient us to the new creation in Christ, and hence to promote genuine human flourishing (in Christ). God, as Creator, knows what is best for us and has provided directions for human flourishing in his Law and Wisdom literature. God's word is authoritative, and works not to limit us in unhealthy ways but rather to authorize us to live with others in ways that are good for us.

Another picture—of an individual interpreting the Bible for himself or herself, without consulting any other authority— holds other modern critics of the Reformation captive. Isn't that what the phrase means: Scripture *alone*? Well, if literal meaning is a function of what its authors meant by the phrase, which in turn is a function of how they actually used the phrase, then the answer is an emphatic *no*.

To interpret *sola Scriptura* as meaning "Scripture is the only theological authority there is" is to rip the phrase out of its original context. The Reformers never intended *sola Scriptura* to exclude the use of secondary sources, for example. They were quite happy to consult, say, grammars and even commentaries in their quest to hear God's word. If there is an exclusionary dimension, it pertains only to what is first and foremost as concerns authority (there can be only one "first"). Yet to say that Scripture *alone* is the supreme or primary authority leaves open the possibility that there are other, secondary authorities. And that is precisely what the Reformers believed, and where church tradition comes in.

Let me therefore propose the following definition: *sola Scriptura* means that Scripture alone, as God's own set-apart discourse, is the only wholly reliable, sufficient, and final authority for the church's life and thought (including imagination). Scripture alone constitutes God's authorized self-presentation in human words. This is why, to use Luther's pithy formula, "Scripture alone rules." Scripture is alone, then, in its *magisterial* authority. *Sola Scriptura* is best understood as both an exclusionary and an exclamatory word: Scripture first! Scripture *above all other earthly powers and authorities!*

So: Scripture alone authorizes, but the Scripture that authorizes is not alone. *Sola Scriptura* is shorthand for a practice of theological authority by a particular kind of theological community (the church) in the context of a broader *pattern* of theological authority, which includes the church's formulation of certain orthodox doctrines (tradition).

One of the concerns about *sola Scriptura* is that it encourages interpretive pride: every individual can act as if they are a chief priest of the Bible's meaning. I see *sola Scriptura* working rather differently, namely, as a standing challenge to this tendency toward prideful certainty. Properly understood, *sola Scriptura* teaches us that Scripture *alone* is authoritative, not our interpretation of it. Jesus Christ alone is Lord, but there are other masters who teach us how to read his word. Scripture clearly shows us the Way of Jesus Christ *and* affords us opportunity to discuss with others what discipleship means for today. What the Protestant Reformers discovered is that reading the Bible with others is itself a means of learning humility. This too is part of our ministry of the word: to facilitate the formation of a "people of the book," a faithful interpretive community—a royal priesthood of bold yet humble readers. It follows that, far from being the source of hopeless division, *sola Scriptura* can serve as a vital means of disciple-making.

THE PROTESTANT PATTERN OF AUTHORITY: SCRIPTURE AS SUPREME, NOT SOLITARY

What Protestants have emphasized when it comes to making disciples is the importance of training people rightly to handle the word of truth. Becoming fit for the purpose of gospel citizenship includes becoming fit to be a priest, that is, a person who can read and minister the word of God. Luther emphasized the priesthood of every believer. It is important to remember, however, that he did not say the "popehood" of every believer. Individual believers do not have the right of say-so when it comes to biblical interpretation. On the contrary: though every believer is a priest, every priest is a member of a company of

priests, as in 1 Peter 2:9: "But you are a chosen race, a royal
priesthood, a holy nation."

What is the nature and function of this royal priesthood, and
what role do pastors play in it? All authority has been given
to Jesus Christ, yet Christ did not count divine authority "a
thing to be grasped" (Phil 2:6), but delegated it to others. Jesus
commissions the apostles to preach (Mark 3:14) and "proclaim
the kingdom of God" (Luke 9:2). He both appoints and *anoints*
the apostles with the Holy Spirit, empowering them for their
authoritative office, to be his witnesses (Acts 1:8).

What about the church and church tradition—do these
have a place in the pattern of theological authority too, or does
sola Scriptura exclude them? May it never be! "Scripture alone"
does not mean "Scripture apart from the community of faith"
or "Scripture independent of church tradition." *Sola Scriptura*
excludes rivals, such as the teaching office of the church or man-
made tradition, only when it's a question of *supreme* authority.
It does not eliminate other sources and resources of theology
altogether. In short, it does not exclude ministers.

However, it does exclude autonomous individuals. Luther
states: "God's word cannot be without God's people and, conversely, God's people cannot be without God's word."[14] The task of
a minister of the word is not simply to teach its contents, but to
teach others how to read it, for themselves, in the context of the
communion of saints. This is why the priesthood of all believers "was at the heart of Luther's reform" of the church.[15] Far
from being a pathology that accords authority to autonomous
individuals, the royal priesthood of all believers is actually part

---

14. Martin Luther, *On the Councils and the Church* (1539), in *Basic Theological
Writings*, ed. Timothy F. Lull (Minneapolis: Fortress, 1989), 547.

15. Paul D. L. Avis, *The Church in the Theology of the Reformers*, reprint ed.
(Eugene, OR: Wipf and Stock, 2002), 95.

of God's plan for distributing authority in the church. *"Royal" signals authority (which resides in the gospel); "priesthood" signals interpretive community (the church as city of God); "all believers" signals that individuals are not autonomous agents but citizens of the gospel.* All believers are priests who minister the word to one another, then, but only some are appointed to the ministerial office (Luther continued to have a place for ordination).

To affirm the royal priesthood is to affirm what virtually amounts to another *sola: sola ecclesia.* While it may be surprising, it is also important to acknowledge a properly Protestant sense in which the church is "alone": *the church alone is the place where Christ rules over his kingdom and gives certain gifts for the building of his living temple.* If we are to retrieve the promise of the Protestant Reformation but not its pathology, we must retrieve not merely the idea but the practice of the royal priesthood of all believers. There is a pattern, a divinely ordered way that Protestants are to be a people of the book, and this pattern helps explain why the church and her traditions matter.

Scripture is the sole magisterial authority—it is both the canonical cradle of Christ and the scepter by which the ascended Christ now rules the church, as Luther said—*but it does not play this role independently of the royal priesthood, which is to say the Holy Spirit working in God's people, including the church's tradition and teaching ministry.* These have *ministerial* authority, like Abraham's servant "who had charge of all that he had" (Gen 24:2). Scott Swain puts it like this: "The Spirit who enables and sustains our reading of Holy Scripture *also provides a community to aid us* in our reading."[16]

---

16. Scott R. Swain, *Trinity, Revelation, and Reading: A Theological Introduction to the Bible and Its Interpretation* (New York: Bloomsbury T&T Clark, 2011), 100.

Neither Luther nor Calvin advocated traditionless interpretation. It is important not to confuse *sola* with "solo" *Scriptura*. The problem with thinking that individuals interpret the Bible alone—that is, by and for themselves, in isolation from the church and tradition—is not only the lack of checks and balances on their readings, but the inevitable ensuing neglect of the gifts the Spirit has provided. In particular, "solo" *Scriptura* denies the importance of reading in communion with the saints. We are now in a better position to see how the church catholic—by which I am thinking in particular of the consensus tradition preserved in the ancient creeds—is the context in which an individual's reading of the biblical text makes sense (thanks to the illumination of the Spirit) and exercises its authority.

This is an important point, so let me be perfectly clear: the Reformers objected to the church magisterium of their day not because it used tradition as a resource, but because it narrowed catholicity to the institution centered at Rome. They were pro catholicity, but contra Rome.[17] Luther and Calvin had no problem appealing to the church fathers as ministerial authorities. When I speak of capital-T Tradition, then, I mean the postapostolic conversation about the meaning and implications of apostolic discourse, a conversation that the Spirit uses to guide the whole ("catholic") church into all truth.

Tradition too is an element in the Protestant pattern of authority that, like the church, exists to nurture the society of Jesus. Think of Tradition as "the church's stance of abiding in and with apostolic teaching through time."[18] I like Herman

---

17. For an expansion of this point, see my "A Mere Protestant Response," in Matthew Levering, *Was the Reformation a Mistake? Why Catholic Doctrine Is Not Unbiblical* (Grand Rapids: Zondervan, 2017), 191–231.

18. Michael Allen and Scott R. Swain, *Reformed Catholicity: The Promise of Retrieval for Theology and Biblical Interpretation* (Grand Rapids: Baker Academic,

Bavinck's construal of tradition as "the method by which the Holy Spirit causes the truth of Scripture to pass into the consciousness and life of the church."[19] *Sola Scriptura* is the practice of attending to the Spirit speaking in the Scriptures *and* to those, equally attentive, who do the same. *Sola Scriptura* is perfectly compatible with this notion, and with what we could call Reformed catholicity, by which I mean a catholicity (Tradition) governed first and foremost by canonicity (Scripture). What God has therefore joined together—canonicity and catholicity—let no one (especially Reformation Protestants or evangelicals!) put asunder.

Interpreters often need help, like the Ethiopian eunuch who answered Philip's question, "Do you understand what you are reading?" by saying, "How can I, unless someone guides me?" (Acts 8:30–31). Tradition at its best is our Philip—the Spirit's provision of community to aid us in our reading. Scripture *alone* is the supreme authority, yet God in his grace decided that it is not good for Scripture to be alone. He thus authorized tradition so that, when he saw it, he said, "This at last is norm of my norm and light of my light; she shall be called postapostolic testimony, because she was taken out of apostolic testimony."

Two examples of how *sola Scriptura* and the royal priesthood function together will suffice. The first is the account of the Jerusalem Council in Acts 15. The issue—do gentiles have to become like Jews, undergoing circumcision when they become Christians?—was controversial, provoking "no small dissension and debate" (Acts 15:2). No one person's interpretation prevailed; instead, they held a council and improvised a solution, building

---

2015), 34.

19. Herman Bavinck, *Reformed Dogmatics*, vol. 1, *Prolegomena*, ed. John Bolt, trans. John Vriend (Grand Rapids: Baker Academic, 2003), 494.

on the premise of God's grace. They reached a consensus, aided by James's reading of Amos 9:11–12, that circumcision of gentile converts was not necessary (Acts 15:16–17), and by the prompting of the Holy Spirit (Acts 15:28).

The Jerusalem Council practiced *sola Scriptura*. The opinion they reached in their royal priestly deliberations was based on what God has said in Scripture and on what they now saw God doing among the gentiles. The council made a theological judgment that indicated a fitting way forward, given both Scripture and the contemporary situation. It was a solution to the problem that was as improvised as it was inspired. Moreover, it was an authoritative decision: "They delivered to them for observance the decisions [*ta dogmata*] that had been reached by the apostles and elders who were in Jerusalem" (Acts 16:4). Here, then, is an example of the royal priesthood improvising authoritative dogma from Scripture.

My second example is another church council, held at Nicaea some three hundred years after the Jerusalem Council. Yet again something vital to the integrity of the gospel was at issue, though this time it was doctrinal: Is it right to say that the Son of God was the highest created being, or must we say the Son shares in the divine nature? Several practical issues are at stake in this doctrine, most of which pertain to the nature of the believer's relation to the Son: Is it right to pray to and worship the Son? Is it right for disciples to confess Jesus as Lord? Is there eternal life in the Son?

How did they proceed? Note, first, that the council was "catholic" in the sense that the whole of Christendom was represented. Second, the church leaders and theologians at Nicaea, like the apostles at the Jerusalem Council, had to improvise a solution to this problem that also fit (that is, was in accordance with) the Scriptures. The Bible itself gave them reason to hope that they could reach an agreement: not only was there the precedent of the Jerusalem Council, but Jesus had promised his apostles that the Spirit would guide the church into all truth (John 16:13). Further, Paul described the church as "the pillar and ground of the truth" (1 Tim 3:15 KJV). As Calvin explains: "By these words Paul means that the church is the faithful keeper of God's truth that it may not perish in the world."[20]

The fathers at Nicaea again improvised a solution: the Son, they said, is *homoousios* (of the same substance) as the Father, in other words, truly and fully God. This new technical term, *homoousios*, did not add something to Scripture but rather made explicit what Christians are authorized to say about the Son on the basis of the prophets and apostles. Here, then, is another example of a church council improvising a dogma that, in making an implicit biblical teaching explicit, is authoritative not just at Nicaea but everywhere and for everyone. Henceforth, the doctrine of the Trinity is an essential part of the disciple's curriculum, something every citizen of the gospel needs to know. We need Scripture and doctrine, and the wisdom of church tradition that is part and parcel of the latter, to make disciples fit for purpose.[21]

In sum: *Sola Scriptura* is not a blank check individuals can cash in to fund their own idiosyncratic interpretations of the Bible, but a call to attend to the broader pattern of Protestant authority and to listen for the Spirit speaking in the history of the church's interpretation of Scripture.

---

20. Calvin, *Institutes* 4.1.10.

21. For a fuller treatment of the doctrine of the Trinity as both biblical and catholic, see Kevin J. Vanhoozer and Daniel J. Treier, *Theology and the Mirror of Scripture: A Mere Evangelical Account*, Studies in Christian Doctrine and Scripture (Downers Grove, IL: IVP Academic, 2015), 113–14.

Like the Nicene Creed, the products of Tradition are sanc-
tified instruments the Holy Spirit uses to lead the church into
all truth, "effects of pedagogical grace."[22] Tradition does not add
new content to Scripture, nor does Tradition have any independent capacity to communicate light. Light is the operative
term. God is light (1 John 1:5), Christ is the light of the world
(John 8:12; 9:5), light from light, and Scripture is the appointed
instrument through which the light of Christ shines—more
light from light. God is light, yet interestingly enough, he
appointed lights in the expanse of heaven to give light on the
earth (Gen 1:15). Genesis 1:16 says, "And God made the *two* great
lights—the greater light to rule the day and the lesser light
to rule the night." Tradition is the lesser light: the moon to
Scripture's sun. What light the moon gives is always and only
a reflection of the sun, yet it is real light. Indeed, a full moon
casts enough light for a pilgrim to find her way—so too with
Tradition. Tradition has a derivative, secondary, ministerial
authority insofar as its creeds and confessions reflect the light
that shines forth from the biblical text.

TABLE TALK: DENOMINATIONS, DISCIPLESHIP, AND DIALOGICAL UNITY

As we have just seen, part of the process of producing mature
disciples is coming to accept your own interpretations of
Scripture as one of the riches of the royal priesthood rather than
the whole treasury. When we look at how Protestant churches
treat the Bible, I want us to see not the despair of pervasive
interpretive pluralism but rather the wisdom of unitive interpretive plurality. This may not be self-evident. When critics look

---

22. Allen and Swain, *Reformed Catholicity*, 45.

at the Protestant church, they see not simply a conflict between various individuals' biblical interpretations, but a conflict of interpretive communities (that is, denominations). That the Protestant church is institutionally not one is a source of discouragement to many, so much so that some well-meaning Bible-believing Christians prefer not to join any church, but to go spiritually solo, not bowling but worshiping alone.

This is most unfortunate. It is difficult for individual Christians to embody things like forgiveness or racial reconciliation or works of love. As I have been arguing, Jesus died, rose, and sent the Spirit to form a holy nation and royal priesthood—a people, not a set of disconnected individuals. Note, too, that discipleship requires churches. As far as I know, there are no books with titles like *How to Be Your Own Disciple*. Of course, it may simply be a matter of time ...

How then should disciples regard the plethora of Protestant churches, confessional traditions, and denominations? Denominations are like houses: they are places where disciples can be sheltered and nurtured. There's nothing wrong with living in a house (it beats homelessness), as long as one practices hospitality to strangers and neighborliness to those who live next door. The scandal is not denominations but denominationalism. Denominationalism is the ideology that only one's tribe displays genuine citizenship of the gospel. Think of denominationalism as a concern more for the house and its structural integrity than the inhabitants or the neighborhood.

The point is that we should train disciples not only in our family traditions, but also to be good neighbors. Please note that each house (each denomination, each local church) is charged with representing *the whole neighborhood*. The local church's first responsibility is to be a royal priesthood that represents Christ, not a particular denomination. In a sense, the various denominations are like different ethnic groups: we're first and foremost human beings, and only secondarily Scottish, French, or Nigerian. Similarly, disciples are first and foremost followers of Christ, and only secondarily Calvinists, Wesleyans, or Lutherans.

If we truly believe the church is one, what should this visible unity look like? This is a challenging question, but at least we can say what it need not look like: it need not be institutional uniformity. In the New Testament, we see something more like an informal network (an organic union) than a formal organization.

One important expression of the Protestant catholicity I'm advocating here is conciliarism: the use of fully representative church councils, like the councils of Jerusalem and Nicaea, to make theological judgments about issues that threaten the integrity of the gospel and the unity of the church. John McNeill argues that conciliarism is the "constitutional principle" of "unitive Protestantism,"[23] or what I like to call "mere Protestant Christianity."[24]

Just as individual heretics are those who choose to go their own way, so too churches need to guard against the temptation of thinking that only their interpretation or way of doing discipleship is biblically authorized. The priesthood of all believers is not a license for epistemic egoism as much as a mandate for epistemic conscientiousness, that is, for acknowledging that other Christian believers in other denominations have "the same natural desire for truth and the same general powers and capacities

---

23. See John T. McNeill, *Unitive Protestantism: The Ecumenical Spirit and Its Persistent Expression* (Richmond, VA: John Knox, 1964).

24. See my *Biblical Authority after Babel: Retrieving the Solas in the Spirit of Mere Protestant Christianity* (Grand Rapids: Brazos, 2016).

that [we] have" in ours.[25] Each church tradition has its blind
spots, cultural, social, and sometimes doctrinal. In this sense,
then, there is no such thing as an "independent" Bible church.
To be a disciple is to follow the Christ of the Scriptures with
others who are doing the same. The Reformation did not sanc-
tion interpretive individualism but, on the contrary, insisted on
keeping *sola Scriptura* and the royal priesthood, canonicity and
catholicity, together.

The Reformers were after what I like to call "table talk," or
dialogical unity. In Calvin's sixteenth-century Geneva, local pastors and others met every Friday afternoon to study the Bible
in what were called *congrégations*. One minister presented,
but it was not a sermon as much as a seminar (they called it
a "conference"). These *congrégations* were times of instruction
and correction, if need be. This required humility, and all the
other dialogical virtues that good listening and conversation
requires. Calvin urged ministers in other towns to adopt the
practice, saying, "This is also the best bond to retain consensus
in doctrine."[26] I submit that this process of conversing together
and corporate submission to the authoritative word of God is
Protestant Christianity at its best.

Table talk does not add new meaning to the text but gives
the dialogue partners a chance to share their respective insights.
Table talk takes time. Time is God's gift to the church: an opportunity to come to a greater unity and deeper understanding.
Time is also necessary for sanctification, and table talk affords
disciples plenty of opportunities for that too! Dialogue requires

---

25. Linda Trinkaus Zagzebski, *Epistemic Authority: A Theory of Trust,
Authority, and Autonomy in Belief* (New York: Oxford University Press, 2012), 55.

26. John Calvin, letter to Wolfgang Musculus, cited in Erik Alexander de
Boer, *Genevan School of Prophets: The Congrégations of the Company of Pastors and
Their Influence in 16th Century Europe* (Geneva: Librairie Droz, 2012), 41–42.

and encourages what I call the conversational virtues, first cousins to the intellectual virtues and the fruit of the Spirit. Pastors need to help disciples become people who learn to listen and accept correction: humble and patient interlocutors who know the Scriptures but want to know what others know as well. Table talk is an excellent curriculum for the disciples, and it provides an excellent opportunity to work for the unity of the church by speaking the truth (as far as one has discerned it) in love.

Local churches must practice table talk in order to be genuinely catholic churches. Pastors have an obligation to help their local churches read in communion with the saints who are in other local churches, in other countries, and in other times. We cannot divorce the authority of Scripture from the interpretive community in which it is read and in which it rules. We can state it like this: a community of disciples discerns the whole counsel of God and thus speaks the whole truth only in the context of the council of the whole church. In the Protestantism that is heir to the Reformation, canonicity and catholicity are equally ultimate. In my dreams, I imagine denominational differences contributing not to deeper dissension but to dialogues that produce a richer, deeper, *dialogical* unity. Or, as J. I. Packer paraphrases it, "Christians should not settle for doing anything separately that they can in good conscience do together."[27]

27. J. I. Packer, preface to *Evangelicals and Catholics Together at Twenty: Vital Statements on Contested Topics*, ed. Timothy George and Thomas G. Guarino (Grand Rapids: Brazos, 2015), viii.

CORE EXERCISES FOR STAYING THE COURSE AND INCREASING ENDURANCE

My thesis in this chapter is that pastors should encourage disciples not only to follow the words of Scripture above all others, but also to follow the milestones and benchmarks of church tradition. Genuine hearers and doers also listen to the long wisdom of church tradition, namely, what the whole church has heard and understood God to be saying in the Scriptures. This is one way of responding to the charge that the Reformation let loose interpretive anarchy upon the world, encouraging each and every Christian to read the Bible for himself or herself.

Church tradition is not an independent source of revelation alongside Scripture; it does not go beyond what is written in Scripture by supplying additional content. Rather, the authority of church tradition derives from Scripture alone and is therefore ministerial only. Tradition neither supplements Scripture nor supplants its authority, for the Tradition I'm thinking of is simply the church's conciliar agreement as to what Scripture actually says, means, and implies. *Sola Scriptura* is "Christianity's dangerous idea" *only when it is untethered from the church's catholic tradition.*

The implication is twofold: First, disciples need to read Scripture both in canonical context and in the context of the whole people of God, spread out over time and space, paying attention especially to those interpretive judgments, like the ones at Jerusalem and Nicaea, that have garnered universal assent. Second, disciples need to read Scripture in light of these catholic doctrines, such as the Trinity. Just as it is necessary to contend "for the faith that was once for all delivered to the saints" (Jude 3), so it is necessary to contend for the faith that was once for all *discerned* by the saints (that is, orthodoxy). The local church is fit for purpose only insofar as it is aware that it belongs to the universal (that is, catholic) church.

If we are to make disciples in accordance with the gospel, then it is not enough to be apostolic; we must also be catholic. When the church turns a deaf ear to Tradition, it is more vulnerable to error: Those who fail to learn the history of heresy are, if not doomed, then more likely to repeat it. Conversely, to catechize believers is to teach them what they need to know to become not simply hearers but also competent doers, active participants in the life of the church, actors who can fittingly improvise the scenes God has given them to play in the drama of redemption. To catechize a disciple, to teach them the basic tenets of the faith, is therefore to *catholicize* them: to integrate them into the faith of the whole church.

Each of the following three exercises in reading the Bible theologically is intended to help pastors train disciples fit for the purpose of staying the course (following in the right way) and increasing endurance (the ability to keep following).

Exercise 1: Playing by the Rules

There is perhaps no better way of socializing disciples into the communion of saints than by teaching them the biblical foundation and historical occasion of the doctrine of the Trinity. Pastors ought to consider seriously the possibility of regular corporate confession of the Apostles' Creed during worship. Several of the Protestant Reformation catechisms go line by line through the Apostles' Creed. It is a wonderful teaching tool for incorporating local saints into the catholic communion of saints. Remember: catechizing = catholicizing.

Paul in Galatians 6:16 commends those readers "who walk by this rule [*kanōn*]," referring to adhering to the dogma of the

Jerusalem Council concerning circumcision. The early church held to a "rule of faith" or "rule of truth" that summarized the story of Scripture and thus what disciples were supposed to believe.[28] Like the Apostles' Creed, this rule has a Trinitarian shape: "I believe in God the Father ... and in Christ Jesus his Son ... and in the Holy Spirit." Today it is important to confess, with the saints at Nicaea and beyond, that Jesus Christ, the Son of God, is *homoousios*, of the same nature as God.

No doubt about it, confessing the creed and playing by the rule in order to make them the social imaginary of the church is a demanding exercise. Yet Paul spoke of "the surpassing worth" of knowing Jesus Christ (Phil 3:8), and ultimately that is why the Trinity matters: to identify Jesus Christ. No pain, no gain. The point of this exercise is to help disciples to understand that they can enter into fellowship with the Father through the Son (in the Spirit) only if Son and Spirit are themselves fully God. The Trinity is not an arcane doctrine, but the lifeblood of the Christian life, and the linchpin of the gospel.[29] If we do not understand the doctrine of the Trinity, we will not be able to read the Bible rightly, nor understand how the work of the Son enables fellowship with the Father through the Spirit. Without the doctrine of the Trinity, it's goodnight, Christianity.

As God separated or distinguished light from dark at creation, so pastors can minister understanding and make disciples

---

28. See further Everett Ferguson, *The Rule of Faith: A Guide* (Eugene, OR: Cascade, 2015). Though formulations of the rule of faith go back to the second century, Augustine in the fourth century equated it with the baptism confession of faith, which was, in Augustine's words, "brief in words but great in content." Augustine, *Sermons vol. 3 (51–94)*, The Works of Saint Augustine: A Translation for the 21st Century, trans. Edmund Hill (Hyde Park, NY: New City Press, 1992), Sermon 59.1.

29. See further Fred Sanders, *The Deep Things of God: How the Trinity Changes Everything*, 2nd ed. (Wheaton, IL: Crossway, 2017).

by making the right distinctions. The key distinction here is between making and begetting. Arius said that the Father *made* the Son (like other creatures); Athanasius insisted that the Son was begotten.[30] Arius appealed to verses like Colossians 1:15, which refers to the Son as "the firstborn of all creation." This exercise in Trinitarian thinking is designed to help disciples respond to challenges like those of Arius, lodged today by Unitarians, Jehovah's Witnesses, and Oneness Pentecostals, among others.[31]

Exercise 2: Global Norming

From the outset, Jesus commissioned the church to be his witnesses "in Jerusalem and in all Judea and Samaria, and to the end of the earth" (Acts 1:8). When twentieth- and twenty-first-century church history comes to be written, surely one of the central emphases will be the globalization of the faith. Perhaps more than ever before, we see the importance of making disciples who are *world* citizens of the gospel. One doesn't need to travel far to do this, for thanks to modern travel and global communications, the world has come to the West. We are on the threshold of a new age of exploration: as the sixteenth-century voyages of discovery rocked the Old World of Europe, so television and immigration and other technologies have shrunk the distances that used to separate one country from another.

---

30. On the importance of this distinction for contemporary discussion of bioethics, see the excellent little book by Oliver O'Donovan, *Begotten or Made?* (Oxford: Clarendon, 1984).

31. There are a number of helpful resources, including entry-level books like Ronald E. Heine's *Classical Christian Doctrine: Introducing the Essentials of the Ancient Faith* (Grand Rapids: Baker Academic, 2013) to more scholarly monographs like Khaled Anatolios, *Retrieving Nicaea: The Development and Meaning of Trinitarian Doctrine* (Grand Rapids: Baker Academic, 2011).

This second exercise may be called "reading in the communion of saints." It involves being intentional about learning how Christians in other cultures are reading the Bible, understanding their faith, and practicing discipleship. There are many ways to do this. Perhaps you have people from other cultures in your congregation. If so, let them share their experience. Another possibility would be to find a sister church in another part of the world, like the sister city program developed after the Second World War that was intended to foster understanding and friendship between former foes.

If the first exercise emphasizes catholicity through time, this one focuses on catholicity over space. One of the things Western Christians have discovered in our newly globalized world is the extent to which our culture affects our biblical interpretation, and thus our discipleship. It has become difficult to maintain the pretense that Western readings are normative for Christians elsewhere. Here is how the authors of *Misreading Scripture with Western Eyes* state their purpose: "The core conviction that drives this book is that some of the habits that we readers from the West (the United States, Canada, and Western Europe) bring to the Bible can blind us to interpretations that the original audience and readers in other cultures see quite naturally."[32]

The benefits of this exercise are a heightened appreciation for the catholicity of the church and a correction of one's own narrow vision when it comes to biblical interpretation. After two thousand years, we seem to have come full circle: the Christian West is becoming increasingly post-Christian, and the countries where Western missionaries evangelized have

---

32. E. Randolph Richards and Brandon J. O'Brien, *Misreading Scripture with Western Eyes: Removing Cultural Blinders to Better Understand the Bible* (Downers Grove, IL: IVP Books, 2012), 15.

become increasingly Christian, so much so that the center of gravity of the worldwide body of Christ has shifted to the global South.[33] Charles Van Engen says that "a healthy congregation of disciples of Jesus lives out its catholicity by intentionally and actively participating in Christ's mission in a *glocal* fashion."[34] "Glocal" means both local and global, a neologism that gets at one aspect of catholicity (spatial wholeness). Here's why it matters: (1) every local understanding of the gospel is partial (we see through a culture, darkly, 1 Cor 13:12); (2) no one understanding grasps everything about the gospel: "We misread because we read alone. ... We often hear only the interpretations of people just like us."[35]

Reading in the communion of saints opens our eyes to our own cultural near-sightedness. At the same time, our local congregation may see something that other churches need to see. For example, some in the African church contend that Jesus is "firstborn over all creation" not because he is *homoousios* but because he is our Ancestor.[36]

I understand that Africans (and many Americans) don't think in metaphysical terms. Nevertheless, the formula "one person in two natures" gets at something right and fitting about Jesus' identity. It is important to remember that the Chalcedonian

---

33. See Philip Jenkins, *The Next Christendom: The Coming of Global Christianity*, 3rd ed. (Oxford: Oxford University Press, 2011).

34. Charles E. Van Engen, "The Glocal Church: Locality and Catholicity in a Globalizing World," in *Globalizing Theology: Belief and Practice in an Era of World Christianity*, ed. Craig Ott and Harold A. Netland (Grand Rapids: Baker Academic, 2006), 157.

35. Richards and O'Brien, *Misreading Scripture with Western Eyes*, 216.

36. On Jesus as our Ancestor, see Victor I. Ezgibo, "Jesus as God's Communicative and Hermeneutical Act: African Christians on the Person and Significance of Jesus Christ," in *Jesus without Borders: Christology in the Majority World*, ed. Gene L. Green, Stephen T. Pardue, and K. K. Yeo (Grand Rapids: Eerdmans, 2014), 49–52.

Council (451) was not Western, but catholic. The global church may yet formulate new legitimate things to say about Jesus, but these improvisational formulas must go on in the same way, or at least not go *against*, the Chalcedon formula. Catholic doctrine remains an important guard against the cultural myopias of West and South alike.

Exercise 3: Enduring Long-Distance Relationships (and Long-Time Differences)

Communication at a distance is often challenging, but catholicity requires nothing less. To read in communion with the saints means being aware of how other Christians, from other times and places, have interpreted Scripture, formulated doctrine, and enacted discipleship. In today's multicultural world, however, "other" Christians may be just next door. Realizing catholicity is often a local challenge.

Congregations should get to know other local churches. If possible, it would be good to explore whether your common gospel fellowship might allow for, say, a joint local mission effort, despite denominational differences. If denominational differences preclude such partnership, it would still be worthwhile coming to understand, and perhaps appreciate, their doctrinal differences. This exercise makes explicit what most hearers already know: no church or church member reads the Bible in the same way. Take a familiar passage and share with your congregation the various ways it has been interpreted over time, and even in places close to home.

It is important that pastors be honest about the differences that distinguish one confessional tradition, or age, from another. It is chronological snobbery to think that we know how to read Scripture better than earlier generations did, as if our GQ (godliness quotient) were higher than theirs.

There are several helpful resources for discovering how others, past and present, read the Bible. In addition to patristic and Reformation commentary series, there are also a number of one-volume works, like C. Clifton Black, *Reading Scripture with the Saints* or the collection in Stephen Fowl's *The Theological Interpretation of Scripture*.[37] In discussing the differences, it will be helpful to keep in mind the reason why the church reads the Bible in the first place. Here, too, there may be differences of opinion, but Augustine's exhortation to read to increase one's love for God and neighbor has to be near the top of the list because it so closely approximates Jesus' Great Commandment (Luke 10:27). The emphasis of the present work is that we read Scripture in the church to make disciples fit for purpose: namely, to live out their citizenship of the gospel, entering into fellowship with the Triune God and with others who are in Christ, thereby cultivating godliness to the glory of God.

There are three lessons to be learned from this exercise of reading the Bible in the broader Christian community. Disciples need to learn, first, that what Paul says in Philippians 2:3 may also apply to reading the Bible: "Do nothing from selfish ambition or conceit, but in humility count others more significant than yourselves." There are sincere Bible believers and competent Bible interpreters in most churches, and it is only interpretive pride that keeps us from acknowledging it. Mature disciples ought to display what we can call interpretive conscientiousness: "When I am conscientious I will come to believe that other normal, mature humans have the same natural desire for truth and the same general powers and capacities that I

---

37. C. Clifton Black, *Reading Scripture with the Saints* (Eugene, OR: Cascade, 2014); Stephen E. Fowl, ed., *The Theological Interpretation of Scripture: Classic and Contemporary Readings* (Oxford: Blackwell, 2007).

have."[38] In matters of biblical interpretation, humility is next to godliness.[39]

Humility in interpretation is a virtue: readers who are in the habit of not exaggerating the importance of their own ideas, and listening to other interpreters, are more likely to grasp what the text is saying. However, and this is my second point, acknowledging legitimate diversity is no excuse for irresponsible reading. That way lies interpretive sloth, the belief that no one can really know what an author is saying, a belief that short-circuits the connection between hearing and doing. Pastors best rid their churches of interpretive sloth by returning to exercise 1 above and reminding congregations of the catholic consensus about doctrines, like the Trinity, that are of first importance.[40]

Finally, disciples learn endurance by living with the second- and third-order doctrinal differences that are behind denominational disagreements. Enduring is an appropriate term to describe the challenge, and sometimes the suffering, that comes with having to live with difficulties and disagreements. Although second-order doctrinal disagreements may preclude church membership and possible shared mission, they need not impede Christian fellowship, and thus they are somewhat easier to endure. Pastors need to help disciples discern which doctrines are essential, requiring unity, and which are nonessential, requiring liberty (and charity). Paul is thinking about first-order, essential doctrines when he writes, "So then, brothers, stand firm and hold to the traditions that you were taught

---

38. Zagzebski, *Epistemic Authority*, 55.

39. For more on interpretive humility, see my *Is There a Meaning in This Text? The Bible, the Reader, and the Morality of Literary Knowledge* (Grand Rapids: Zondervan, 1998), 462–66.

40. On the difference between first-, second-, and third-order doctrines, see Vanhoozer and Treier, *Theology and the Mirror of Scripture*, 125–26. Catholicity characterizes the first-order or essential doctrines on which there is unity.

by us" (2 Thess 2:15). This is the faith for which disciples need
to contend (Jude 3) and endure.

CONCLUSION: COORDINATING THE BODY— WHY PROTESTANT PASTORS SHOULD BE MAKING CATHOLIC DISCIPLES

Are *sola Scriptura* and the royal priesthood of all believers a dangerous Protestant formula that strikes terror into the communion of the saints? Did the Reformers want believers to read the
Bible for themselves as individuals? Is it true that the priesthood of every believer leads to the dismembering of the body of
Christ? Into what kind of Bible readers are we making disciples?
This chapter has proposed that we encourage disciples to read
the Bible for themselves, but in the contexts of the local and the
catholic church—with the whole people of God.

As we have seen, there is plenty of Protestant precedent for
corporate Bible study. Indeed, this is something the Reformers
may have retrieved from Scripture itself, where we see Jesus and
Paul and the other apostles reading the Bible in the synagogue
(Luke 4:16–21; Acts 13:14–44).

Glenn Paauw, mentioned in chapter 4, believes the church
today can learn three things from the ancient synagogue: (1) the
importance of prioritizing public Bible reading; (2) the importance of having pastor-theologians who are familiar with both
the biblical text and the Great Tradition and can minister real
understanding of what is read; (3) the importance not only of
Bible study but of vigorous biblical interpretation in which
small groups learn both how to indwell the text and to listen in

humility to other interpreters.[41] The alternative to charitable dialogue is church hopping until we find a like-minded community. And the problem with church-hopping disciples is that they fail to read the Bible for the purpose God gave it, namely, to form a holy nation.

I have argued that Protestants too care about catholicity. Protestants propose a kind of wholeness, unity, and universality centered not on an imperial structure (the domain of Rome) but an imperial gospel (the domain of God's word). Protestants who affirm *sola Scriptura* ought also to affirm catholic tradition *as a Spirit-guided embodiment of right (that is, illumined) biblical understanding.*

Philip Schaff appreciated the unitive possibility of the Reformation in his 1844 inaugural address to his seminary at Mercersburg, Pennsylvania, when he declared the Reformation to be the "greatest act" of the catholic church.[42] Schaff thought that the greatest threat to "the Protestant Principle" was not the Church of Rome but an exaggerated subjectivism that so focused on an individual's personal relationship with God that it failed to acknowledge the objectivity of the church. Evangelicals are good about asking, What does this passage mean for me and my life? They are not so good at wrestling with the civics question, What does this passage mean for our community and our life together? It's also important to keep in mind that "our community" is a local representation of the universal church. The way forward according to Schaff was the marriage of two minds: "protestant" and "catholic."

---

41. Glenn Paauw, *Saving the Bible from Ourselves: Learning to Read and Live the Bible Well* (Downers Grove, IL: InterVarsity Press, 2015), 176–78.

42. Philip Schaff, *The Principle of Protestantism* (Eugene, OR: Wipf & Stock, 2004).

For the record, Protestants never wanted a divorce. The Reformation was a plea for a deeper and wider catholicity. The Lutheran theologian Carl Braaten puts it like this: "The Reformers made their protest against Rome on behalf of the whole church, out of love and loyalty to the truly catholic church. ... The Reformation was a movement of protest for the sake of the one church."[43] The Reformers' main objection to Roman Catholicism was not its *catholicity* but its narrow focus on *Rome*. Calvin says as much in his 1539 letter to Cardinal Sadoleto: "Our agreement with antiquity is far closer than yours ... all we have attempted has been to renew the ancient form of the Church."[44]

Take a moment to let that sink in. Both Luther and Calvin have a high regard for catholic tradition as long as such catholicity is defined not by Rome but by Romans—that is, the gospel that Paul says is "the power of God for salvation to everyone who believes" (Rom 1:16). Luther does not violate *sola Scriptura* when he acknowledges the usefulness (but not infallibility) of church councils, provided that they are truly (and not narrowly) catholic. Jaroslav Pelikan summarizes Luther's position: "As a Protestant, he subjected the authority of church councils to the authority of the word of God; as a Catholic, he interpreted the word of God in conformity with the dogmas of the councils. ... Catholic substance and Protestant principle belong together."[45]

We must hold together protestant principle (the supreme authority of Scriptures) and catholic substance (the consensus reading of the Scriptures worked out through time and across

---

43. Carl E. Braaten, *Mother Church: Ecclesiology and Ecumenism* (Minneapolis: Fortress, 1998), 12.

44. John Calvin, *A Reformation Debate: Sadoleto's Letter to the Genevans and Calvin's Reply*, ed. John Olin (Grand Rapids: Baker, 1987), 62.

45. Jaroslav Pelikan, *Obedient Rebels: Catholic Substance and Protestant Principle in Luther's Reformation* (London: SCM, 1964), 76.

space). Disciples are never more biblical than when they too work and pray for the dialogical unity the Spirit is creating out of the many members. A disciple of Jesus Christ is a person of both one book (*sola Scriptura*) and one church (*sola ecclesia*): the church alone is the place where Christ gives ministers of the word for the building up of his body (Eph 4:11–13). We *may* be Baptists, Presbyterians, or something else, but we *must* be catholics. There is therefore now no condemnation for those who wholeheartedly affirm both canonicity (the supreme authority of Scripture as a rule for Christian faith and life) and catholicity (the divinely appointed nurturing role of the church and her consensual tradition).

Scripture is never absolutely "alone" because it is never without the communal domain about which it speaks and over which it rules: the people of God. "Catholicity" belongs in the pattern of theological authority too: minimally, as the proper context for reading Scripture; maximally, as a first earthly step in the Triune mission "to unite all things in him, things in heaven and things on earth" (Eph 1:10). The church's catholicity—the scope of the company of the baptized "in Christ"—is a parable of the cosmic unity that will obtain in the kingdom of God. *Mere Protestant Christianity uses the resources of the* solas *and the priesthood of all believers to express the unity-in-denominational-diversity that local churches have in Christ.*

The kind of Protestantism that needs to live on is not the tragic caricature that encourages individual autonomy or corporate pride but the catholic original that encourages the church to hold fast to the gospel, and to one another, in Christ: "The followers of Jesus are a new *polis*, a people whose citizenship is now in God's realm."[46] The only good Protestant is a

---

46. Paauw, *Saving the Bible*, 182.

catholic Protestant—one who learns from, and bears fruit for, the whole church.

Pastors help disciples to learn how to read the Bible rightly when they teach them both Scripture and the consensus tradition of the whole church. How else can disciples realize their membership in the one, holy, and apostolic church, and thereby become "fit for purpose" of gospel citizenship? Protestants therefore can, and should, sing *sola Scriptura*—as long as they don't confuse it with the lyrics of *'o sole mio* ("my own sun"). Neither the sun, nor the Scriptures, belongs to individuals only, but to individuals who make up the one, holy, apostolic, and *catholic* body of Christ.

Churches are the place to make disciples who, not least by exhibiting their union and communion with Christ, can together glorify and enjoy God. The local church, a people with canon sense and catholic sensibility, is the true end of the Protestant Reformation.

8

CHILDREN OF GOD

The Disciple as Fitting Image of Jesus Christ

I n the last three chapters we've seen that pastors should train believers to be biblically rooted, liturgically formed, and catholically guided improvisers who are able to be faithful to the text in the contemporary cultural context. We have talked in general about the shape and criteria of discipleship, but not enough about what it looks like on the ground, its concrete substance. It is not enough to tell someone to be good if we don't know what goodness means or looks like in practice. Nor is it enough to tell someone to be godly unless we have some image of godliness.

Thankfully, the New Testament gives us such a picture. Paul calls Jesus "the image of God" (2 Cor 4:4) and "the image of the invisible God" (Col 1:15). God's plan of salvation includes God's foreknowledge of those who will "be conformed to the image of his Son" (Rom 8:29). Just as we have borne the image of Adam, "the man of dust," so "we shall also bear the image of the man of heaven" (1 Cor 15:49). This is something future for which we can hope, but it is also something happening in the present in which we can participate: "And we all … beholding the glory of the Lord, are being transformed into the same image from one degree of glory to another" (2 Cor 3:18).

Christian discipleship involves more than intellectually agreeing with Jesus, even more than trying to obey his commandments. Discipleship is ultimately about becoming more like Jesus: "It is enough for the disciple to be like his teacher" (Matt 10:25). Christlikeness is the goal of discipleship. It is not only a way of walking but a state of being.[1] To be more precise, it is the state of being-in, and abiding with, Christ.

MIRRORING JESUS? IMAGES OF DISCIPLESHIP

Christ is the image of God and disciples are to be images of Christ. But what kind of images? Mirror images? We have come across mirror imagery before. Those who hear the word of God but do not do it are like people who look into the mirror and forget what they look like. By way of contrast, those who look into the law of liberty—the gospel of freedom in Christ—are not hearers who forget but doers who act (Jas 1:22–25). What I now want to add is that being a doer means realizing one's being "in Christ." Pastors make disciples by reminding them to look to Scripture to see Christ, and their new identities in Christ. This, after all, is how we become naturalized citizens of the gospel: the Spirit unites us to the Son through the faith that comes from hearing.

When Jesus encourages his disciples to stay awake (Mark 13:37; Luke 21:36), he is encouraging them to stay *alert* and *aware*. Of what, exactly? In chapter 6 I argued that disciples must be aware of what drama they are in so they can act accordingly. The drama of redemption is a theodrama in which disciples respond to

---

1. See Rowan Williams, *Being Disciples: Essentials of the Christian Life* (Grand Rapids: Eerdmans, 2016), ch. 1.

divine initiatives. Just as the Son sees what the Father is doing and does likewise (John 5:19–20), so the disciples are to be alert to and aware of what the Father is doing in the Son, and in us, through the Holy Spirit.

It is not that disciples have to do *exactly* what the Son did (as Hebrews tells us, the Son is superior to all other beings and his sacrificial death was "once for all"), but they should be doing the *same kind* of thing they see the Son doing, and in the same power, namely, the Holy Spirit. As we shall see, this is the solution to what we could call the problem of the "one and the many" as it concerns discipleship: every disciple is to be like Christ—his image—but not every disciple is like Christ in exactly the same way. Disciples are not spitting but *fitting* images of Christ.

DOCTRINE AS THE DISCIPLE'S DIET: CHURCH AS EVANGELICAL FITNESS CULTURE

The church is not an assembly line that turns out cookie-cutter images of Jesus. Even in the New Testament we see how unlike the disciples were from one another. One has only to think of the difference between Peter and John. How, then, should a pastor help disciples to "put on" Christ? Is it more like a one-size-fits-all or a tailor-made outfit? When disciples look at themselves in the mirror, to what extent do they see themselves, that is, their own faces, rather than that of Jesus?

In this chapter I want to pursue two related answers to this fundamental pastoral challenge. In the first place, pastors are *fitness trainers* who help church members to become "fit for purpose," both individually and corporately, the purpose being active gospel citizenship. Second, pastors are *workers in fitting-ness* who help disciples offer the unique gifts of their own lives as they seek to participate fittingly in the drama of redemption. Pastors lead and love their congregations best when they minister Scripture and doctrine, helping each person in the church to become fit for the purpose of imaging Christ, embodying his mind and heart, everywhere, to everyone, at all times.

The Diet of Doctrine

Throughout this book, I have argued that everyone is a disciple. Everyone has been indoctrinated by certain words and teachings. In chapter 2 we examined some of the diet and exercise programs that over the years have attracted disciples who literally try to live by every word that comes out of their preferred dietician's or trainer's mouth in a quest for health, beauty, and longevity. Diet and exercise programs are disciplined ways of living.

Do you hear the connection between "discipline" and "disciple"? There are parallels between becoming physically and spiritually fit. In both cases, what matters is becoming a certain kind of person. We have to want it. We have to be hearers and doers. We have to want to enjoy and glorify God the way Jesus wanted it: "My food is to do the will of him who sent me" (John 4:34).

Christian doctrine is the disciple's meat and drink. You may think I'm overemphasizing the role of doctrine in the Christian life because I'm a theologian, but *doctrine is biblical*. The Greek term *didaskalia* (teaching; doctrine) occurs twenty-one times in the New Testament. Fifteen of these occurrences are found in the Pastoral Epistles alone, which strongly suggests that doctrine finds its fitting place in the church, as a means to pastor congregations and teach disciples. Indeed, Paul says Timothy's duty is to teach (*didaskō*, 1 Tim 4:11; 6:2).

Disciples need sound teaching because false doctrine abounds, and always has. Jesus warns about false prophets

(Matt 7:15; 24:11), as does John (1 John 4:1). For his part, Paul warns his readers about the "teachings [*didaskaliais*] of demons" (1 Tim 4:1). The antidote to false teaching is true teaching. Yet, interestingly enough, the term Paul chooses is not "true" but "sound," as in "sound doctrine" (1 Tim 1:10).

The mention of "sound doctrine" brings us to the crux of my argument. I have argued that doctrine serves the project of making disciples, and is therefore an eminently pastoral concern. Given my emphasis on making disciples "fit for purpose," Paul's use of the term "sound" (Greek: *hygiainō*) to qualify "doctrine" (*didaskalia*) is striking. In classical Greek, *hygiainō* meant "to be healthy" (the adjectival form meant "healthy, well"). Our English term *hygienic* derives from the Greek. The point is that doctrine is "sound" not simply because it is true, but because it is *health-giving*.

Doctrine is health-giving to the body of Christ when it exercises pastoral functions, such as correcting error, deepening understanding, and fostering wisdom. Robert Gundry translates "sound doctrine" as "healthful teaching" in his commentary on the Pastoral Epistles.[2] It's true that we speak of a "sound" or "healthy" mind to indicate mental stability. Yet, strikingly, what Paul says is "contrary to sound doctrine" are not heresies but sinful practices, ways of living (1 Tim 1:10). This reminds us that doctrine is only health-giving if it is heard *and done*.

Doctrine is "sound" because it is indicative of reality. Right teaching directs disciples in the Way of Jesus Christ, the Way of truth, wisdom, and life. By way of contrast, it is not healthy

---

2. Robert H. Gundry, *Commentary on the New Testament: Verse-by-Verse Explanations with a Literal Translation* (Peabody, MA: Hendrickson, 2010), on 1 Tim 1:10; 2 Tim 4:3; Titus 1:9; and 2:1.

to be oriented toward illusions, nothingness, and foolishness. Idolaters cannot be of sound mind. Paul urges pastor-theologians to rebuke false teachers (Titus 1:9, 13) who seek to persuade others to go chasing after wind.

Sound doctrine is reliable, then, because it is reality-indicating. Sound doctrine ministers understanding because it indicates the meaning and significance of what God has done in Jesus Christ. Sound doctrine is an essential ingredient in the disciple's diet because it is "in accordance with the gospel" (1 Tim 1:11). Sound doctrine demands to be heard and done, for it tells us how things are in the light of Christ and what must be done to walk in its light. To use the Latin, sound doctrine instructs us what to believe (*credenda*), what we may hope (*speranda*), and what we must do (*agenda*). As such, it provides direction for disciples to participate fittingly in the drama of redemption with faith, hope, and love.

The notion of health-giving doctrine reminds us that faith is more than intellectual assent to revealed propositions. As James says, "Even the demons believe" (Jas 2:19). Intellectual assent— theoretical knowledge—falls short of true faith if unaccompanied by "works" (Greek: *ergon*) (Jas 2:20–22). This is the ultimate purpose of evangelical theology: to build up disciples who will be not "hearers who forget" but "doers who act" (Jas 1:25), where the kind of acting in question pertains to doing things that accord with gospel citizenship.

It is one thing to assent to the truth, another to be transformed by it. Dieting is a good example of how information alone is not transformative. For doctrine truly to be sound, we must do more than store it away in our memory. If we could be transformed simply by intellectually assenting to the truth, no doubt we all would weigh a few pounds less! No, in order to become fit, one must first have the right diet, and then follow its prescribed discipline. Spiritual fitness is equally demanding.

Willpower alone is not enough to stay on a diet of sound doctrine. We need the indwelling Holy Spirit. The Holy Spirit uses Scripture and doctrine to renew our minds (Rom 12:2). How do we renew our minds? By following the diet of sound doctrine that ministers the reality of the gospel. Paul often spends half his letters telling his readers how things are, in the indicative mood (for example, "our old self was crucified," Rom 6:6). He typically pivots in the middle with a significant "Therefore," then follows up with imperatives. It's important to get the order right: first the indicative (what God has done in Christ), then the imperative (what we must do in Christ). The indicative is grace; the imperative is gratitude. Everything disciples do follows from a prior divine enablement: "For freedom Christ has set us free [indicative]; stand firm therefore [imperative]" (Gal 5:1).

It is important to remember that one of the most important ways Scripture transforms us is by opening our eyes not only to what God is doing in Christ but also to what is happening in culture. Scripture wakes us up to what is really going on in our world. Here we may recall Jesus' urgent exhortation to his disciples not to fall asleep. Too many people are sleepwalking their way through life, going through the motions of existence but not really paying attention to what they're doing, what it means, and the consequences of their actions. They're inattentive to what they are doing and oblivious to the presence, activity, and judgment of God.

The sobering truth is that much of what is going through our heads is not the story of Jesus but some other story. I fear, for example, that many people spend more time viewing videos than reading Scripture. In February 2017, YouTube announced that people around the world watch a billion hours of content on the site *every day*.[3] Many of the video games and apps for your smartphone are designed not only by software architects, but by applied psychologists and behavioral economists too. Some of Silicon Valley's app designers study how to create obsessive-compulsive patterns of behavior in the Persuasive Technology Lab at Stanford University. The lab was founded in 1998 by B. J. Fogg, the founder of a new field of study called "captology," which is derived from the acronym for "computers as persuasive technology."[4] Captologists look for ways to capture people's attention and cultivate compulsive patterns of behavior that center on using the app, putting a new and more insidious spin on Paul's warning about not being taken captive by "empty deceit" (Col 2:8). This fast-food diet is not health-giving. Consuming the cultural equivalent of junk food is not good for the human spirit. Like junk food, apps, games, and videos are pleasant to consume, but also like junk food, they do not nurture the soul.

Disciples who want to follow Jesus in the twenty-first century need to wake up, and to stay awake. They need to become aware (mindful) of the nature and effects of consuming cultural products, of trying to live on a diet of cultural doctrine: stories, practices, imaginaries. Christians need to understand what modern communication technology, and the media culture as a whole, is doing to us—what kind of humanity it is cultivating and what kind of spirits it is forming.[5] Here's my point: Scripture

---

3. "You Know What's Cool? A Billion Hours," *YouTube Official Blog*, February 27, 2017, https://youtube.googleblog.com/2017/02/you-know-whats-cool-billion-hours.html.

4. "What Is Captology?," Stanford Persuasive Tech Lab, http://captology.stanford.edu/about/what-is-captology.html (accessed February 26, 2018).

5. Two helpful recent studies are Tony Reinke, *12 Ways Your Phone Is Changing You* (Wheaton, IL: Crossway, 2017), and Andy Crouch, *The Tech-Wise Family:*

and sound doctrine set the captives free by waking them up to reality, freeing them *from* enslavement to cultural fast food— patterns of behavior and values that do not yield ultimate satisfaction—and, in conjunction with the Holy Spirit, freeing them *for* living for God and one another. The wellness, health, and fitness we should ultimately be seeking must first and foremost be defined by the gospel, not by secular culture.

"You are what you eat." This piece of proverbial wisdom entered into the English language about a hundred years ago, about the same time that various nutritionists were trying to win the hearts and minds (and stomachs) of the general public. I am concerned more with spiritual than physical fitness, but if the proverb holds true—and I believe it does—then pastors must do everything they can to ensure that their disciples are fed the right diet, namely, sound doctrine.

The Church as Evangelical Fitness Culture

Tell me your diet, and I'll tell you your culture. As we saw in chapter 2, large swaths of society are obsessed with physical wellness, beauty, and health, the main ingredients of our contemporary fitness culture. Yet different pictures of what "total fitness" consists in circulate and compete in the arena of social imaginaries.

Pastors need to wake up congregations to the cultural forces that are forming their spirits, and perhaps clouding their vision. The church is in the world, a holy nation in the midst of another nation; hence, our congregations are not immune to these cultural stories about how to live well, or what it means to be saved. Perhaps the most spectacular, and appalling, illustration of this

---

Everyday Steps for Putting Technology in Its Proper Place (Grand Rapids: Baker Books, 2017).

cultural conditioning is the so-called health and wealth gospel, which some see as a Christianized version of the American Dream.[6] A 2006 poll conducted by *Time* magazine indicated that 17 percent of American Christians identified with the movement.[7] It has also gone viral, infecting churches in other countries, such as Brazil, Nigeria, and Singapore. This prosperity theology, with its presumption that God's will is for his people always to be not simply well but *well off* (that is, medically and financially fit), is the polar opposite of the theology of the cross.[8]

Jesus calls disciples to follow him. We get our term "vocation" from the Latin *vocare* (to call or summon). Pastors help make disciples by serving up a steady diet of Scripture and doctrine. The Great Commission (to make disciples) is related to the Great Commandment: "You shall love the Lord your God with all your heart and with all your soul and with all your mind" (Matt 22:36–37). This is the disciple's ultimate vocation, for this is what makes a person Christlike. Jesus says: "My food is to do the will of him who sent me and to accomplish his work" (John 4:34). Will we respond to our vocation as Christians or not? This question is what puts the drama into discipleship: Will we answer the call to become Christlike by loving God and neighbor, and if so, what will our answer look like?

---

6. Antonio Spadaro and Marcelo Figueroa, "The Prosperity Gospel: Dangerous and Different," *La Civiltà Cattolica*, July 18, 2018, https://laciviltacattolica.com/the-prosperity-gospel-dangerous-and-different/.

7. David Van Biema and Jeff Chu, "Does God Want You to be Rich?," *Time*, September 10, 2006, http://content.time.com/time/magazine/article/0,9171,1533448,00.html.

8. For an insightful history of the movement, see Kate Bowler, *Blessed: A History of the American Prosperity Gospel* (Oxford: Oxford University Press, 2013). For a critical analysis, see Gordon D. Fee, *The Disease of the Health and Wealth Gospels* (Vancouver, BC: Regent College Publishing, 1985); and David W. Jones and Russell S. Woodbridge, *Health, Wealth, and Happiness: How the Prosperity Gospel Overshadows the Gospel of Christ* (Grand Rapids: Kregel, 2017).

Evangelical theology is not simply theology done by evangelicals. The deeper sense of "evangelical" means "corresponding to the gospel." Evangelical theology, in the sense of theology that sets forth in speech the truth of the gospel and its implications, exists to help us understand what God is saying and doing in Jesus Christ, and in the Scriptures that attest to him, so that disciples can act *out* what is *in* Christ. The church is thus a fitness culture, a nurturing environment that encourages Christly gestures and Christlike behavior. Pastors minister God's word in order to train disciples to be fit for the purpose of walking in ways that correspond to the truth of the gospel and their citizenship in it.

LEARNING CHRIST

Scripture and doctrine may be the disciple's curriculum, but the subject matter is Jesus Christ, and the course aim is "building up the body of Christ" (Eph 4:12). Becoming a disciple means learning Christ.

Jesus, the rabbi, is the disciple's principal teacher. He came proclaiming the kingdom, then taught about it through parables. Yet in learning Christ, we also learn God. No one knows God the Father except the Son "and anyone to whom the Son chooses to reveal him" (Matt 11:27). Immediately afterward Jesus tells his disciples: "Take my yoke upon you, and learn from me" (Matt 11:29). This is no textbook learning. To take Jesus' yoke is to adopt his way and follow his example; it is a figure of speech for becoming his disciple. To take Jesus' yoke involves becoming a hearer and doer.

Learning Christ is an important Pauline theme. The modern academy privileges knowledge that can be quantified and observed theoretically, from a critical distance. But learning *about* Jesus is not the same thing as learning Christ. When Paul

says, "But that is not the way you learned Christ!" (Eph 4:20), he
is referring to the kind of behavior that accompanies the futility
of mind and hardness of heart typical of those who are alienated
from the life of God (Eph 4:17–19). Learning Christ means more
than acquiring knowledge *about* him.

Calvin's commentary on this passage highlights the special
kind of learning in view: "He whose life differs not from that
of unbelievers, has learned nothing of Christ; for the knowledge of Christ cannot be separated from the mortification of the
flesh."[9] Paul then specifies how the Ephesians *did* learn Christ
(Eph 4:21–24), namely, by *hearing* about him and then by *doing* him,
that is, by putting off the old self with its characteristic behavior
and putting on the new (that is, the regenerated self in Christ).

It is no mere lexical coincidence that the Greek term Paul
uses for "learning" Christ (*manthanō*) is related to the term for
disciple (*mathētēs*), or that the Latin root of "disciple" (*discipu-
lus*) resembles the term academic *discipline* and means "student."
This explains why Jesus can say to his disciples both "Learn from
me" (Matt 11:29) and "Follow me" (Matt 4:19). "A disciple ... when
he is fully trained will be like his teacher" (Luke 6:40).

Learning to read the Bible in order to follow Christ requires
something more than transmitting information. One does not
become a "Christ person," however, simply by learning one or
two new facts. Doctrine that is merely informative is nothing but
a noisy gong or a clanging cymbal. Learning Christ involves the
ability not simply to recall information but, more importantly,
to make judgments that display "the mind of Christ" (1 Cor 2:16;
Phil 2:5). This may seem a bit abstract, so Paul makes it more
concrete: "Be imitators of me, as I am of Christ" (1 Cor 11:1; cf.

---

9. John Calvin and William Pringle, *Commentaries on the Epistles of Paul to
the Galatians and Ephesians* (Bellingham, WA: Logos Bible Software, 2010), 294.

1 Cor 4:16; 1 Thess 1:6). To imitate someone is to walk in their way. It is not a matter of mirror-imaging or exact replication but rather of recontextualizing Jesus' attitudes and reflexes, which is what "mind of Christ" means. In brief, to imitate Christ is to improvise his way in new situations.

This is not the place to enter into debates about Christian education. The basic point is that we learn Christ by hearing and doing, that is, by discerning and then following his way—what Scripture calls the way of wisdom (Prov 4:11), righteousness (2 Pet 2:21), truth (2 Pet 2:2), and life (Jer 21:8). Scripture is profitable for teaching (*didaskalion*) and training (*paideia*) in righteousness (2 Tim 3:16). As we have seen, it is also profitable for training in wisdom, truth, and life by imparting the big imaginative picture of why God created humans in the world and how, in Christ through the Spirit, God is accomplishing his original purpose despite human sinfulness, the devil, and death. Similarly, Christian doctrine is profitable for training in discipleship. Doctrine is not an end in itself but a pedagogical tool for making disciples. The whole of Calvin's *Institutes* serves this practical purpose: "For Calvin, discipleship is *paideia*, 'formative education.' "[10]

As I mentioned in chapter 5, Calvin compares the Bible to "spectacles," corrective lenses that retrain the eyes (of the mind, of faith, of the heart) to see things correctly, which is to say, by the light of the gospel of Jesus Christ. Scripture is a pedagogue that helps us see things—God, the world, and ourselves—as they really are, and as they come together in Jesus Christ.

Scripture and doctrine both help disciples to discern how things fit together in Jesus Christ, and thus what is fitting for

---

10. Matthew Myer Boulton, *Life in God: John Calvin, Practical Formation, and the Future of Protestant Theology* (Grand Rapids: Eerdmans, 2001), 4.

Christians to say and do. Scripture trains our faculties "to distinguish good from evil" (Heb 5:14), not simply by stating moral principles, but also by giving us the storied framework that give "good" and "evil" their sense. At the end of the day, what is most important in learning Christ is not having bits of information but rather the big picture. Only when they understand the whole drama of redemption are disciples able to make right judgments about things—in particular, judgments about the form their discipleship should take here and now. We demonstrate our understanding by what we do.

The canon leads readers *to* Christ and then forms the life of Christ *in* them so that they can continue walking the way *of* Christ. Learning Christ is a matter of following—or we could say *practicing*—Christ. It is by reading God's word, illuminated by the Spirit, that disciples learn to think rightly, see rightly, judge rightly, and act rightly, that is, in a Christlike manner. Scripture is more than the "spectacles" of faith: it is the Oculus Rift that enables us to see and experience not virtual but eschatological reality, the real in Christ. It is by becoming apprentices to Scripture—to its canonical pedagogy—that we learn the mind of Christ (Phil 2:5), including his own way of reading Israel's Scriptures.[11] Disciples are apprentices to Scripture, biblical interpreters who receive not simply information about but formation in truth and righteousness—in other words, formation in Christ.

Knowing how to read the Bible to learn Christ requires biblical literacy, canonical competence, and interpretive excellence. It is ultimately about becoming wise, which involves more than theoretical knowledge. One can get knowledge by hearing alone.

---

11. For a helpful expansion of this point, see David I. Starling, *Hermeneutics as Apprenticeship: How the Bible Shapes Our Interpretive Habits and Practices* (Grand Rapids: Baker Academic, 2016).

By way of contrast, wisdom and understanding are forms of practical knowledge and require practice.

What is wisdom? Here, too, the way forward is to take our bearings from Scripture, in which wisdom pertains to a life that flourishes because it is in harmony with the created order and issues from the fear of the Lord. Here, too, disciples must learn Christ in order to gain wisdom, for Jesus Christ is wisdom incarnate (1 Cor 1:24, 30). Wisdom means *knowing what to do in particular situations* in order to glorify God and follow Jesus in ways that befit faithful disciples. In a word, theological wisdom means knowing *how to improvise the mind of Christ at all times, everywhere, and to everyone.*

PUTTING ON CHRIST

Paul commands his Roman readers to "put on the Lord Jesus Christ" (Rom 13:14). What does putting on Christ have to do with learning Christ? Just this: both require doing, and not hearing only. Putting on Christ admits of two meanings: First, it is a way we talk about getting dressed (we put on our pajamas). Second (at least in English), it has a theatrical meaning, as in staging a show. I want to think about putting on Christ in both senses, as costume and performance.

As Individuals

When Paul exhorts his readers, "Have this [Christ's] mind," he is urging them to adopt in their inner being ("spirit") Christ's habitual attitude of humility, his disposition to look to the interests of others before his own (Phil 2:3–4). Paul asks his readers to put on Christ only because he views them as those who have already been baptized into Christ. Indeed, what was issued as an imperatival command in Romans 13:14 is elsewhere stated as indicative fact: "For as many of you as were baptized into Christ have put on Christ" (Gal 3:27).

Baptism has something to do with putting on Christ, but what? The short answer is that water baptism is a sign and sacrament of the believer's baptism with the Holy Spirit, a dramatic elemental representation of our participation, through faith, in Jesus' death and resurrection, and thus of our being born again, made new.

In Romans 6, Paul strikingly catches up his readers' imagination by explaining their baptism as their being caught up in Jesus' life story: "We were buried therefore with him by baptism into death, in order that, just as Christ was raised from the dead ... we too might walk in newness of life" (Rom 6:4). This is why baptism is a moment of high drama in the church, an act literally dripping with meaning and significance. It is also a clue to what it means to put on Christ.

Putting on Christ is not an exercise in moral striving, something we do, but something made possible only by a prior work of the Triune God. Baptism is thus a key scene in the drama of discipleship: on the one hand, only God can bring about our participation in the death and resurrection of Jesus Christ; on the other hand, we participate in our incorporation into Christ precisely by acting out, with water, what God has accomplished through faith by the Holy Spirit. Baptism dramatically represents the disciple's union with Christ.

The Spirit's role in the drama of redemption is essential. As Calvin says, "As long as Christ remains outside of us ... all that he has suffered and done for the salvation of the human race remains useless."[12] Disciples can act out Christ only if Christ is first in them, and getting disciples into Christ, and Christ into disciples, is arguably the whole point of the Spirit's mission, as

12. John Calvin, *Institutes of the Christian Religion*, ed. John T. McNeill, trans. Ford Lewis Battles, Library of Christian Classics (1960; repr., Louisville:

well as the climactic Pentecostal scene where God creates a new people. The Spirit is the "giver of life" because he unites us to Christ. It is thanks to the Spirit that the life of Christ is formed within us. The Spirit is the theatrical "dresser" who clothes disciples with the righteousness of Christ (Eph 4:24; cf. Isa 61:10), the one who assists disciples with putting on Christ and maintains costume quality throughout the performance.

For those who by faith through the Spirit have been united to Christ, putting on Christ is not a fiction (what *if*) but a reality (what *is*). Disciples do not act like Christ in order to approximate an exemplar *outside* them. Rather, disciples put on Christ *from the inside out*.

To be in Christ through the Spirit is to have been transferred into his kingdom (Col 1:13) and thus to enjoy citizenship in heaven (Phil 3:20). This change in citizenship may not be empirically verifiable, but it is neither fantasy nor pretense. On the contrary, doctrine is simply the attempt to spell out (indicate) *what is* in Christ.

To say what is in Christ is to describe what is "already" and "not yet." To put on Christ is therefore to begin to act out *now* our participation in the age *to come*. In acting out the life of Christ, disciples are neither relying on their moral efforts nor pretending to be something they are not; they are rather participating in what is eschatologically the case, namely, that disciples "are his workmanship, created in Christ Jesus for good works" (Eph 2:10).

Thanks to the Spirit, those who confess Jesus Christ as Lord really do have a share in his life, and this includes his sense of sonship, desire to do God's will, and compassion for others (that is, his "mind"). Through faith disciples come not only to believe but also to *experience* the reality of "we in Christ" and

"Christ in us." The Spirit ministers the biblical word and so renews their imagination, their ability to both *taste* and *see* the glory and excellence of the unfolding drama in which they have been transferred.

To be in Christ is to be in the process of being restored to true humanity, a process that requires our active involvement. To put on Christ means to act out his life in us. As Paul says: "I have been crucified with Christ. It is no longer I who live, but Christ who lives in me" (Gal 2:20). If we did not live out the life of Christ in us, our *doing* would fail to correspond to our *being*. To act out what is in Christ is to be an answerable self who can respond to God's call like Samuel ("Here I am," 1 Sam 3:4) and Mary ("Let it be to me according to your word," Luke 1:38). It takes a faith-formed imagination to participate in this evangelical reality, to taste and see what is already but not yet in Christ. The drama of discipleship is all about acting out—dramatically representing in earthbound bodies and everyday practices—the new humanity that is in heaven, yet ours in Christ.

As Church

A good biblical commentary does justice to the historical, literary, and theological aspects of the text. In an important sense, however, the life of the disciple, and in particular of the local church, is the most appropriate form our biblical commentary takes: "What we do as the people of God is our interpretation of the Bible."[13] The ultimate aim of theological education is to help disciples be living commentaries, "a letter from Christ" (2 Cor 3:3).

---

13. David Scott, "Speaking to Form: Trinitarian-Performative Scripture Reading," *Anglican Theological Review* 77 (1995): 145.

In chapter 5 we examined why it takes not simply individuals but a gathered community—a "company"—to be a theater of the gospel. The gist of my argument there was that, in order to bear witness to the new creation that is in Christ, and to exercise a ministry of reconciliation, the church has not only to talk about but also to exhibit this new creation and reconciliation in Christ. The church does this by being itself: a community of sinners and a communion of saints.

Disciples gather together to represent Christ in their time and place.[14] It takes a community to represent Christ, for it takes at least two to act out forgiveness; it takes a multicultural company fully to act out social, racial, and interpersonal reconciliation in Christ. The church is a place where people who were formerly strangers to one another act out the new reality of their common citizenship in the gospel (Eph 2:19). In Ephesians 6, Paul speaks about the armor of God Christians are to put on together. There are also things we are to put off, such as anger, malice, and slander (Col 3:8), and especially the "old self with its practices" (Col 3:9).

The church is most itself at Table, for it is in partaking Christ's body that the church becomes Christ's body: one. In all its activities, especially the Lord's Supper, a local church in its corporate life "puts on" the spectacle of reconciliation in Christ, and not only acts out but also becomes a parable of the kingdom of God.

14. So Uche Anizor and Hank Voss, *Representing Christ: A Vision for the Priesthood of All Believers* (Downers Grove, IL: IVP Academic, 2016).

CORE EXERCISES FOR
STRENGTH TRAINING
IN CHRIST

What we can do with our bodies depends in part on our core fitness. Here we examine core strength. Strength pertains to the energy needed to bring about changes, to do things. The body of Christ, the church local and universal, must have the strength necessary to fulfill its calling and mission.

The apostles were concerned with the church's core strength—its ability to accomplish its mission—from the very beginning, hence the emphasis on "strengthening" (Greek: *sterizō*). After evangelizing in Lystra, Iconium, and Antioch, Paul and Barnabas returned, "strengthening the souls of the disciples, encouraging them to continue in the faith" (Acts 14:22). Elsewhere, Judas and Silas "strengthened the brothers with many words" (Acts 15:32). Paul's whole ministry could be described in terms of "strengthening the churches" (Acts 15:41) or "strengthening all the disciples" (Acts 18:23). Strengthening here means supporting, stabilizing, establishing, and firming up.

We see, then, that the ministry of the word, which pastors are to exercise today, has been and continues to be the chief means of strengthening disciples and the church. Yet it is important to remember that, though pastors are secondary causes and thus means of grace, it is ultimately God who strengthens, as we see in Paul's doxology to Romans: "Now to him who is able to strengthen [*stērixai*] you according to my gospel" (Rom 16:25; see also 1 Thess 3:13; 2 Thess 2:17; 3:3; 1 Pet 5:10).

The other Greek terms to note in this connection are *dynamis* (power) and *endynamoō* (to strengthen). Jesus Christ is the "power of God" (1 Cor 1:24), which is why Paul can use *endynamoō* to describe how Christ is able to strengthen those who believe in and follow him. Christ is the disciple's strength, just as he was

Paul's: "I can do all things *through him* [Christ] who strengthens me" (Phil 4:13). This is crucial. We do not grow as disciples through our own efforts alone. It requires grace. It is thanks to the Spirit—the life of Christ in us—that we have the strength to follow Christ.

At first, we take baby steps, but if we continue to walk in the Spirit we will be able to endure more and more. Like weightlifters, we become stronger by doing reps, that is, the same exercise repeatedly, like carrying one another's burdens. Christ strengthens disciples to do reps of love.

Throughout this book, I have insisted on the importance of cultivating a biblically informed and transformed imagination that sees this world as the stage for what God is doing in Christ to make all things new (Rev 21:5). In order to see the world as it is, we need to view it eschatologically, as the site of the breaking-in of the kingdom of God in the person and work of Jesus Christ.

Faith originally comes from hearing the report about Christ (Rom 10:17), and one way to strengthen disciples' faith is to help them read all of Scripture as in one way or another a witness to Christ. Moreover, we have seen that doctrine spells out the meaning and implications of this witness. Luke tells us that, when Paul and Timothy communicated the "dogmas" reached by the Jerusalem Council to other churches, these churches "were strengthened in the faith" (Acts 16:5). Faith becomes stronger the more we come to know the reality that is in Christ through Scripture and doctrine alike.

Exercise 1: "Take/Read; Come/See"

As Augustine tells it in his *Confessions*, a child's singsong voice saying "take and read" led him to Romans 13:13–14 ("Let us walk properly as in the daytime, not in orgies and drunkenness. ... But put on the Lord Jesus Christ"), and his conversion, that point at which he become not only a hearer but a doer. Augustine experienced the transforming power of the text. As Jesus explains, the power of the (biblical) text is the power of God (Matt 22:29; cf. Mark 12:24). Of course, Jesus is himself "the power of God and the wisdom of God" (1 Cor 1:24). Perhaps this is why Philip encourages Nathanael to "come and see" what Jesus was saying and doing (John 1:46). Pastors help disciples experience the power of God when they too "come and see" the Christ lying in the manger of the Scriptures.

One of the best ways to do this is to preach Christ from the Old Testament. In light of the centrality of the ministry of the word in strengthening faith, it is only fitting that we return again to the centrality of preaching in disciple-making. The gospel is "the power of God for salvation" (Rom 1:16). This is significant: to preach the gospel is to do more than commend moral principles. The gospel is not a principle but a proclamation of something that has happened, and what God is doing in Christ is ultimately unintelligible apart from the Old Testament. For the gospel is part two of the story of Israel, in which Jesus is the climax.[15] Seeing Jesus' story against the backdrop of the story of Israel reminds us that salvation in Christ is about more than the fate of individual souls; rather, it is about the fate of a holy nation.

Pastors may perhaps be squeamish about "finding" Christ in every Old Testament passage. This is not quite what I am advocating. I am simply proposing that we read all the Scriptures keeping in mind Jesus' own exercise with the disciples on the road to Emmaus: "And beginning with Moses and all the Prophets, he interpreted to them in all the Scriptures the things concerning himself" (Luke 24:27; cf. 24:44). I believe this was

---

15. See further Starling, *Hermeneutics as Apprenticeship*, 107–17.

not a heavy-handed allegorical reading that made use of fanciful connections between incidental details and the life of Christ, but rather an interpretation that discerned the through-line, the central dramatic thrust, of divine redemptive history—namely, the way in which the prophets, priests, and kings anticipated aspects of Christ's own work, and the way in which God's repeated delivery of the people of Israel from their enemies (and ultimately from themselves) anticipated his delivery of the church from sin, death, and destruction.

To take, read, and preach the Bible in the church, with an ear for the word of God to the people of God, is to read it as testimony to Christ, his person and work, his suffering and glory. To read the Bible in the church, with faith, is to read it as a divinely authored, unified story about God's attempt to bless all nations through the seed of Abraham by forming a multiethnic family to be his own treasured possession, a people incorporated in his Son through his Holy Spirit. Take, read the whole Bible. Come, see how it is all about Christ.[16]

In order to come and see how Scripture speaks of Christ, I encourage pastors to take and read Luther's *Prefaces to the Bible*. In addition to writing prefaces to each Testament, Luther also penned prefaces to individual Old and New Testament books. As Luther explains, the preface is a teaching tool intended to help the biblical reader to know "what he is to look for in this book."[17] For example, in his *Preface to the Gospels*, Luther says to

---

16. For examples of "Christ-centered" reading, see Bryan Chapell, *Christ-Centered Preaching: Redeeming the Expository Sermon*, 3rd ed. (Grand Rapids: Baker Academic, 2018); Edmund P. Clowney, *The Unfolding Mystery: Discovering Christ in the Old Testament Scriptures*, 2nd ed. (Phillipsburg, NJ: P&R, 2013); Graeme Goldsworthy, *Christ-Centered Biblical Theology: Hermeneutical Foundations and Principles* (Downers Grove, IL: IVP Academic, 2012).

17. Martin Luther, *Prefaces to the New Testament*, in *Martin Luther's Basic Theological Writings*, ed. Timothy F. Lull (Minneapolis: Fortress, 1989), 112.

the prospective reader, "Before you take Christ as an example ... accept and recognize him as a gift."[18] As for the Old Testament, Luther gives this advice: "If you would interpret well and confidently, set Christ before you, for he is the man to whom it all applies, every bit of it."[19]

Luther's *Prefaces* are important clues to understand his biblical hermeneutic. To those who worry that discovering Christ in the Old Testament violates grammatical-historical interpretation, I would say, first, that in light of Jesus' own statements mentioned above, we should be wary of reducing the meaning to the human authorial intention alone. Second, and more to the christological point, I commend William Marsh's study of Luther. Marsh shows that Luther reads the Bible as Christian Scripture (that is, as divine address) and that he views Christ as the literal sense of the Old Testament. How? By viewing the promised Messiah as the intended referent of the divine author expressed in the words of the human authors of the Law, Prophets, and Writings.[20] Pastors today should go and do likewise.

Exercise 2: "Take Up Your Cross"

When it comes to strength training, one of the most challenging assignments is the exercise Jesus gave his disciples: "If anyone would come after me, let him deny himself and take up his cross and follow me" (Matt 16:24; Mark 8:34), to which Luke adds "daily" (Luke 9:23). Disciples must not only take and read;

---

18. Martin Luther, *A Brief Instruction on What to Look For and Expect in the Gospels*, in Lull, *Basic Theological Writings*, 106.

19. Luther, *Preface to the Old Testament*, in Lull, *Basic Theological Writings*, 130.

20. See William M. Marsh, *Martin Luther on Reading the Bible as Christian Scripture: The Messiah in Luther's Biblical Hermeneutic and Theology* (Eugene, OR: Pickwick, 2017).

they must take up their cross (not Jesus') in order to follow him in an exercise in everyday martyrdom.

When I was teaching at Wheaton College several years ago, there was a student who went from class to class dragging a life-sized cross. This is one interpretation of what Jesus meant. Other Christians signal their allegiance to Jesus by wearing smaller crosses around their necks. These varying responses represent what we might call the maximum and minimum literal interpretations of Jesus' words.

In context, Jesus is likely speaking of the importance of remaining loyal to him even at the cost of persecution, for the next verse reads, "For whoever would save his life will lose it, but whoever loses his life for my sake and the gospel's will save it" (Mark 8:35). As Jesus' cross was a shameful death, so those who follow Jesus must be willing to expose themselves to shame, ridicule, and persecution. This is precisely what happened to Paul, who describes his own suffering as "a spectacle [*theatron*] to the world" (1 Cor 4:9). The verbal form of *theatron* appears in Hebrews, where the author reminds his readers that they too endured "a hard struggle with sufferings, sometimes being publicly exposed [*theatrizomenoi*] to reproach and affliction" (Heb 10:32–33).

Paul speaks of sharing in Christ's sufferings, and thus becoming like him in his death (Phil 3:10; cf. 2 Cor 4:8–10). Jesus' death was sufficient for the remission of sins, so disciples take up their own crosses not to complete but to attest to Jesus' redemptive work. Disciples must be prepared to take up their crosses daily, demonstrating their willingness to suffer for the truth of the gospel, until such time that there is no more evangelism to be done.

Disciples must be ready to follow a daily diet of martyrdom, by which I mean, first, a readiness to bear witness to the gospel and, second, a willingness to suffer for bearing witness. Such suffering may range from ridicule and social ostracism to (depending on where one lives) legal prosecution and physical persecution. Nevertheless, disciples must be prepared to speak and act as people who are so caught up in the story of Jesus that they cannot help but participate in it. This is what it means for pastors to train disciples who are fit for purpose—fit, that is, to participate fittingly in the ongoing story of Christ in the world, to say and do the kind of thing that befits a citizen of the gospel. To learn Christ is to learn his patient endurance and steadfast faithfulness in suffering as a witness to the gospel. Taking up the cross is not a burden, however, for those who are lost in wonder, love, and praise of the one who "became what we are in order to make us what He is."[21]

Exercise 3: "Practice Death (and Resurrection)"

In today's secular social imaginary, this life is all there is, which means that death presents a technological problem that needs to be solved. It is in learning to deal with death and dying that disciples undertake what is perhaps the most challenging course of their curriculum.

The apostle Paul declares: "I die every day" (1 Cor 15:31). Disciples who act out the life of Christ must prepare to play their death scenes. Medieval Christians familiar with the Black Death that ravaged Europe used the *Ars moriendi*, a manual on the "art of dying." Reformation Christians had Luther's 1519 "Sermon on Preparing to Die." In our times, dying has largely been outsourced to the medical professionals and typically happens offstage. Pastors need to think of ways to update Luther's sermon

---

21. Irenaeus, *The Scandal of the Incarnation: Irenaeus Against the Heresies*, trans. John Saward (San Francisco: Ignatius Press, 1981), 55.

to help disciples confront death and dying with the hope, joy, and power of Christ's resurrection. Paul was keenly aware of his mortality, which he likened to a fragile jar of clay (2 Cor 4:7). Like Jesus, Paul suffered corporeal punishments for his witness to the gospel, so much so that he says he is "always carrying in the body the death of Jesus" (2 Cor 4:10). And yet Paul the disciple was so caught up in the story of Jesus that he was able to display not only the suffering of Jesus' cross but also the power and life of the risen Jesus: "For he was crucified in weakness, but lives by the power of God" (2 Cor 13:4; cf. 4:11).

The paradox of discipleship ("For when I am weak, then I am strong," 2 Cor 12:10) is an indication of grace: "Therefore I will boast all the more gladly of my weaknesses, so that the power of Christ may rest upon me" (2 Cor 12:9). Union with Christ involves participation in his death and resurrection. Disciples have to play their death scene (unless and until the Lord returns), yet to play it rightly they also need to communicate the life, joy, and power of resurrection.

Here, too, pastors need to train disciples in reading Scripture in order to strengthen the eschatological eyes of their hearts, that is, the eschatological imagination that discerns both the "already" and the "not yet." First Peter 1:3–5 speaks of a "living hope" that comes through Jesus' resurrection, a hope in an imperishable inheritance reserved in heaven for the children of God. This is no pie-in-the-sky fantasy. Rather, it is the object of faith, and faith itself is evidence of God's power (1 Pet 1:5). Faith is God's protecting power because it establishes disciples in reality: what God has done, is doing, and will do in Jesus Christ.

Discipleship, I have been insisting, is the process of learning to get real, in Christ. This includes not flinching from the harsh reality of physical death. Yet we see death as it truly is only in the light of Jesus' death and resurrection, namely, as something

Christ has defeated: "O death, where is your victory? O death, where is your sting?" (1 Cor 15:55). In his aforementioned sermon, Luther stresses the importance of believing that Christ conquered death, sin, and the devil on the cross. Luther believed that the dying person "could overcome the evil images [that is, despair] by contemplating these images of Christ."[22]

In an age where people are living longer, though not necessarily better, the church needs to retrieve the art and craft of dying well. Fortunately, there are a number of helpful recent testimonies, some from saints at the end of their mortal coil,[23] other from those who have accompanied the dying as hospice volunteers.[24]

Is there an "art of dying" that pastors can teach present-day disciples? The fifteenth-century self-help manual listed the temptations a dying person faces (such as fear, anger, despair, even a sense of betrayal by God) and then recommended the virtues necessary for resisting them. It also "commended" death as the soul's release from the body and from earthly cares.[25]

A gospel-centered vision of the risen Christ provides direction for playing one's death scene. In the first place, it addresses our medicalized social imaginary, insisting that "the victory over

---

22. Austra Reinis, *Reforming the Art of Dying: The* Ars Moriendi *in the German Reformation (1519–1528)* (London: Routledge, 2016), 247.

23. See, for example, Billy Graham, *Nearing Home: Life, Faith, and Finishing Well* (Nashville: Thomas Nelson, 2011); and J. I. Packer, *Finishing Our Course with Joy: Guidance from God for Engaging with Our Aging* (Wheaton, IL: Crossway, 2014).

24. See, for example, Rob Moll, *The Art of Dying: Living Fully into the Life to Come* (Downers Grove, IL: InterVarsity Press, 2010); and Marilyn Chandler McEntyre, *A Faithful Farewell: Living Your Last Chapter with Love* (Grand Rapids: Eerdmans, 2015).

25. The high point in Protestant texts is probably Jeremy Taylor's 1651 *The Rule and Exercises of Holy Dying* (New York: Arno Press, 1977).

death is a divine victory, not a technological one."[26] Second, the confidence that nothing, even death, "will be able to separate us from the love of God in Christ Jesus our Lord" (Rom 8:39), helps disciples to imitate the patience and courage with which Jesus faced his own death.

We should not blame the medical establishment for making it difficult to know how to die well. It is simply filling the vacuum left by the church. It is part of the pastor's remit to instruct disciples in the art of dying. Disciples are formed to practice death and resurrection through the regular life practices of the church, in particular, the ministry of the word, the celebration of the Lord's Supper, corporate prayers, and funeral services. Paul does not want the Thessalonians to be "uninformed" about the fate of the dead, so that they "may not grieve as others do who have no hope" (1 Thess 4:13). Paul reveals the end of the drama to his Thessalonian readers: Christ will return and the dead in Christ will rise. Knowing the ending turns what might otherwise be a tragedy into a divine comedy, which is why Paul concludes, "Therefore encourage one another with these words" (1 Thess 4:18). Here too, the church's social imaginary is to be transformed in accordance with the gospel.

The way we play our death scenes ought to be consistent with how we play our life scenes, namely, as an opportunity to embody our belief that we can do all things, even die, through Christ who strengthens us.

---

26. Allen Verhey, *The Christian Art of Dying: Learning from Jesus* (Grand Rapids: Eerdmans, 2011), 277.

CONCLUSION:
CONFORMING DISCIPLES
TO CHRIST

When disciples view themselves in the mirror of Scripture, they see that their truest and deepest identity is a function not of their gender, career, or ethnicity, but of their being in Christ. To be in Christ is both gift and task. It is a gift in the sense that God has united us to the Son through the Spirit, and those in Christ have all the privileges of children of God (Rom 8:15, 23; Eph 1:5). It is a task in the sense that we are called to live out and act out our identity in Christ. This is the Pauline imperative that follows the Pauline indicative: you have the life and Spirit of Christ in you; therefore, act out Christ's heart and mind.

The goal of discipleship is conformity to Christ. It is also the culmination of God's plan of salvation: "For those whom he foreknew he also predestined to be conformed to the image of his Son" (Rom 8:29). Paul never sounds more like a pastor than when he addresses his readers as his own children: "My little children, for whom I am again in the anguish of childbirth until Christ is formed in you" (Gal 4:19).

A pastor is a kind of midwife who assists in the formation of Christ in the disciple. Christ is formed in the disciple as disciples are conformed to the image of Christ. This is Paul's hope: "Just as we have borne the image of the man of dust, we shall also bear the image of the man of heaven" (1 Cor 15:49). Disciples mature as they get more real, that is, as they actualize their eschatological reality as images of Christ. Moreover, the community of disciples, the church, is a parable of the kingdom—a lived enactment of how God's will should be done on earth as it is in heaven.

Pastors may make one disciple at a time, but they should do so in the context of a local church. It is in and with the church community, the company of the gospel, that disciples best learn how to participate in the drama of redemption: to identify with Christ, endure suffering, experience the transforming presence of God, walk the way of wisdom, and imitate mature examples.[27]

At the beginning of this chapter I asked whether disciples had to be mirror images or exact duplicates of Christ. The answer should now be clear. Conformity to Christ is not the same as uniformity. Even in the New Testament it is evident that Jesus' disciples had different personalities, backgrounds, interests, and gifts. Against such diversity there is no law. At the same time, we have seen that all disciples are to have the mind of Christ—the same set of fundamental dispositions, most notably the willingness to respond to God's call with faith and obedience—to be a hearer who does.

To identify with Christ is not the same as to confuse oneself with Christ. Rather, it means to acknowledge our union with Christ (through the Spirit), and our communion with others who are likewise in Christ. A disciple's identity is "in Christ," but this identity can be lived out in many ways.

In particular, being in Christ means that our careers should not be at the center of our lives. The center belongs to Christ. Career belongs on the periphery, an outworking of our response to Christ's call. Jesus' call on our lives is deeper than our line of work: it means that "everything we are, everything we do, and everything we have is invested with a special devotion and dynamism lived out as a response to his summons."[28] Our calling is to love God *in* and *as* we go about our daily life and work.

---

27. I take these points from James Samra's fine study, *Being Conformed to Christ in Community: A Study of Maturity, Maturation and the Local Church in the Undisputed Pauline Epistles* (New York: T&T Clark, 2006), 152–65.

28. Os Guinness, *The Call: Finding and Fulfilling the Central Purpose of Your Life* (Nashville: Thomas Nelson, 2003), 4.

Each day affords disciples plenty of opportunities to act out what is in Christ by presenting their bodies as living sacrifices. Through reading Scripture, learning doctrine, corporate worship, and communal life, disciples discern how they are called to embody the mind of Christ in all times, places, and circumstances.

In the final analysis, God is not shaping individuals only, but a people. It's a long-term project: Israel had to spend forty years wandering in the wilderness in order to be formed into a people who knew who to obey and worship rightly. (They never learned.) Paul says their story was written for our instruction (1 Cor 10): let's not repeat their mistake! The purpose of Scripture is to prepare a people to be God's own treasured possession: a "holy nation" (Exod 19:6; 1 Pet 2:9). God treated the people of Israel as his son ("Out of Egypt I called my son," Hos 11:1). Israel disappointed, and Jesus had to come to be the son God always wanted. But this is our ultimate calling, our highest privilege and responsibility: to live into our adoption as sons and daughters of the Father. This is our destiny (and our predestination, Eph 1:5), to be adopted as sons and daughters through Jesus Christ.

The whole of Proverbs can be read as parental instruction to a son who was being groomed to become king. But this is also the story of humanity: Adam was given a royal mandate to rule the earth in God's place. In one sense, the whole of Scripture functions like the book of Proverbs, inasmuch as it gives us direction for walking the Way of Jesus Christ, and for giving instruction as to how disciples should live out their adoption as royal sons and daughters. Scripture's ultimate purpose is to train sons and daughters to display the same filial obedience as Jesus, loving God the Father with all their heart, soul, mind, and strength. In this sense, the pastor who makes disciples functions in loco parentis.

Teaching Scripture and doctrine involves more than theory. The proper end of reading Scripture and doing theology is to help disciples mature into men and women who are ready for solid food (1 Cor 3:2; Heb 5:12–14), a long walk, and the rough and tumble of daily life.

Remember, in helping disciples act out the life of Christ, we are not encouraging them to rely on their own moral efforts but on God's reliable word. Discipleship is not a how-to self-help project. On the contrary: "We are *his* workmanship, created in Christ Jesus for good works" (Eph 2:10). It is God who reforms, restores, and renews, but he has given to pastors the privilege and responsibility of participating in this work of conforming disciples to Christ in community. Discipleship is a growing-up project, where men and women in Christ "grow up in every way into him who is the head, into Christ" (Eph 4:15).

Conclusion

"NOW WE ARE FIT"

Discipleship to the Glory of God

If you abide in my word, you are truly my disciples. (John 8:31)

So glorify God in your body. (1 Cor 6:20)

I began with a reference to popular culture (the films *Wall-E* and *Cold Souls*), and I end with one too: Frank Sinatra's signature song "My Way." Unlike *David Copperfield*, in which the narrator wonders whether he will be the hero of his life story, Sinatra is in no doubt. He *has been* the hero of his story, and he has also been its author. "My Way" was released as a single recording in the United Kingdom and stayed in the Top 40 from April 1969 to 1971 for a record seventy-five weeks. It was also a hit in the United States. Clearly, it struck a chord.

The lyrics of the song are instructive, for they lay out the course of the kind of life considered heroic in the light of the modern social imaginary, which celebrates freedom as individual expression. The song begins by setting the stage for something like a deathbed confession, then goes on to speak of a life lived following (allegedly) one's own course. In the final stanza, Sinatra waxes positively philosophical:

> For what is a man, what has he got
> If not himself, then he has naught
> To say the things he truly feels
> And not the words of one who kneels.[1]

"My Way" is a picture of someone who is so self-sufficient that he has no need to speak to God (I'm assuming that "kneeling" in the last line is either an acknowledgment of authority or a veiled reference to prayer). Yes, he did it his way, but where exactly did it get him?

MINISTERING SCRIPTURE AND DOCTRINE TO MAKE DISCIPLES

Much of what I have been doing in this book is best described as vision casting. In particular, I've been challenging some familiar pictures of what theology and doctrine are in order to recover what I take to be a more biblical, and healthy, picture of the role of theology, and theological interpretation of Scripture, in the church. The big picture: God is forming a holy nation by taking captive every thought, imagination, and practice of the disciple in order to make them more like Christ.

It is no little thing to facilitate a person's becoming more like Christ. There is arguably nothing more important that pastors, or any of us, should be doing than growing up into the fullness of Christ (Eph 4:13), "in whom are hidden all the treasures of wisdom and knowledge" (Col 2:3), not to mention eternal life,

---

1. "My Way," English lyrics by Paul Anka; original French lyrics by Gilles Thibaut; copyright 1967 Chrysalis Standards, Inc.

peace, and friendship with God. Receiving these blessings in Christ is a matter of *getting real*. The risen Christ gives us a fore-taste of the new creation and the new humanity we have in him, and we are never closer to being real than when we live in ways that correspond to our being "in Christ." Pastors have the great privilege and responsibility of helping disciples to get real as they become more like Christ, the archetype of Real Humanity.

The primary way we get real, and become more like Christ, is through Scripture and doctrine—or better, through reading the Bible theologically as the true story of what God is doing in our world. The more we can see history, the church, and our own lives as the field of God's presence and activity, the more we will be able to reclaim the church's unique biblical imaginary. Reading the Bible theologically takes place in the church, by the church, for the church, yesterday and today, for the sake of tomorrow, when we shall be like him (1 John 3:2) and see him face-to-face (1 Cor 13:12). I'm not forgetting about the importance of worship, but as we've seen in previous chapters, corporate worship, both the ministry of the word and the celebration of the Table, is itself a way of forming disciples to become the sort of persons who fit rightly into the drama of redemption.

In this book I have been trying to shape our understandings of several key concepts for the purpose of encouraging pastors to see reading the Bible theologically (that is, with the help of doctrines that take us higher up and further in), and teaching others to do the same, as a central part of their task. Let me now survey the ground we've covered.

First, what is Scripture? Scripture is the true story of who we are, why we're here, and where we're going. Some people accuse Christianity of being the opiate of the people, a fantasy island, but the truth is that Scripture gives a good long dose of reality. God's word, Scripture, is truth, a mirror in which we see ourselves as we really are and God as he reveals himself to be toward us in Jesus Christ. Everything else—all those other cultural images, myths, and social imaginaries—is only smoke and mirrors.

Second, what is the gospel? "Gospel" means "good news." Our world is awash in news. We have CNN and other news networks twenty-four hours a day. And no matter what the time of day, there is *always* "breaking news": somewhere, something urgent is happening at every moment—or so they would have us think, so that we stay tuned. Disciples must resist this tyranny of the immediate. The gospel too is breaking news, of a different and altogether more urgent kind. It is the news that the kingdom of God has broken and continues to break into our world in and through the person and work of Jesus Christ.

That God has acted and spoken in history is ultimately news-worthy. Everything in Christianity depends on these two presuppositions: God has acted (there is news to report); God has spoken (the news is reliable because God is the source of the report). Extra, extra! Read all about it (in the Bible): God has put the world right.

It's not enough to hear this news or even to believe it. The gospel is the kind of message, if we really understand it, that demands a response. The purpose of spreading the news that God is renewing the creation in Christ is to summon us to participate in this process of renewal—to be *doers*. As we have seen, Christianity is not a system of ideas but a way of truth and life.

Third, what is discipleship? A disciple is a follower: of words written and, ultimately, the Word made flesh, Jesus Christ. When we interpret a text, we "follow the way the words go." We also speak of following arguments, or of following directions for how to get to a certain place. We also speak of following a story. We ask, "Are you following me?" if we aren't sure someone has got the story right. We can get lost in long stories, which is why since ancient times the church has held to the rule of faith, a kind of CliffsNotes to the story of the Bible.

Reading the Bible theologically is vital for discipleship because Scripture alone tells us who we're following, and how to follow. We need to follow these words, this story, and the accompanying arguments about the meaning of the story in order to follow the one who ultimately commissioned them, who is also the one to whom they ultimately refer: Jesus Christ.

I used the theatrical model in chapter 6 to remind us that the most important way of following Scripture's story is not simply to say what we think it means but to respond to God's address with our entire person, body and soul. Interpreting the Bible theologically means responding to the living and active word of God. Here we would do well to speak of the *drama* of discipleship. Discipleship is dramatic because God's word summons us to follow, and that means that readers have a decision to make ("Choose you this day whose script you will enact"). When the word of the Lord comes to a person in a biblical story, it often provokes a crisis: "Samuel, Samuel!" requires a response. So does Jesus' "Follow me" (1 Sam 3:10; Matt 4:19). Whatever else it says, the word of the Lord poses a question: Will you hear and obey? Will you faithfully follow and improvise? Discipleship is dramatic because there is something enormous at stake. Will we be faithful actors, or will we live out and enact some other script?

Fourth, what is theology? Despite its apparent home in the academy, theology is first and foremost a ministry in and for the church. It is a teaching ministry that helps believers grow by increasing their understanding of who God is (and who humans are before God) and of what God is doing in Christ to renew the whole of creation, particularly human hearts. As a ministry of understanding, theology deals with the relationship of whole (that is, the unified biblical story of creation, fall, redemption, and consummation) and parts (that is, the key persons and events in the story, like the meaning of Jesus' crucifixion). As such, theology addresses the intellect and the imagination, taking captive both thoughts and social imaginaries.

Fifth, what is Christian doctrine? Doctrine is a primary form of the teaching of theology. Doctrine sets forth in speech the church's understanding of Scripture's account of who God is and what God is doing in Christ through the Spirit to form the people of God. Knowing doctrine strengthens the body of Christ. It helps members of the church, Christ's body, to "grow up in every way into him who is the head, into Christ" (Eph 4:15). Learning doctrine is an exercise in bodybuilding. Doctrine is vital for the Christian life, for it is only when we understand the drama of redemption and our own parts in it that we can respond to Paul's exhortation: "So, whether you eat or drink, or whatever you do, do all to the glory of God" (1 Cor 10:31).

Sixth, what is a pastor? A pastor does many things, but I have argued that most of these things are forms of ministering God's word: either by speaking (preaching, teaching, counseling, praying) or enacting it (celebrating the Lord's Supper, visitation). The particular focus of the present work has been on the pastor as disciple-maker, or what I have described elsewhere as "public theologian"—one who does theology with and for *people*.[2]

Strictly speaking, only the Triune God can make disciples, for as Jesus says, his followers are "born of the Spirit" (John 3:8). Pastors do not have the capacity to regenerate or sanctify. However, God in his wisdom has decided to make disciples by using what Thomas Aquinas calls "secondary causes": factors

---

2. See further Kevin J. Vanhoozer and Owen Strachan, *The Pastor as Public Theologian: Reclaiming a Lost Vision* (Grand Rapids: Baker Academic, 2015), ch. 4.

that assist the primary causes; or the means through which the primary cause becomes efficacious.

I have already mentioned Paul's statement that the ascended Christ gave pastor-teachers as gifts to the church (Eph 4:11–16). The Bible, the church, including her tradition and ministers, together with Christian doctrine are all precious aids to discipleship—helps for "building up the body of Christ" (Eph 4:12), for growing "up in every way … into Christ" (Eph 4:15), and for learning Christ (see Eph 4:20).

An engine is an agent or instrument of a particular process, a machine that converts power into motion. Pastors are engines who convert the hearing of God's word (the power of truth) into the doing of God's word (walking in truth). It is the privilege and responsibility of pastors to help disciples walk in truth by ministering the word of God and its understanding. When pastors help believers to hear with understanding, and then to demonstrate this understanding by doing what is fit, pastors become secondary causes and means of grace, a saving grace leading to spiritual health and an everlasting wellness.

THE CHURCH AS THEATER OF GLORY

"I did it my way" is hardly a fitting thing for a disciple to sing, or say. According to the Westminster Shorter Catechism, the chief end or highest good of human life is not to do it my own way, in order to magnify my own name, but rather "to glorify God and to enjoy him forever."[3] The chief end for training disciples to be fit for the purpose of gospel citizenship, Christlikeness, and godliness is indeed that of glorifying God.

---

3. Westminster Shorter Catechism, Q. 1, "What is the chief end of man?"

To glorify God is not to add one more item to the disciple's "to do" list. Glorifying God is not another activity *in addition to* all the other things a disciple does. On the contrary, we glorify God in, by, and through everything else we do by yielding up these activities and deeds as a heartfelt offering to the Lord: "So, whether you eat or drink, or whatever you do, do all to the glory of God" (1 Cor 10:31).

Just as glorifying God is not a separate activity, so God's glory is not a separate divine attribute. God's glory is rather a publication, a setting forth in public, of the magnificence of all his perfections. Jesus is "the radiance of the glory of God" because he revealed the character of God (Heb 1:3). As the Son of God who took on humanity, everything Jesus said, did, and suffered displayed some divine attribute, thereby glorifying God: "And the Word became flesh and dwelt among us, and we have seen his glory" (John 1:14). Disciples who follow in Jesus' steps similarly glorify God in proportion to their Christlikeness.

And this, finally, is the end purpose of the other kinds of fitness. The reason for building up the church, living a life worthy of our citizenship in the gospel, cultivating godliness, and becoming Christlike is ultimately to glorify God.

The great privilege and responsibility of pastor-theologians is making disciples who glorify God in everything they do. In the same way, the work of pastor-theologians in making disciples is also to the glory of God. What other response to a person's growth in godliness is there but to give God the glory?

Of course, the path of discipleship is never-ending: as long as we are alive, there is always one more step to take. So, no, we are not there yet: "Christian maturity in this life finds its realization in conformity to Christ's perfect human nature in the world to come."[4] But we are on the way, and the end is already ours, in Christ. It is because the finisher of our faith indwells us that we can run with patient and joyful endurance the race that is set before us (Heb 12:2). There is glory not only at the finish line (Col 3:1–4) but also along the way: "And we all, with unveiled face, beholding the glory of the Lord, are being transformed into the same image from one degree of glory to another" (2 Cor 3:18).

Here is a marvel. "God draws supreme glory to himself, in part, by glorifying us."[5] God's plan is to glorify himself through the glorification of disciples: "Those whom he predestined he also called ... justified ... glorified" (Rom 8:30). Disciples glorify God when they realize the purpose for which they were originally created, namely, to image God. God alone is light, and Christ alone is the light of the world, but when disciples follow Jesus to the point of becoming like him, they become little lights, that is, those who share in God's light: "He called you to this through our gospel, that you might share in the glory of our Lord Jesus Christ" (2 Thess 2:14 NIV).

What does it look like in practice? Good citizenship in our earthly city is not to be despised, but it is not our ultimate vocation. As the author of Hebrews puts it, "Here we do not have an enduring city, but we are looking for the city that is to come" (Heb 13:14 NIV). This is why Paul exhorts the Colossians to "set your hearts on things above, where Christ is" (Col 3:1 NIV). We glorify God when we live lives worthy of citizens of heaven, and the new Jerusalem. Yet, even now, when disciples heed Scripture and doctrine, their life together as a company of the

---

4. Bernard Ramm, *Them He Glorified: A Systematic Study of the Doctrine of Glorification* (Grand Rapids: Eerdmans, 1963), 89.

5. David VanDrunen, *God's Glory Alone: The Majestic Heart of Christian Faith and Life* (Grand Rapids: Zondervan, 2015), 25.

gospel becomes a theater of glory, and anticipates the greater glory to come.

Disciples become fit for purpose by following the Way of Jesus Christ: the way of truth and life, wisdom and flourishing. It is a good way, indicated by the good news. In his Third Letter, John says, "Beloved, I pray that all may go well with you and that you may be in good health, as it goes well with your soul" (3 John 2). This is the wellness I have had in mind from the beginning. The Greek term for "go well" is *euodoō*. It's the same *eu-* prefix that we find in *euangelion* (gospel). As such, it is a fitting conclusion to the present book, for it reminds us that disciples will "go well," and be well, only when they hear and do the message of the gospel.

Not "I did it my way," but rather, "I did it his way, through him who strengthens me." This is the fitting response to the Great Commission, and to Jesus' call to each and every Christian: "Follow me." This is the fitting response, that in turn will elicit an even better response, Jesus' "Well done, good and faithful servant" (Matt 25:21).

SUBJECT AND NAME INDEX

SCRIPTURE INDEX

OLD TESTAMENT